Grace and the Human Condition

A THEOLOGY FOR ARTISANS OF A NEW HUMANITY

Volumes 1 & 3-5

The Community Called Church

Our Idea of God

The Sacraments Today

Evolution and Guilt

ORBIS  BOOKS

VOLUME TWO

Grace and
the Human Condition

BY JUAN LUIS SEGUNDO, S.J., IN COLLABORATION
WITH THE STAFF OF THE PETER FABER CENTER
IN MONTEVIDEO, URUGUAY
TRANSLATED BY JOHN DRURY

MARYKNOLL, NEW YORK

Abbreviations Used in This Volume

AA *Apostolicam actuositatem*. Vatican II. Decree on the Apostolate of the Laity. November 18, 1965.

Denz. Denzinger-Schönmetzer, *Enchiridion Symbolorum*. Fribourg: Herder, 1963.

DV *Dei Verbum*. Vatican II. Dogmatic Constitution on Divine Revelation. November 18, 1965.

ES *Ecclesiam Suam*. Encyclical of Pope Paul VI. August 6, 1964.

GS *Gaudium et spes*. Vatican II. Pastoral Constitution on the Church in the Modern World. December 7, 1965.

LG *Lumen gentium*. Vatican II. Dogmatic Constitution on the Church. November 21, 1964.

NAB The New American Bible. New York: P. J. Kenedy & Sons, 1970.

PL *Patrologiae cursus . . . Series latina*. Paris: Migne, 1844–1864.

Biblical citations are taken from The New English Bible, with the Apocrypha (New York and London: Oxford University Press and Cambridge University Press, 1970).

Citations of conciliar documents, unless otherwise indicated, are taken from Walter M. Abbot, S.J. (ed.), *The Documents of Vatican II* (New York: Guild-America-Association, 1966).

Wherever possible, other church and papal documents are cited on the basis of translations in *The Pope Speaks* Magazine (Washington, D.C.).

ORIGINALLY PUBLISHED BY EDICIONES CARLOS LOHLÉ, BUENOS AIRES © 1968

COPYRIGHT © 1973, ORBIS BOOKS, MARYKNOLL, NEW YORK 10545

LIBRARY OF CONGRESS CATALOG CARD NUMBER: 72–85794

ISBN 088344–480–1   088344–482–8

DESIGN BY LA LIBERTÉ & RAYNER

MANUFACTURED IN THE UNITED STATES OF AMERICA

SECOND PRINTING

With deep roots and firm foundations, may you be strong to grasp, with all God's people, what is the breadth and length and height and depth of the love of Christ.

EPHESIANS 3:18

VOLUME TWO

Contents

Grace and the Human Condition

INTRODUCTION

What Name Do We Give to Christian Existence?

In the modern world no environment can give us Christianity ready-made. If what we possess has been handed over to us in this fashion, then we have good reasons to believe that it is not truly Christianity at all but rather an oversimplified substitute. In any case today we would think twice before making a decision which many of us may never have recalled making at all.

In truth the "habitual" way of being a Christian is being jolted every day: by the changes and tensions occurring within the Church, by the radical decisions being made by many in the name of Christianity, and by the criticisms coming from Christian circles about conceptions of society that have always been associated with Christianity.

There is only one mature way of facing up to this situation. At least once in our life we must try to make the hypothetical mental journey that precedes the decision to be a Christian. Putting this more concretely, we must try to ask ourselves this question: What content would my life acquire if *today* I were to decide to become a Christian? What new dimensions would open up in my life?

For the contemporaries of Jesus who accepted his person and message, the transition to the new existence was quite gradual and had no special name. Their Christian life was intermingled with the memories they treasured about the Master, his words and his deeds.

Some like John, however, wanted to explore things more deeply. They examined themselves and their memories, trying to figure out what specifically characterized the new existence that had begun with Christ. The first four chapters of the fourth Gospel reply precisely and explicitly to this question. For this reason some exegetes have called them "the book of new beginnings."

Others like Paul had an obvious additional reason for posing this question to themselves. They were converts. They had not followed

3

Christ step by step and gradually come to understand what it meant to live with Christ and "in Christ." The Christian life had been presented to them in one fell swoop as a choice to be made *in toto*.

We could say that Paul posed no other question but this one throughout his life. His whole life involved working out the conclusions and consequences of the "now" that began with his conversion and was separated from his life "before." One need only read his epistles to see how these two contrapuntal terms keep cropping up: *before–now*.

By "now" Paul clearly meant his Christian existence. But when we call it "Christian existence" we are describing the reality superficially from the outside. We are simply saying: the existence that Paul lived from the time he became a Christian. But what does this new existence consist of intrinsically?

Perhaps because Paul was the one who most employed the counterpoint between "before" and "now," the name that he used most to designate the internal reality of this "now" is the one that has prevailed in Christian tradition. The fact of its use is certain anyway. And that name was *grace.*

To give this word all the meaning and connotations it has, we must use our imagination and go back in history to the time when Christians, faced with a new reality, tried to find within human language the word that said most about its essence. Here in this introduction we are going to try to do that. We are going to try to get back to the original process of creating one of the most essential words in early Christianity, to capture all its significance when it was freshly made.

Section I

The word *grace* comes from Latin *gratia* and translates the Greek term *charis,* which was employed by the first Christian authors in their writings. Far from being simple, the reality designated by this term is extremely complex; and it is evidenced even in our modern way of speaking. We say such things as this: "she walked with charm and grace"; "they graciously granted him the favor of"; "he was graced with . . ."; "how gracious of you!" And Spanish-speaking peoples say "muchas gracias" to express their thanks.

At first glance the different uses of the word may seem to have nothing to do with each other. But they do indeed possess a common root and a common primitive nucleus. And most of these connotations were in use at the time when the first Christians took over the word *grace* to express the reality of Christendom.

In the *Iliad* (14, 183) and the *Odyssey* (6, 237), Homer uses the word in the sense of beauty and charm; and this meaning runs through all of Greek literature. We also find many instances where *charis* connotes benevolence: e.g., *"charin pherein eis tina"* (Euripides, *The Phoenician Maidens,* 1, 757). There are also many instances in Greek usage where *charis* has the meaning of gratitude, right from Homer on (*Odyssey,* 4, 695).

The other wellspring of Christian language, the Old Testament, presents an equivalent of the Greek word *charis* in the Hebrew word Qèn. The latter term has a meaning that is somewhat more specific than the Greek term, almost always referring to the benevolence of a superior toward an inferior. For example, when Esther is received favorably by King Ahasuerus despite the prohibition, she talks about having found "favor" (i.e., grace) in his eyes (Esther 8:5). Other examples can be found in Genesis (18:3; 19:19; 30:27), in Proverbs (more than twenty times), and in the Book of Wisdom. In the last book mentioned there are two instances where this benevolence is even more gratuitous, if that is possible, because it is shown toward the lowly and wretched (3:9; 4:15). So we see an equivalence being established between grace and *mercy*.

Thus when the first Christian writers decided to use the word "grace" to designate this new, unique reality, the word combined such different connotations as charm, benevolence, mercy, gratitude.

Now in the formation of speech idioms, especially of terms that describe states or properties of the soul and spirit, we must normally look for a poetic origin. And it is a poetic origin that starts from a simple, corporeal experience which is then applied analogously to a spiritual quality or state. Starting from there, we will be able to retrace the road that leads to each of the connotations and frame them with a human connotative unity.

In our case, the initial experience is undoubtedly that of bodily charm. We spontaneously relate charm to children and young people. If we call an old person "charming," it is because he has retained a bit of youthfulness within himself. Something that is old in every respect can be beautiful, solemn, and sublime but not enchanting in this sense. Thus in order to designate something as charming, we require that it be totally lacking in rigidity and full of life. What is rigid, what is subject to rules, what remains immutable is not charming. Nor is that which is niggardly, circumspect, and opaque; that which lacks the impetus that wells up from interior fullness. Hence only that which is young, recent, fresh, and pure can be charming.

It is easy enough to transpose these qualities poetically to the soul on the level of the individual. To use the words of Péguy:

The germ is the minimum of residue, the minimum of readymade, the minimum of habit and memory. Hence it is the minimum of decrepitude, rigidity, hardening, and lifelessness. And, on the other hand, it is the maximum of liberty, playfulness, agility, and grace. The germ is the least habituated thing that exists. It contains the least possible amount of hoarded material already fixed by memory and habit. It contains the least possible amount of matter consecrated to memory. It contains the least amount of file papers, memories, paperwork, bureaucracy. Or, to put it better, it is that which is closest to creation and most recent in the sense of the Latin word *recens*. It is the most recent and fresh thing that has truly come from the hands of God.[1]

In trying to work out the present-day concept of grace, however, it is even more interesting to consider this charm on the plane of human relationships. After all, on the level of the individual its identification with bodily charm is evident enough.

Taken in general, human relationships can be beneficent, harmful, or simply nonexistent. In other words, a human being can do good to his fellow man, do harm to him, or simply do nothing at all out of indifference. Obviously enough we would not use the word grace to refer to the last two attitudes; we would apply it to beneficent acts. But not every beneficent act is grace, for not every beneficent act is charming. Let us try to find out wherein lies the grace, the charm, of a good deed.

Every beneficent act surely involves giving to the beneficiary something that he did not possess. But if he had a right to it, we would never call it a gift or a present; indeed we could scarcely call it a benefit, since having a right to something is like possessing it. So the charm resides solely in that which is a gift, a gratuitous benefit. I would never apply the word "charming" to a person who pays me what he owes me, since he is obligated to do it. The payment may indeed be accompanied by a charming smile, since the smile is not obligatory and I have no right to it. But the simple deed of repaying me the debt is in no sense charming. All this could be concluded from what we said above about bodily charm. There is no charm in anything that is rigid, predetermined, mediocre, just, or circumspect. On the contrary, charm always involves abundance, liberty (since liberty is essentially an abundance of being that goes beyond what is merely necessary and foreseeable), gratuitousness. In his *Rhetoric* (2, 7), Aristotle himself pointed out that grace is synonymous with gift, because every gift is simultaneously synonymous with abundance, liberty, and gratuitousness.

Finally, through a simple process, we derive from this the third connotation of the word "grace." Today we say that a person should "give thanks" for a gift received. Actually the original expression was more logical: a person had to "return" or "repay" thanks. In other words, he had to return something equivalent to the gift received and something equally gratuitous: e.g., a gift of the same value or an expression of acknowledgment that was equivalent to the gift. Thus gradually the word *grace* alone, which originally made sense only together with the verb "return," came to signify the fulfillment of a debt of *gratitude:* i.e., of a debt not required.

This connotation, too, is important if we are to understand what Christianity wanted to invest in the theological expression contained in the word *grace*. But it was the first two connotations—charm and gratuitousness—that had the most influence on the choice of the word.

Section II

Bonnetain points out that "the word *grace* apparently did not form part of our Lord's vocabulary." [2] In truth it is not used in the Gospels of Matthew and Mark. The Gospel of John, which together with his epistles seem to be the latest writings of the New Testament, does not put the word *grace* on Jesus' lips either. But since that word was already known and used by Christians, John shows us that the word "life" was the one used by Christ to express the same reality.

The Gospel of Luke does use the word *grace*. This is understandable in view of the relationship between Luke and Paul. But something is worth noting in his Gospel too. In the four most important passages, where the word *grace* has a meaning that goes beyond ordinary usage (Luke 1:30; 2:40; 2:52; 4:22), it is not Jesus who utters it but the evangelist or the angel of the Incarnation. By contrast, in the two cases where Saint Luke puts the word on the lips of Jesus, the word has its ordinary connotations. But these passages are interesting because in them we find an echo of the analysis we have just made and an explanation of the word's use to designate the new reality. In the sermon on the mount (Luke 6:32-34), Jesus says: "If you love only those who love you, what *credit* [i.e., grace] is that to you? Again, if you do good only to those who do good to you, what credit is that to you? . . . If you lend only where you expect to be repaid, what credit is that to you?" Even in this new English translation, one can see that the underlying word has connotations of gratuitousness and superabundance, presuming that Christ uttered it. And even if he did not, it certainly does in the mind of Luke.

There is no *grace* in giving if the person has a right to what you give
(i.e., in loving those who love you, doing good to those who do good to
you), or if there is a possibility that you will be able to exercise your
right in return (i.e., getting your loan repaid). There is nothing spontaneous, gratuitous, or superabundant in that; hence it does not merit
the favor or recompense that is due to something given "gratis." The
equivalent passages in Matthew's Gospel confirm this outlook (Matt.
5:46–47). There is nothing gratuitous or spontaneous in something that
is the result of an obligation or a social mechanism.

Thus we can see that even if *grace* did form part of Christ's vocabulary, it did not have any special or new connotations; but it did possess
the fundamental elements that help to explain why it was used to designate the new reality proclaimed by his message.

Now we come to the other four passages in Luke's Gospel where the
word *grace* appears but is not attributed to Christ. Does the word have
its common meaning or a new connotation in these passages? Before we
answer this question, we do better to examine the new connotation in
Paul's letters, some of which are certainly prior to Luke's Gospel. Moreover, if we recall that Luke was Paul's disciple, we may understand better
by starting with the disciple's master.

Paul does use the word *grace* frequently in his letters. And by it he
means the new reality that Christ brought into the world. What is this
new reality exactly? Rousselot says: "Saint Paul seems to see grace, above
all, as a divine aid which heaven grants out of pure mercy. It heals our
wounded will, changes it, and draws it away from evil to good—with
gentleness, yes, but above all with wondrous force." [3]

Now one might wonder what led Paul to choose the term *grace* for
the new reality. Among the several elements already mentioned, which
one or which ones, insofar as they were analogous with the common usage
of the word, prompted Paul's choice of the term? Apparently only one,
which Rousselot describes this way: "an aid granted *out of pure mercy.*"
In short, grace is a gift, something gratuitous and unmerited, something
to which man has no right and hence cannot lay claim to.

With all the connotations and elements it contained, why was this
and only this connotation behind Paul's choice of a word to designate
the total reality? We find our answer in Paul's conversion. Perhaps even
more specifically we find it in the circumstances surrounding it: the
vision at the gates of Damascus that drove him to the ground and transformed him suddenly and violently from a persecutor of the Church into
a vessel of election and a preacher of the gospel to the gentiles. Let us
read his own account of the happening in Galatians: "You have heard
what my manner of life was when I was still a practicing Jew: how

savagely I persecuted the church of God and tried to destroy it" (1:13). This is the first element in the picture. As he had already pointed out in a preceding verse, nothing in himself presaged a coming change. Everything he did was the consequence of an enthusiastic attachment to a given culture and internal conviction. "But then in his good pleasure God, who had set me apart from birth and called me through his grace, chose to reveal his Son to me and through me, in order that I might proclaim him among the Gentiles" (1:15-16).

Paul is aware that nothing of his own had anything to do with the conversion. Everything came directly from God, as we can surmise from the last passage. Thus his conversion is truly a gift, a "grace," as he says. And he puts stress on this fact by tracing this grace back to the very moment when his existence began. If indeed nothing in his life could have called or prepared for this grace, the gift of God had to be a personal gift, a favor done to the *person* of Paul rather than a reward for his virtue. Paul wants to underline this by tying the word *grace* with the phrase "from birth." He thus stresses that this whole new reality, which transformed his life in the Damascus encounter with Christ, was something supremely gratuitous. Says Rousselot: "What Paul related to us is a spiritual experience, the interior story of a convert . . . For a convert (especially one in Paul's circumstances), it is natural that grace be, first and foremost, a pardon. Grace is always mercy . . . But he feels more keenly in himself what is true for all." [4]

So if the word *grace* has become Christianity's classical expression for the new life brought by Christ, it is because of this sudden, explosive, illuminating personal experience of Paul, the first Christian theologian, in his encounter with Christ on the road to Damascus.

Centuries later a terribly technical word would crop up in the vocabulary of theology: "supernatural." But its content is the same. It is that which is impossible for our nature to acquire, demand, or even prepare for. In the later term, however, the vivacious stress has disappeared. And the reifying tone of the new word would unfortunately dilute the power of the old word.

Section III

It is now clear that the reason why Christian existence has been called *grace* derives from an awareness (Paul's preferably) of its *gratuitousness* from the viewpoint of the giver. In short, it signifies God's free gift.

Thus it might seem that the second connotation of the word *grace* has been the determining one here. It might seem that the first connotation (of charm, youthfulness, freshness, and spontaneity) was absent or overlooked in choosing this word for the new reality. Indeed this might seem to be quite logical in view of the word *grace* itself: since it is a gift, the charm would reside in the person who makes the gift, who is capable of this gratuitousness. In other words, if God gives us his gift and it is nothing less than his own life, then he by his action is the unpredictable and superabundant and youthful one who is "full of grace" (John 1:14). By contrast, we would have to say of man, as Paul does, that he "has been an object of grace." And in fact when we look at the original Greek of Luke's Gospel, we find that Mary is not "full of grace" but "has been filled with grace." Grace has filled her.

On the other hand, however, we know[5] that this gift from God is his own life. Is it not meant to make man capable of grace, of gratuitousness? Is it not meant to introduce into him this attitude, this quality, this potency? Is not the grace received supposed to be converted into a fount of life and spontaneity for man, rather than into a personal asset?

While Paul does indeed designate the new existence as grace, we find other synonyms in his letters and in other parts of the New Testament, especially in the writings of John. The main ones are: life, spirit, new creation, filial adoption, the interior man.

All these words point precisely to the fact that God's gift, his grace, converts man's existence into a grace. In other words, it gives man's deeper life the features of gratuitousness and charming graciousness. The logic which ties these words together as synonyms will be seen more clearly and precisely in the chapters that follow. Here we shall merely touch upon it briefly.

It is clear that possessing God's life is a creative summons to a new life in love (1 John 2:5–6). In that life John and Paul point to the features which proceed from God's own life: opposition to death (Rom. 6:12–14), to literalism (Rom. 7:5–6), and to the legalism centered on works (Rom. 8:3–13). This life is Spirit, the great divine breeze or breath (Lat. *spiritus*) that blows in us and bears us up (John 3:8). This new existence has all the freshness of an absolutely new start; it is a new creation (2 Cor. 5:17; Gal. 6:15), a new birth (John 3:3). But in order for this new reality to open up in man's existence, within a universe that dominates and overwhelms it, the Spirit that gives breath and life must transform us from slaves into free and operative creators. It does this by giving us and making us feel the spirit of sonship (Rom. 8:14–21; Gal. 4:6; 1 John 3:1–3), and by establishing us, not juridically but existentially, as heirs and lords of the universe (Gal. 4:1–3). Only in this way will we cease to be dominated by external things and by fear. Only in this way does our inner self open up to full spontaneity (Rom. 7:21), so that gratuitousness wells up in man as well.

That is how the synthesis of *grace* is achieved. Vatican II describes it thus: "This likeness reveals that man, who is the only creature on earth which God willed for itself, cannot fully find himself except through a sincere gift of himself" (GS 24).

This is the general theme of our reflections in the following chapters. What we have seen already simply helps us to recognize and comprehend the language which the first Christians used to talk about the great happening that had burst in upon their lives. But even this cursory introduction will help the reader to begin associating the traditional word *grace,* the key word in this book, with another term that sums it up: *man's liberation.*[6]

NOTES TO INTRODUCTION

1. Charles Péguy, *Nota conjunta sobre Descartes y la filosofía cartesiana* (Buenos Aires: Emecé, 1946), p. 102.

2. *Supplément du Dictionnaire de la Bible,* III, col. 716.

3. "La grâce d'après saint Jean et d'après saint Paul," *Recherches de Science Religieuse* (1928), p. 87.

4. *Ibid.,* p. 98.

5. *Cf.* 1 John *passim,* and the main article in Chapter II, Volume I of this series.

6. While this volume forms part of a five-volume series, it can also be read and understood on its own. But it was composed and it can be utilized in the same general way that applies to the series. For this reason we are reproducing a part of the general introduction to the series, contained in Volume I, in the appendices of subsequent volumes. It will show the reader how the volumes arose and how they were used in practical seminars. See Appendix I in this volume.

CLARIFICATION

THE TWO APPROACHES OF CHRISTIAN LANGUAGE

The themes of a theology imbedded in real life are sufficiently interwoven to rule out separating one set of problems completely from another set. Thus this volume on grace and its dimensions will of necessity pick up themes that were dealt with in Volume I on the Church.

The reader will notice this at once. He will also notice that the two represent lines of thought that are opposed to some extent.

In the first volume we were interested in finding out what this community called Church came to do for a world that was already there before it. We considered and questioned the Church with this underlying conviction: God could not have abandoned most of the human race, leaving them without help or salvation, in order to establish a small nucleus of privileged souls. In this volume, by contrast, we start right out by asking what makes up Christian existence. And we are doing this from within this reality, so to speak: i.e., out of the conviction that this existence is a gift, a grace.

These two points of view, or better, these two points of departure complement one another. If we follow the pathways they point out, we should arrive at the same point. Neither is false, so long as we do not leave out of account the reality that may be relegated to second place at the start of our inquiry.

When we spoke about the Church in the previous volume, we started out by establishing the work of salvation and grace in the midst of the whole human race. And we saw how this salvation, in the process of being expanded and realized, posed questions by virtue of which revelation and the Church as its herald acquired meaning and service-value.

In this volume we begin with what revelation and the Church have to say about the existence of those who believe in revelation and live within the Church. And this existence is presumed to be a human one. In this process of trying to understand this particular existence, there will come a point in our inquiry when another question crops up: And what about others?

In the same way *Gaudium et spes* (n. 22) attempts to describe Christian man. And when it has done this, its own description seems to force it to open up the panorama infinitely wider: "All this holds true not only for Christians, but for all men of good will in whose hearts grace works in an unseen way."

There will almost certainly be a feeling of unease among some readers of this volume from the very outset, as they read about the origin of the word *grace* as the designation of Christian existence. This is more likely to be true to the extent that they have taken to heart the lessons of Volume I. For Paul applies the word *grace* to his conversion, which caused him to move from one human group to another, from one community to another. Is it perhaps that he thought this passage converted him into a privileged person? And if he recognized that this passage did not separate him from his first community, why did he apply the word *grace* to the second and not to the first?

Let us repeat that this criticism would be valid, if the thinking of Paul or the Church went no further. For the stages of a journey, whatever be the departure point, are always limited and limiting. Every conversion presents itself as an encounter with the Truth. Only later and gradually does it become capable of looking back and asking whether the whole preceding journey might not have been an encounter with the Truth as well. And also wondering whether the road ahead might not be an infinitely richer encounter with that same Truth.

So there is nothing wrong about following the dialectical rhythm of this approach, even though a line of thought more attuned to the objectivity of world history would have followed a more logical approach and would have undoubtedly given another name to what Paul calls *grace*. But if this other approach had paid attention to revelation, it too would eventually have had to agree that this universal reality, according to the Christian message, is essentially *gratuitous*.

What is more, there is certainly no question of a preference here. The Christian cannot spare himself the task of operating with these *two languages*. What is revealed cannot be deduced from his existence, and he does not encounter the Christian message in terms that he already recognizes and that seem to well up from his reality and continue it. There is work to be done. By the same token, it will do him little good to understand revelation if he wants to apply it as such to the solution of human problems. A second effort is needed. He must translate it in such a way that it will allow us to point up the pathways to fully human solutions in the very warp and woof of activity in history (GS 11).

Nevertheless many important elements, meant to pass from the Christian faith to human practice, do not reach this goal because people are too quick to raise the final question: When all is said and done, what does this contribute to my social, political, and economic activity?

Indeed one pole of the Church's activity is the elaboration of the revealed message, while the other pole is the elaboration of human language. But we would be immature to close ourselves up in one of them exclusively. Each of the two languages has its rationale, value, and rhythm. And there must be some minimum of manipulating effort in trying to synthesize them. In this sense, the first and second volumes of this series represent the two pathways for the one and only task incumbent on the same community.

CHAPTER ONE

Length: The Pre-Human, the Human Condition

God's gift transforms human existence, providing it with new dimensions. Our purpose in this volume is to locate the grace of God, to give concrete content to this transformation, and to find it in our own lives.

The first step in this process, then, is to go as far back in our existence as we have to in order to find the point of departure in it for this transforming force.

Jesus himself told Nicodemus that the gift which comes to man from above is like a wind that picks us up and carries us forward. Chesterton wrote a book (*Manalive,* 1912), in which the ordered and solemn life of the boarders at Beacon House is transformed by a series of unforeseen, outrageous, and juvenile events produced by a sudden windstorm. Much later the boarders reflected on the love, enthusiasm, aggressiveness, and creativity that these events prompted. And then they recalled what their lives were like before the "great wind of Beacon House."

We too can and should reflect on what our lives would have been without the "great wind" that has taken possession of us. But there is a difference. No matter how far we go back toward the beginning of our lives, experience alone will not tell us when we felt the first stirrings of this dynamism that we are trying to locate.

In reality it is no good for us to ask what was or is our life without the gift or grace of God. For the simple reason that it is not something external that appears and disappears, thus allowing us to make comparisons and conclusions. We cannot ask: What am I like without grace? What am I like *with* grace? As the Council tells us, grace is a reality intimately bound up with every human life that appears in the world. Hence not even comparison with other human beings will help, because in the concrete order of history as we know it there does not exist any human being who is totally alien to God's grace. So in our experience there does not exist any term of comparison that would enable us to know what concrete transformation in us is due to God's grace.

Thus if we are to answer the question we have posed, both experience and faith are required. Our answer represents a convergence of the two. Faith will tell us what God wishes to do in us and with us. Our experience will help us to understand how we oppose this divine intention. It will show us our basic difficulty, our adherence to something else which grace must overcome, the situation which it snatches us from in order to get us going. In other words, if we are to understand the *length* of Christian existence, we must go back far enough in our lives, through faith, to understand and appreciate the human condition which grace encounters and transforms.

Section I

We will proceed by stages in our reflection. Indeed these stages match the stages in the formation of Christian thought. So we will start with the data provided by the New Testament itself: i.e., with the faith-experience of the first Christians.

What does Paul see as the condition in which God's grace encounters the human being? Perhaps we can sum it up briefly with two or three passages in Romans. "We know that the law is spiritual [i.e., comes from God], but I am not; I am unspiritual [i.e., a creature], the purchased slave of sin. I do not even acknowledge my own actions as mine, for what I do is not what I want to do, but what I detest . . . For I know that nothing good lodges in me—in my unspiritual nature, I mean—for though the will to do good is there, the deed is not . . . In my inmost self I delight in the law of God, but I perceive that there is in my bodily members a different law, fighting against the law that my reason approves . . . Miserable creature that I am . . ." (Rom. 7:14–24). Using the first person singular, Paul brings all men into the picture. It is the human condition that he is describing in these words.[1] There was a time before when we had only our frail power as a creature to enable us to carry out the law. Now another reality exists in us. In order to make the transition tangible to us, Paul presents this reality at the conclusion of his description of man's wretchedness: "Miserable creature that I am, who is there to rescue me out of this body doomed to death? God alone, through Jesus Christ our Lord! Thanks be to God!" (Rom. 7:24–25).

So the New Testament gives us a picture of the human condition as the departure point for grace. It is a picture of a being who is divided within. There is a profound tension in man between that which he desires and decides within himself and that which he ends up doing externally.

Let us note right here that this is not the *whole* man. For Christian faith the human condition is not man but that which conditions every man. And in calling this conditioning factor "before," as opposed to the "now" of grace, Paul is not trying to make a radical distinction between two different points in time. He is not implying that human beings in another epoch were framed simply and wholly in this condition. *Before* is simply a way of saying that to this basic element there is added that which comes from God's gift.[2]

This *before* maintains its solidity in the face of the *now*. It is not a reality that has disappeared; it is a force that perdures and gives opposition. In Paul's terms, it is the "old man" who does not wish to be converted into the *new* man through the transforming power of grace (Eph. 4:22–24).

Section II

Now let us move on to a second level, a second stage in Christian thought. The data of the New Testament were assimilated and developed by the Church in subsequent epochs, mainly through the controversies that arose concerning the theology of grace.

How were we to picture the potentialities of man without grace? What would human life be if God had not made a gift of his own life? This problem presented itself in history when two fundamental interpretations of man met head on. They were Christianity and Stoicism.

The clash was foreseeable for more than one reason. First of all, there did exist in the Church an ascetical current that could be labelled voluntaristic and that found its home in the communities of monks.

Monasticism was born in the Church when the tension which had provoked persecution disappeared. After the peace of Constantine, the Church made herself at home in the world. The number of Christians grew considerably and Christianity began to become a sociological reality. No longer did one have to risk his life for the faith, and Christianity became a bourgeois affair—if we can use that anachronism. Faced with this situation, nonconformists began to withdraw into the desert in order to devote their lives wholly to God. Using asceticism, they regained the whole situation of risk that had once been provoked by persecutions.

Setting out on the path of asceticism and bodily penance, these people managed to set real records. Some anchorites spent years in caves or on the top of a column. Then the isolated anchorites became the spiritual fathers of other young people who wanted to live the gospel with the same intensity. So monasteries were formed, and stress was placed on the ascetical aspect. One was supposed to gain victory over the passions and the forces of concupiscence. As time went on, however, even the monks lost some of their austerity and fell into spiritual sloth; they forgot their primitive fervor. Now in all the reactions against this new drift, stress was laid on the power of the human will, on self-control, on merit and the painful quest for eternal life. In a word, stress was laid on man's activity in his quest for salvation.

Thus within itself Christianity found a certain complicity with one of the deepest tendencies of the Western world: Stoicism. And in fact both tendencies were destined to meet. Other theories of human life either involved nothing more than ritual religious practices (the mystery religions) or else lacked a total vision of the universe that could depict man within a universal perspective (e.g., Epicurean philosophy).

The Stoic ideal was beautiful, and it possessed real moral force even though it was incomplete. I am part of a whole which is ruled by an abstract law. There exists a fundamental harmony among all things, a supreme law that rules everything. Man's effort and goal is to bring himself into conformity with this truth. He does this first on the level of knowledge, and then on the level of action (by acting in accord with what he knows to be true). To accomplish this, man has at his disposal reason and will. Reason may not have physical dominion over the passions: i.e., a dominion that is immediate and decisive. But it does have a "political" dominion over them: i.e., by rational exercise of the virtues, it can ultimately impose its control over them and prevent them from moving away from the universal law that rules the whole.

If we recall Paul's vision of man described above, we will realize that Stoicism and Christianity are irremediably opposed when carried to their ultimate conclusions. But such deep thinking was not to be expected of the Christian people in general. Sooner or later there were bound to be infiltrations of Stoic practice into the spirituality of concrete, historical Christianity. And indeed this is what happened in the first years of the fifth century, the Stoic-Christian current being called *Pelagianism*. Pelagius, a British monk whose real name was Morgan, was the most well known defender of this current.

The key document in this controversy is the letter of spiritual direction that Pelagius sent to Demetriades, a young Roman maiden who had just taken the veil of virgin and wanted to orient herself aright with regard to the spiritual life. This letter is one of the most interesting documents in the history of Christianity, and it retains its relevance today. Here we shall quote some of its more important passages in full.

Whenever I must speak of moral formation and the habits of a holy life, I usually stress before anything else the power and character of human nature and all that it can do. And in this way I try to excite the soul of my hearer with the beauty of the virtues, because it is no use to be called to things that are regarded as impossible . . . Take, then, as the first and foremost foundation of a holy spiritual life this dictum: the virgin must know her powers, so that she may be able to exercise them once she has understood what she has.

Pelagius then goes on to intone what we could call a hymn to human nature:

The first thing to do is to measure the goodness of human nature in terms of its author, i.e., God, of whom it is said that he made the universe and everything in it not only good but very good. How much more true this must be with regard to man, for whom we know he created everything else. . . . Secondly, God made subject to him all the animals, many of whom surpass man in bodily size and strength . . . Did God not thus indicate the superior beauty of man and force him to appreciate the dignity of his nature? For he did not leave man naked and defenseless before these animals, exposing him to danger without any weapons. While he created him defenseless on the outside, he armed him interiorly with reason and prudence, so that with his understanding and mental activity he alone would recognize the Creator of all; so that he would serve God with the very things that gave him dominion over every other creature. God willed that man carry out this righteousness voluntarily. For this reason he left man in the hands of his own free will; and he placed before him life and death, good and evil. Whichever he would choose would be given to him.

And where can we see better the wondrous power of human nature in action than in pagans, since we assume that they, lacking faith, do not have access to the supernatural plane?

Have we not read and heard and seen that many philosophers were chaste, patient, modest, generous, abstinent, and kind? That they spurned the honors and delights of the world and loved justice no less than wisdom? Where did they get these good qualities, if not from the goodness of their nature? And since all these things exist—whether it be all of them in one person, or one of them in each individual—and since the nature of all of them is one, doesn't their example show us that all of these things can be in every person? And if human beings show us what God has created them to be even without the aid of God, what are Christians capable of doing? For their nature and life has been better endowed by Christ, and they are aided as well by the help of divine grace . . . For I tell you that there exists in our souls what we might call natural sanctity. It presides over the temple of the soul, judging good and evil. It fosters good and upright acts and condemns evil deeds. And it judges everything as if it were a law within in accordance with the testimony of conscience.

But this hymn to human nature is meant to be realistic. It does not identify nature with the good. It identifies nature with liberty, with a liberty that invariably stands at an equal distance from two different possibilities like the needle of a balance scale. The two possibilities are pure, precise, and complete: good and evil. "We do not uphold the goodness of nature to the point of saying that it cannot commit evil, for we are capable of both possibilities. We simply want to acquit it of the charge that through its fault we are impelled to evil. If we do good, we do it voluntarily, and the same holds true if we do evil. *We will always be free to choose one of the two, and both are equally in our power.*[3]

As you can see, this is one of the most interesting documents in the history of Christianity. To be sure, we could find passages in earlier Greek literature (for example) that celebrated man, his power, and his situation in the universe. But the interesting thing here is the position of our text within the atmosphere of Christianity, within the real, concrete life of Christianity. We might say that it is the greatest and ultimate attempt to transmit this hymn to man into the Christian mentality, to transmit an outlook that sees in the human condition something limited, to be sure, but something perfect and complete within its limitation.

The Church condemned Pelagianism for the first time at the regional Council of Carthage in 418. It summed up and rejected the doctrine of Pelagius in these terms: "If anyone says that the grace of justification is given to us so that we may more easily do that which we are commanded to do freely, as if we could carry out the divine commandments without it, even though only with difficulty, let him be anathema" (Denz. 105).

Nevertheless a difficulty remains. We have seen that the internal division within man, already present in Paul's conception and repeated by later theology against Pelagius' hymn to natural man, was translated concretely into a weakness of liberty. I want to do good but I do not carry it out. Now then, although the teaching of Augustine, the great opponent of Pelagianism, was very clear in describing this weakness of our liberty, it was not so clear in picturing how the grace of God made it possible for man in reality to put himself in harmony with what God demanded of him.

Grace was undoubtedly an attraction toward good. But is liberty healed by virtue of the fact that God puts a supplementary attraction, a special delight, in the good? This question puts us right in the eye of one of the most fundamental and topical questions in the theology of grace. Does grace actually come to help *liberty* or to help the *law?* In other words, does it make man more free or less a sinner?

This latent ambiguity would show up much more clearly in a group

of later theologians who claimed to be following Saint Augustine. This
was the Jansenism of the seventeenth and eighteenth centuries.

For Bishop Jansen, grace was a delight that the Holy Spirit puts into
good things and actions. Man always obeys that which affords him more
pleasure. Without grace, it is evil and law-breaking that afford this
greater pleasure. Hence man without grace is not strictly free, in the
sense that he sins and keeps sinning continually. Grace comes to endow
good with the delight it lacks. When grace is greater, that is, when it
affords a greater delight than evil does, it is also victorious; and man
then does good voluntarily but infallibly. When grace is less, man will
lose—voluntarily again, but infallibly—in his combat against evil.

In condemning Jansen and his followers on several occasions, the
Church defended liberty. But in a way the Church seemed to defend it
not only against concupiscence (the inclination to evil) but also against
grace (the inclination to good). In 1653, for example, she condemned
this proposition taken from Jansen's book on Saint Augustine: "In the
state of fallen nature, interior grace is never resisted" (Denz. 1093). Sixty
years later, the Church likewise condemned these propositions of Pasquier
Quesnel: "Without grace . . . the sinner is free only to do evil(!)" (Denz.
1351); on the other hand, "grace is nothing else but the all-powerful will
of God which ordains things and carries out what it ordains" (Denz. 1361).

As one can see, in both condemnations of Jansenist ideas the Church
was insisting that grace and liberty are not and should not be opposed
to each other.

But the problem crops up again and again, both then and now, because deep down in Christians there persists a key outlook and image
from the erroneous views on this topic. As they picture it, upon his arrival in this world every man encounters a law that is already there to
pinpoint the good actions he should perform and the evil deeds he
should avoid in order to gain salvation. In such a setup, salvation seems
to reside in the fact that one actually does perform good deeds, deeds
that are in conformity with the law. So no matter what one may say,
liberty can only seem to be a useless risk, to which we give mere lip
service. It would seem that the holier a person is, the less he would
know what to do with his liberty.

The situation would still be tolerable if we could be sure of what
Pelagius said: what a man chooses will be given to him. But it turns out
that even that is apparently not so; that we must agree with the Anti-
Pelagians when they say that wounded human liberty tends necessarily
toward evil. So when I am faced with the intervention of grace, would it
be logical for me to hope that it would heal my liberty? Since grace

comes to further my salvation, and since liberty is as fragile as it is, would it not be more logical to hope that grace would rid me of my liberty?

It would make sense to say that grace heals my liberty and to combine these two realities in one ideal, if my liberty were in fact more important or valuable than the good or bad actions I choose to do with it. But is that really the case?

Section III

The problematic issue of man in the past two centuries, focused on the themes of person and liberty, has allowed the theology of grace to take a further step and to put itself in deeper contact with Christian wellsprings—with the thought of Paul in particular.

This is the third level on which we shall study the question, examining a third stage in the development of Christian thought with regard to the human condition as the starting point for grace.

We said that God's gift heals man. By this we did not mean Christian man specifically in the act of being converted to Christianity. It is not as if the non-Christian human being could be equated with man-without-grace. We are not comparing historical realities. We are inquiring into our faith to find out what God's gift to us consists of. And we began by asking what we would have been like if God had not given us his gift.

Now according to our faith, man in the concrete without God's grace would not be a human being fully capable of carrying out his life. He would be an infirm, divided, tragic being. He would be dominated or enslaved by a force or tendency that is labelled *concupiscence* by theology (Denz. 806, 832).

But this element is not one which we know only through faith. And even if grace allows us to conquer it, it does not enable us to eliminate it. Hence concupiscence is something we *experience*. We encounter it in our everyday existence, even though it is only God's revelation that enables us to discern its meaning. And through this obstacle, which we must overcome to carry out the good we decide to do, there is revealed by contrast the gift of God which makes this good possible for us.

Now let us read again, only this time more attentively, Paul's commentary on this fundamental human experience. We shall simply add, in parentheses, the modern terms that will help us to comprehend a point expressed in the images of an older day and a different culture:

We know that the law is *spiritual* [i.e., a demand of God], but I am not.
I am *unspiritual* * [i.e., have a human condition], the purchased slave of
sin. I do not even acknowledge my own actions as mine, for what I do is
not what I want to do, but what I detest. But if what I do is against my
will, it means that I agree with the law and hold it to be admirable. But
as things are, it is no longer I who perform the action, but sin that lodges
in me. For I know that nothing good lodges in me—in my *unspiritual
nature*†[i.e., my human condition], I mean—for though the will to do good
is there, the deed is not. The good which I want to do, I fail to do; but
what I do is the wrong which is against my will; and if what I do is against
my will, clearly it is no longer *I* who am the agent, but sin that has its
lodging in me. I discover this principle, then; that when I want to do the
right, only the wrong is within my reach [i.e., my condition]. In my inmost
self I delight in the law of God, but I perceive that there is in my bodily
members a different law, fighting against the law that my reason [i.e., my
inmost self] approves and making me a prisoner under the law that is in my
members, the law of sin. Miserable creature that I am, who is there to rescue
me out of this body [i.e., condition] doomed to death? God alone, through
Jesus Christ our Lord! Thanks be to God! (Rom. 7:14-25)

Now if we compare this passage of Paul with the outlook described at
the end of the last section, it is obvious that the two presentations are not
at all equivalent. Let us first consider the central image in the erroneous
outlook. Under the influence of Greek philosophy, theology unwittingly
simplified the overall picture of the human condition. The law would
determine what was good and what was evil. Man's free will would stand
equally balanced between the two, that is, it would be fully free, if it
were not for the fact that evil (i.e., that which is prohibited by the law),
by virtue of concupiscence (a remnant of original sin), had an additional
allure. With grace man would once again be capable of freely doing good.

Paul would admit the correctness of the conclusion, the last sentence,
but he would not agree with the oversimplified image presented. As he
sees it, there are two desires, two tendencies, in man. One is interior,
the other comes from outside the individual. Liberty is not total because
he cannot carry out what he decides to do within himself in accordance
with his innermost desire. As he moves outside himself to carry out what
he inwardly desires to do, he falls under the spell of his bodily members:
i.e., of the very instruments he has at his disposal. The end result is an
action, a deed, a way of life that does not correspond to his innermost

---

* Translator's note: The NAB here has "weak flesh" rather than "unspiritual," and the Spanish text focuses on this term in Paul. See especially Chapter
II, CLARIFICATION I in this volume.

† Translator's note: NAB has "flesh" here.

pression of that which he seeks to be as a person. That is to say, free choice should envelop his spontaneous action, adapting it and conferring its own character on it so that even the reality of the spontaneous act will no longer be purely natural but *personal*." [7]

Note the last word, which crops up repeatedly. It, as opposed to *natural* (here designating an order that is wholly determined), will represent the key word in translating Paul's talk about the liberation of grace into modern terms.

Paul's statement that "everything belongs to you" (1 Cor. 3:21), insofar as it refers to something not only juridical but concretely real, represents the task of a whole lifetime. The reality of our experience would seem to tell us that everything is foreign to us. If it is to be *ours*, we must make all of it a reflection of our person, of what we are, think, and desire in our innermost self. And here the obstacle is not others. Inside us and outside us, as Paul says, there exists a law governing bodily things. Operating on the principle of minimum effort, it leads us to convert ourselves into just another material thing, to reify ourselves. According to Rahner, it is from this that the essence of concupiscence is derived. "In the concrete human person who exists within the present order, free decision and self-determination is incapable of operating perfectly and totally . . . In the process of self-determination, the human person suffers opposition from the nature that exists prior to liberty. He never manages to succeed fully, to see to it that everything he is realizes and expresses what he feels himself to be in the core of his person. The fact is that in man there is much that always remains in some way impersonal, impenetrable, and opaque to his existential decision; it is merely endured, not freely fashioned." [8]

2. Now this brings us back to the question we raised at the end of section II in this chapter. If all this is true, what is the story with good and evil, with what is permitted and what is prohibited by the law? Well, if what we have said so far is true, the radical result of concupiscence is to "de-absolutize" man, to prevent him from pouring himself out totally and finding himself once again in any decision he makes and carries out. And this holds true whether he decides to break the law or to obey it. So it is not that man can sincerely recognize himself in his licit actions and disown himself when he is faced with his illicit impulses and deeds. On the contrary, the upshot of concupiscence is that vice and virtue are not *his* own even though they come from him.[9] This is what Rahner means when he writes: "Man never becomes wholly absorbed either in good or in evil." [10]

The formula is concrete and expressive. And what was said above permits us to give it due value. But Rahner's terminology departs from

that which Paul used in his image. We must no absolutization" of man is something that Paul ider while for him only free interiority is identified understand and accept what Rahner says, his for is not a Pauline one. Paul would have said that himself as a whole, hence he does evil.

Paul would not deny what Rahner says. Th minimum effort is that both virtue and crime he is bad at being a saint and at being a criminal much akin to inert beings and quite different fro aspires to be; that it costs him to be consisten fulfilling the law and in violating it.

It is not certain that forbidden fruit is permitted fruit. But it is certain that it costs m oneself, than to let oneself be carried along by i says and does—either for or against the law.

3. What is it, then, that permits Paul to say his governing law decide upon the *good,* but th governing law perform *evil?* Would we not h good confront each other in both realms, in t the realm of performance?

To understand this point, which is funda anthropology, we must recall Paul's conception For him there no longer exists within the Chri independent of us, fixes what is licit and illici law of the Christian is to love, and to do this i of us must fashion a unique and novel love in novel needs of our neighbors—that is, those existence with us.

Thus all love is good if it is true, auth Why does this seem strange to us? Precisely perceptibly shift from self-giving love to a that is no longer self-giving at all. The superf we apply the same word, love, to the two di sin come on the scene within the Christian such and such a person, but when authenti tism *so that it may be carried out more easil* ble way that which started out as love is li siderations of ease.

Let us consider an example. Two man Each seeks the welfare of the other. Over th task and becomes more and more demandi

decision. So his innermost decision was the good. It is the falsified, irreconcilable execution that is the evil.

Let us now try to pursue the logic of this second image further.

1. Right off we are led to a revision of the theological notion of *concupiscence*. As Paul sees it, it is not a question of forbidden fruits being more attractive than permitted ones. What, then, is the nature of the existential force which is opposed to grace? Of what sort is the infirmity, the congenital weakness, from which grace rescues us? [4]

To begin with: What experience is Paul taking into account when he describes man's condition? Fundamentally it is this: While it is certain that there exists in every human being a personal principle of liberty, a desire and an exigency to determine for oneself what one aspires to be rather than to be handed this readymade, it is no less certain that the natural order of the universe seems to be unaware of this principle of liberty and treats man as just another cog in its mechanism.

What is even worse, however, is the fact that not only the things around him but man himself belongs to this mechanism. Nature works in man and *on* man. Liberty does not regulate his biological functions, for example, except in their most superficial and contingent aspects. Whereas man's creative ability, his capacity to think, his disposition depend on his digestion, the latter operates without the intervention of the faculty which pretends to rule the human universe. And the same holds true on other planes, such as the psychic, the social, and the economic ones.[5]

Thus it is not strange to find that when man aspires to carry out the good he has planned, his instruments—subject to the law of nature rather than to his own law, betray him; and the end result does not correspond with his desire (at least not with his *innermost* desire). For nature works on man, even determining his desires—perhaps not those which express a deep, deliberated decision but certainly those that are instinctive and spontaneous.[6]

We are right at the center of Paul's picture. All of us human beings possess an incipient liberty that seeks fulfillment. But in the power of nature that invades us and dwells within us, our incipient liberty encounters something which belongs to us and conditions all our executions even though it is indeed alien to the innermost core of our own ego.

"Hence," says Rahner, "we can now begin to say what *concupiscence* is in the theological sense. As we said, man's free decision tends toward the goal of each man being at his own disposal as a total reality in God's eyes and actively fashioning himself into what he freely chooses to be. Thus free choice is geared toward the aim that everything in man (nature), including therefore his involuntary acts, be the potency and expression of that which he seeks to be as a person. That is to say, free choice should envelop his spontaneous action, adapting it and conferring its own character on it so that even the reality of the spontaneous act will no longer be purely natural but *personal*." [7]

Note the last word, which crops up repeatedly. It, as opposed to *natural* (here designating an order that is wholly determined), will represent the key word in translating Paul's talk about the liberation of grace into modern terms.

Paul's statement that "everything belongs to you" (1 Cor. 3:21), insofar as it refers to something not only juridical but concretely real, represents the task of a whole lifetime. The reality of our experience would seem to tell us that everything is foreign to us. If it is to be *ours*, we must make all of it a reflection of our person, of what we are, think, and desire in our innermost self. And here the obstacle is not others. Inside us and outside us, as Paul says, there exists a law governing bodily things. Operating on the principle of minimum effort, it leads us to convert ourselves into just another material thing, to reify ourselves. According to Rahner, it is from this that the essence of concupiscence is derived. "In the concrete human person who exists within the present order, free decision and self-determination is incapable of operating perfectly and totally . . . In the process of self-determination, the human person suffers opposition from the nature that exists prior to liberty. He never manages to succeed fully, to see to it that everything he is realizes and expresses what he feels himself to be in the core of his person. The fact is that in man there is much that always remains in some way impersonal, impenetrable, and opaque to his existential decision; it is merely endured, not freely fashioned." [8]

2. Now this brings us back to the question we raised at the end of section II in this chapter. If all this is true, what is the story with good and evil, with what is permitted and what is prohibited by the law? Well, if what we have said so far is true, the radical result of concupiscence is to "de-absolutize" man, to prevent him from pouring himself out totally and finding himself once again in any decision he makes and carries out. And this holds true whether he decides to break the law or to obey it. So it is not that man can sincerely recognize himself in his licit actions and disown himself when he is faced with his illicit impulses and deeds. On the contrary, the upshot of concupiscence is that vice and virtue are not *his own* even though they come from him.[9] This is what Rahner means when he writes: "Man never becomes wholly absorbed either in good or in evil." [10]

The formula is concrete and expressive. And what was said above permits us to give it due value. But Rahner's terminology departs from that which Paul used in his image. We must not forget that this "de-absolutization" of man is something that Paul identifies simply with evil, while for him only free interiority is identified with good. Even if we understand and accept what Rahner says, his formula as quoted above is not a Pauline one. Paul would have said that man never disposes of himself as a whole, hence he does evil.

Paul would not deny what Rahner says. The effect of the law of minimum effort is that both virtue and crime go badly for man; that he is bad at being a saint and at being a criminal; that he is a *poor man,* much akin to inert beings and quite different from the creative being he aspires to be; that it costs him to be consistent with himself, both in fulfilling the law and in violating it.

It is not certain that forbidden fruit is more appetizing than permitted fruit. But it is certain that it costs more to be a person, to be oneself, than to let oneself be carried along by instinct, by what everyone says and does—either for or against the law.

3. What is it, then, that permits Paul to say that the inner man and his governing law decide upon the *good,* but that the outer man and his governing law perform *evil?* Would we not have to say that evil and good confront each other in both realms, in the realm of decision and the realm of performance?

To understand this point, which is fundamental in all of Christian anthropology, we must recall Paul's conception of Christian moral life.[11] For him there no longer exists within the Christian outlook a law which, independent of us, fixes what is licit and illicit, good and bad. The only law of the Christian is to love, and to do this in a creative way. Each one of us must fashion a unique and novel love in the face of the unique and novel needs of our neighbors—that is, those around us who share our existence with us.

Thus all love is good if it is true, authentic love: i.e., self-giving. Why does this seem strange to us? Precisely because we readily and imperceptibly shift from self-giving love to a superficially similar reality that is no longer self-giving at all. The superficial similarity explains why we apply the same word, love, to the two different realities. When does sin come on the scene within the Christian outlook? Not when we love such and such a person, but when authentic love is converted into egotism *so that it may be carried out more easily;* when in some imperceptible way that which started out as love is limited and restricted by considerations of ease.

Let us consider an example. Two married people love each other. Each seeks the welfare of the other. Over the long haul this is a difficult task and becomes more and more demanding. Even while they maintain the same forms of affection, they can grow weary of love with its incessant demands for fresh creativity and deeper intimacy. It is often obvious that it is easier to replace creative intimacy with homey comfort and superficial gifts that make living together easier—but on a more superficial level. An automobile can often be used to replace the costly effort at deeper understanding. And they may have to choose between an automobile and a baby.

It is at this point that the evil *becomes apparent*. But let us make no mistake, it was already there. It was not a matter of using or not using the pill, but of renouncing the demands of authentic love and replacing them with facile solutions dictated by egotism. Even a baby can be the facile solution of egotism, as Vatican II indicates when it says that parents have a responsibility to plan their family.

Another area where true love is transformed into facile egotism quite readily is the area of social reform. A person wants social reforms but prescinds entirely from the welfare of other people. Authentic love sees the societal arena as a precondition for the human fulfillment of those it loves. To love others authentically means to give them a society in which they can develop and reach fulfillment. To impatiently tear down the foundations of the society in which other men live, out of supposed love for them, is either a mistake or a sin. Not *in spite of* love, but precisely *on account of* love and its demands. And the same holds true when we cling to a law that favors us or protects us unjustly.

What is even more important to realize here is that while love may penetrate our being forcefully, egotism by contrast quietly takes control of our love. It is not expressed clearly and openly in denial of love. It is expressed obscurely in our *bad faith*, whereby we maintain the forms and expressions and gestures of love even though we have already said no to its spirit and its demands.

This is what Paul is referring to. In reality man has no original, interior, personal motivation that does not impel him toward love: i.e., to take what he is and give it to another person. This is the authentic *law*, the divine law, which Paul calls "spiritual" to differentiate it from a law that specifies what is permitted and what is prohibited. In the inner heart of man this divine law is the one and only law. On this level man does not decide between good and evil. The whole inner man agrees with this law that comes from God.

But then comes the task of *carrying out* love, of translating it into an external reality, not just talk, but something real and active, as John puts it. And it is there that the law of minimum effort offers egotism a thousand opportunities to take control of love and, under the pretext of carrying it out, to restrict and eliminate it. It is very easy to terminate our efforts at loving while pretending we are still working at it. It is very easy to box love in routine and to evade resolving its difficulties in a creative way. And when we reach this point, we are saying no to love and doing evil—whether we are within the law or outside it, whether we are doing permitted things or forbidden things.

In other words, man decides between being truly *free* and personal by choosing love and the good and *letting himself be alienated* by the law of nature through setting limits on love and practicing egotism and evil.

To be sure, not every consideration of ease is egotistical. Like everything natural it can and should serve love. But it tends to betray us when we use it. No sooner have we started out, no sooner have we set our hands on this instrument, than we allow ourselves to be taken over by it. No longer are we doing what we chose to do, no longer are we ourselves. We are alienated from ourselves, we are no longer free. And the proof of this is that when we look at the end result, we do not understand what we have done with our love. We do not recognize it, it is not ours. That is precisely what Paul is saying.

4. For Paul, then, liberty—not the mere capacity to choose but the positive quality of determining one's own existence for oneself—is *the good*. Non-liberty—allowing oneself to be taken over by egotism and ease, which is the law that, ruling us from outside our being—is *the evil*.

And this should enlighten us about something else in the New Testament that would otherwise seem strange to us. We find it especially in the epistles of Paul and the Gospel of John. According to these sources, what is it that is opposed to the work of Christ in us? It is not this or that specific "sin," this or that concrete, deliberate infraction of the law. From a much more radical and structural point of view, it is the three elements whose significance we have just discovered: (1) *the flesh,* which for Paul does not signify sex but the weight which the human condition brings to bear on our liberty; (2) *the world,* which for John signifies the vicious circle of easy egotism that hems in love; (3) *the father of lies,* since lying is precisely the inauthenticity with which we hide the truth from ourselves, denying love and alienating ourselves while we pretend to be continuing on the pathway of love.

We must recognize something essential here. While gratuitousness is an essential aspect of God's grace (that is why it is called grace), even more essential is the fact that it makes us too capable of gratuitousness, creation, and liberty (which is another reason why it is called grace, as we pointed out in the Introduction).

Thus grace and personality, grace and liberty, grace and youthfulness, grace and creation, are synonymous. And, on the other hand, impersonality, alienation, decrepitude, and routine are synomyms for what man in the concrete is without grace. They form an experiential description of the starting point from which grace takes us in order to heal us and make us fully human. The *length-dimension* of grace and its dynamism is the point at which we cease to be mere things and begin to be human beings.

One final question. We try to examine our conscience before God, a God who "plumbs the hearts of men." In doing this, is it right to catalogue our "sins" without going on to consider that which truly sets us up in opposition to God's grace in a much more thoroughgoing way: namely, the inauthenticity of our love or of our loves? Perhaps we would do well to turn a prayer that was formerly used on Tuesday of Holy Week into our permanent petition: "O God, by your mercy cleanse us of the deceitfulness of our old selves and enable us to increase in new holiness."

NOTES TO CHAPTER ONE

1. We do not feel it is worthwhile here to get into the centuries-old debate between exegetes on the meaning of the "I" which appears in Paul's text as the subject of this divided existence. It could be the personification of a universal human experience; the description of Paul's own existence prior to becoming a Christian; or even a description of his existence as a Christian, provided it is understood that the painful division has already been overcome *in principle*. Paul has this to say about the ultimate realities which are already present but still unseen and subject to our option. "In baptism also you were raised to life with him . . ." (Col. 2:12). "Even we, to whom the Spirit is given as firstfruits of the harvest to come, are groaning inwardly while we wait for God to make us his sons and set our whole body free" (Rom. 8:23).

In any case every Christian will readily recognize himself in Paul's description. As we shall see in Chapter IV, even though grace has transformed us, the basic human condition is not part of some past that has been abolished completely.

2. We are aware that we are using reified language here. The knowledgeable reader in this area will be uncomfortable with talk about one thing being "added" to another, and with good reason. But there is no way to avoid such language at the start. Gradually as our thinking on this topic proceeds and deepens, we shall talk instead about a reality from above being "inserted" into a living framework. Then the language will change again, and we shall talk about a divine, personalizing reality that lays hold of our nature, masters it, and makes use of it.

3. *Cf.* St. Augustine, *Opera Omnia: Appendix ad Epist. XVII*, Migne, PL.

4. The principal elements in the present-day analysis of concupiscence can be found in an article by Karl Rahner entitled, "The Theological Concept of Concupiscentia," which can be found in *Theological Investigations*, I, (Baltimore: Helicon Press; London: Darton, Longman & Todd, 1961), pp. 347–382.

Translator's note: This Spanish series cites the Spanish translation of this particular volume. I translate the Spanish texts here, with an eye on the fine

English translation by Cornelius Ernst, O.P. Since this series is aimed at a broader range of people than Rahner's writings themselves, direct translation of the Spanish translation of Rahner's articles ensures a style more in keeping with the whole tenor of the volume. But the title of the article in English is cited for the reader who wishes to tackle the full text.

5. Rahner writes: "What is certain is that all nature which precedes liberty offers resistance to the total and free self-availability and self-disposability of the person," *ibid.*

6. "In terms of the distinction just made [i.e., nature versus person, see previous note], the spontaneous appetitive act belongs to nature," *ibid.*

7. *Ibid.*

8. *Ibid.*

9. With these words Paul is not seeking to diminish man's moral responsibility. What man is responsible for here is precisely evading his responsibility. Liberty is lost "freely." On the language difficulty here, see CLARIFICATION I in this Chapter.

10. See note 4. "From what has been said it is clear that in a theological sense concupiscence as such cannot be qualified in moral terms. Speaking in strict theological terms, therefore, we should not talk about 'bad' concupiscence. Considered in terms of its full theological import, concupiscence can also operate positively; it can be the resistance of nature to an evil moral decision, which makes it less absolute" (*ibid.*).

11. See Volume I, Chapter V, in this series. For this reason we cannot accept the explanation offered by one approach to the natural law which seeks to decipher the licitness or illicitness of an action in itself and isolated from the context of man's intended plan. That approach is not justified in claiming to be a faithful rendition of Paul's teaching on liberty. It would be in the case where a person spontaneously carries out what has been commanded without taking note of the fact that a law exists. This would be nothing more than the fulfillment of the messianic prophecies uttered by Jeremiah and Ezekiel. But the Gospel and Paul go much further. Man is no longer under the law, not only because he does not feel he is but also because he should not feel he is by right. He must now make himself lord of the universe in fact; and it is a universe wherein he no longer questions the licitness of things but rather their usefulness for a love that is ever original and personal.

CLARIFICATIONS

I. IN SEARCH OF A TERMINOLOGY

A basic element in understanding Christian existence is the work of pinpointing the inner struggle that divides man. This being the case, we cannot be indifferent about efforts to find equivalents in today's vocabulary for Paul's talk about the "inmost self" and the "law of our bodily members."

What is more, we have good reason to believe that this theme has been greatly enriched by current thinking in philosophy, theology, and literature. That is all the more reason why we should avoid verbal confusion and establish the foundations of a terminology which will give us access to these riches.

1. A few years ago Jean Paul Sartre popularized a definition of existentialism in which "existence precedes essence." By this he meant that man does not carry the being that he will be at the end of his life as something already inscribed in the essence with which he is born. On the contrary, he freely defines his being in the process of existing. It is not that man *wills* in accordance with what he is; he *is* what he wills. In other words, an undefined range of pathways opens up before man at the start. He freely enters certain pathways which will bring him, at the end, to *his* pathway, to the unique, irrevocable pathway he has chosen: his definitive essence.

It is easy to criticize the element of unreality and exaggeration in this conception, which is a reaction to the equally unreal and exaggerated element in the opposite position. The latter sees the final pathway already defined for man, physically or morally, by a law that was his specific essence and that dictated power and value to him. In the best of cases, his existence was nothing more than the actualization or fulfillment of the essence that dominated him from the beginning. Essence, in short, preceded and defined existence.

As we just said, it is easy to point out the element of exaggeration in both positions. That is precisely what Paul does in his description. Liberty, particularly in the beginning, does not possess the measure of power that the first outlook attributes to it. Nor does essence, particularly at the end, define the existence of a human being so definitively and totally as the second outlook would maintain.

The reality is more complicated. But what concerns us here is not the reality but the terminology involved. In the duality which is my human existence, there certainly is something which precedes and limits my liberty, which does not come from me, which has been imposed on me and which, even though it belongs to my being, I cannot recognize as my deepest and most authentic ego. This is what Sartre calls *essence*. Current philosophy uses a more up-to-date term: *nature*. It is the "law of my bodily members" in Paul's terminology.

But whether it is realized or not, there is also something which I will to be, which corresponds or claims to correspond to my more inner and personal reality, which is the valuable thing for me toward which everything must be oriented. This is what Sartre calls *existence*. Current philosophy again uses a more up-to-date term: *liberty*. It is the "inmost self" in Paul's terminology.

These are the two elements that struggle with each other to determine the existence of man. Man cannot eliminate either of them, for the simple reason that they are not only opposed but also complementary.

An example will help us to understand this, and it will bring us to another important term in this matter: *determinism*.

Human plans and projects require instruments for their carrying out. And the reader will recall that it was here, in the transition from planning to carrying out, from interior decision to the members charged to carry it out, that Paul saw man's work turn into something incomprehensible to its very author. It slipped out of his hands and became something strange and alienated.

Suppose I need a horse to get from one place to another. Now the horse has a life of his own. He has his own internal mechanism and his own "intentions," and my desire to get someplace does not directly enter here at all. One must get these different things to *coincide*. A balance must be established between the natural needs of the horse, his natural fidelity to his master, or his fear of punishment on the one hand, and my intention to travel on the other. Now this presupposes in me, the rider, some knowledge of the horse and, what is more, some measured pampering of the horse's own life if I am to achieve my objective. I certainly will not achieve this objective by using the law of minimum effort, which would leave me at the mercy of my horse's "intentions."

So we have opposition and complementarity, analogous to that between essence and existence, nature and liberty, interior man and law of the bodily members. As a result of this opposition-complementarity, there is always a compromise in the end result. In other words, the end result is something different from my initial plan. To use the horse example again: I may have to decrease my speed, or take detours, or trust blindly to his sense of direction in order to get where I want to go. And it might even turn out that I don't get there because my instrument gets control over me.

In reality this often happens imperceptibly. The difficulties involved in maintaining control over my instruments lead me to "forget" my original project or to cut it down to suit the amount of effort I am willing to expend. Hence the enigma that our own labor often presents to us. The unhappy fact is that every project we envision must be carried out with "borrowed" instruments that have a life of their own, that have dynamisms which ignore our pretended claims to utilize them. And these borrowed instruments are not only the things outside me. They include my own body and mind and emotions, as well as the physical and social structures in which I am inscribed.

What is more, we must do more than admit an opposition between essence, nature, and law of our bodily members on the one hand, and existence, liberty, and interior man on the other. We must also confess that the odds are heavily weighted on the side of the former. I can will the good but I cannot carry it out, as Paul says.

In other words, nature has on its side the power of the systems that make it up. And I am within nature, with only my faculty for understanding and willing.

Thus liberty does not constitute a spiritual zone that is threatened by the power of the senses and the material world. It is the capacity to bestow meaning and value on elements which, both inside me and outside me (i.e., in both the sensible and the spiritual realm),[1] constitute systems that are independent of my free will. My process of digestion is one example. My class mentality with its concepts, explanations, and prejudices is another.

2. Now if this is the case, then at this point our terminological problem arrives at two other terms that must be clarified: *determinism* and *free will*.

We all agree now that nature for us means all that which conditions liberty—on whatever level or plane of human existence it may be. And we know what "conditions" means: to make possible and to limit at the same time. There is no liberty without these forces of primary nature (both those of my own being and those of my environment) and of our cultural "second nature" (again both those of my own being and those of my environment); it is these forces that constitute its only instruments for carrying out its work. And there is no liberty that does not clash and compromise with them.

If we want to be honest, then, we could say that at first glance nature seems more like the complex of *determinisms* that makes our liberty illusory. There is in fact nothing wrong with describing the natural dynamisms, both within and outside me, as determinisms. For the fact is that they are not neutral forces that stand passively at the disposal of some dominating will. But there is a great difference between talking about determinisms and propounding *determinism* (i.e., the nonexistence of liberty). To say that liberty is confronted with determinisms is the same as Paul saying that the inner man is confronted with the law of his members. That does not mean that my liberty is illusory, that it is nothing and cannot be anything. It simply means that it is not a "faculty" (like memory or the senses) which, starting with the use of reason, produces free acts as man gets used to operating reflectively and deliberately rather than on the basis of first impulse.

We can prove from our own experience that this is not the case. Even if willing is easy, the very first step toward carrying it out is not. The very attempt to express what I will involves a struggle against the mechanisms that control the formation of images, concepts, and ultimately the content and organization of words in logical language. All this being quite aside from the fact that saying is one thing and doing is another.

Besides, all of us have surely experienced the situation we mentioned earlier. We tend to "forget" our initial plans; or to cut them down to suit the amount of effort we are willing to put into them. Have we not often told others, and even convinced ourselves, that we have arrived right where we planned to go, when in fact we were stranded there by a horse we could not control? Translate the image to the political plane and you will find the same thing. We often choose not to see something that would mean too costly an expansion of our own ideological horizons.

So in other words liberty operates, first and foremost, in the realm of truth. It operates against bad faith and the deceitful tendencies whereby we pass off, as our own, things that are in fact imposed upon us by the determinisms with which we work, think, and feel. One of the most fundamental phrases in the Christian message concerning man's life is that in John 8:32: "The truth will set you free."

Thus the struggle for truth—and liberty—is a struggle to *interpret* in all our end results that which truly comes from us; to separate it from that which is spuriously presented as ours. The primary victory of liberty will be to separate what is ours from that which "lodges in us" (Paul).

Our cultural world today has discovered, explicitly and systematically, the scope and irreplaceable value of this *hermeneutic;* i.e., the process of interpretation in every domain of the human, in order to de-alienate man and put him back on the pathway of truth and liberty.[2]

Hermeneutics, stripped of its false limitations and antagonisms, is many things. It is Marxism, criticizing ideologies and looking for social truth that lies buried in structures that alienate man. It is the whole effort undertaken since Freud to unmask the real motives behind human conduct and to restore man to the truth of his projected aims. It is also phenomenology in its deeper sense and its study of inauthentic phenomena.

Perhaps it may help to point out here that in our concrete life such liberating interpretation is never the result of mere laboratory work. To repeat once again: bad faith is the product of one or a few determinisms that work on us through the law of minimum effort. Suppose, for example, that I do not see certain realities which go beyond those that are present or admitted in my own social class. I will continue in this blindness until some other determinism comes along to balance the weight of the earlier ones. This new force could come from any number of "systems": e.g., sexual attraction, changed economic picture, aggressiveness toward some type of political or parental authority.

So what do we conclude from this? Precisely this: That determinism does not exist to the extent that *determinisms* in the plural do exist and operate.

And there is something else that is important. Liberty is not ready-made. It is not some liberated, spiritual, numinal zone wherein man is able to construct his own existence. Liberty is a *possibility* given and a value to be won by handling an ever increasing number of determinisms.

Education does not consist in "habituating" someone to perform determined things. The only authentic human education is an education in liberty, one which opens up a broad enough range of human interests so that the person being educated can combine them and balance them off in an ever richer and more complete way—presuming that he chooses freely to be an active participant in his education. The man of only one interest, one passion, one determinism is a slave.

Now from the viewpoint of terminology, how would we define the situation of this slave (to the senses, to some ideology, or whatever)? Would we say that he does not possess *liberty?* Certainly he always possesses some minimal possibility of broadening his system of motivations and progressing to a new form of equilibrium. That is why some prefer to apply the term *free will* (*liberum arbitrium*) to this basic remnant inherent in every human psyche, and to reserve the term *liberty* for the value that this type of person certainly does not possess. Indeed no one really possesses the latter except to a certain degree, this always depending on what his free will decides. For a person can freely refuse to be free, and liberty is nothing else but a liberation that is freely realized. *Liberty is chosen.* And it must be chosen constantly.

But there is no break in continuity between enslaved free will and operative liberty that is ever jeopardized. For this reason we prefer to take the terminological risk of calling both *liberty.* We apply the term both to the basic faculty we possess and to what we actually choose. Context will indicate when we are referring to the basic underlying possibility and when we are referring to the noblest human task: that of man making himself master of his own destiny.

3. Finally the reader may be inclined to ask another question here. If we take *nature* to mean the opposite of liberty, to mean all the determinisms that condition and limit man's freely chosen projects, are we then referring to the same reality which theology sets up in opposition to the notion of the *supernatural?*

At first glance the answer would seem to be no. Why? Because here both nature and liberty are taken in their philosophical sense and therefore seem to be part of the natural realm, in terms of the traditional theological distinction.

However, everything that we shall see in this book will lead us to make an ever closer identification between liberty and grace: i.e., between liberty realized and the divine, supernatural gift. Thus, in parallel fashion, we can say that the nature which is surpassed by God's gift is the same nature that is ruled by real liberty which is exercised and turned into self-giving love. Even more clearly than in Volume I we shall see that nature and the supernatural are inextricably bound together in every human action, even though the two notions are not at all confused with each other.

Even now we can appreciate something that will be treated in greater detail further on. We can see how nature can show up as "fallen" with respect to liberty and God's gift. Insofar as we allow things to drift instead of imprinting our liberty on the forces at our disposal, we immerse ourselves once again in the natural and the pre-human. We revert to the *natural plane of things.* Realized liberty can only be a gift of self, love. Egotism, even when it is freely chosen by liberty, represents a surrender to the impersonal, the easy way out. To the extent that egotism is introduced into love, the human person is transformed into a thing desired and love is transformed into an appetite. The interpersonal relationship is replaced by a relationship between things.

In reality, then, man's free will chooses between free, personal, supernatural love and the natural, pre-human egotism that is devoid of liberty and personality. In Paul's conception of man, the image of "slavery" is as central and essential as the image of "redemption." Indeed the latter is the slave's return to freedom and self-mastery.

Now to talk about slavery is to talk about *alienation*. And this certainly means alienation with regard to liberty, alienation within history. In other words: the economic alienation discussed by Marx and the psychological alienation discussed by Freud cannot be alien to the Christian conception of redemption. The Christian way of life must always begin with a process of *interpretation* that eliminates the alienation. Without such an interpretation Christianity itself—in its verbal, dogmatic, and communitarian expression—could turn into an obstacle to Christ's redemptive work.

II. APPROACHING FREUD'S TERMINOLOGY

We cannot conclude our discussion of terminology without taking note of another vocabulary that is bandied about in many educated circles today. Freud's terminology is interwoven with the terms that we tried to clarify in the preceding section. In Volume V of this series, entitled *Evolution and Guilt,* we shall try to look directly at Freud's interpretation of individual and cultural psychic evolution. But here we should like to say a few words about his vocabulary. Hopefully they will help the reader who is familiar with Freud's terminology to orientate himself to our theological effort here. Hopefully they will also help the Christian who wishes to approach Freud's work from the starting point of the theology of grace.

This is no easy matter. What is more, certain ideological presuppositions in Freud's work would rule out any *formal* attempt to find a common vocabulary. But any great work opens up broader perspectives than those which are canonized in what might be called its "official system." We feel there is room for a richer and deeper interpretation, and that such an interpretation can provide the keys for an enriching dialogue. Such an interpretation is attempted by Paul Ricoeur in his book, *De l'Interpretation: Un essai sur Freud.* His interpretation is based on Freud's doctrine, but it goes much further than what Freud himself explicitly states. For this reason, and quite understandably, it is the subject of much debate. But because it has been worked out from within a Christian perspective, it lends support to our effort here.

As most people know, one of Freud's principles divided psychic phenomena into three zones (or systems): the unconscious, the subconscious (or preconscious), and the conscious. In reality the degree of consciousness does not affect our opposition between Paul's "inmost self" and the law of our bodily members. It is evident, however, that everything unconscious *in se* and of its very nature must be set up in opposition to man's liberty.

The same holds true for Freud's second division: *id, ego,* and *super-ego.* As Ricoeur says quite rightly: "The question of the ego is not the question of consciousness because the question of becoming conscious, which is the central theme of the first division, is not identical with the problem of turning oneself into an I. Freud never confused these two questions . . . The real problematic issue of the ego . . . goes beyond the alternative of being loved or hated. It finds its fundamental expression in the alternative of dominating or being dominated, being the master or being a slave." [3]

Thus in his discussion of the *ego* Freud approaches Marx's problem of alienation, Nietzsche's problem of weakness[4] and, we would say, Paul's problem of the inner man who is stripped of control over his efforts by a law that is more powerful than his ego. Thus it is possible to open up a pathway to our theme through Freud's theme dealing with the *ego*.

What is more, the other two terms (*id* and *super-ego*) can be framed more precisely from within this standpoint. In terms of domination and alienation, they are precisely the things that deprive the ego of ownership and personality with regard to its works. We could say that they represent the two elements which unite against liberty: (1) the primary nature that suffuses man by virtue of his biological and instinctive life; (2) the secondary nature introduced into man through cultural imperatives, an ethical code that is regarded as natural,[5] and a religion conceived as a magical illusion.[6]

Hence Freud himself states: "The *super-ego* is always close to the *id*, and it can operate as the latter's representative in the face of the *ego*. It is rooted in the *id* and hence is further from consciousness than the *ego*." [7] In terms of domination and liberty, "the *super-ego* and the *id* belong to the same system." [8]

In terms of vocabulary we find a difference here that might seem to be an opposition. But it is more apparent than real. Freud describes the *super-ego* as an "alien land within." [9] The term "alien" refers to the alienation of the *ego* already mentioned. The contrast between *interior* and *exterior*, however, is used by Freud in a sense that is directly opposite to Paul's contrast between the *inner* and *outer* man. But the opposition is not irreconcilable. For Freud exteriority is synonymous with the authenticity of a fully realized *ego*. It is the *ego* whose liberty is verified in and by external reality. And Paul too sees the inner man as truly real only when he can externalize his intentions in concrete fulfillments. He is truly free only in the exterior world. If he measured his liberty solely in terms of enunciating his plans, then he would be alienated.

In like manner, what is called liberty encounters a nature which in some obscure way opposes man, with the result that he is surprised to find that he cannot recognize his original intention in what he actually does. He allows himself to get lost in obscurity rather than controlling and verifying his plans with hard reality. Freud focuses on the mental process here and calls the whole thing "internal." Paul calls it the "law of our bodily members" or the "exterior man," meaning that ultimately the world of external reality takes over man's activity and snatches it from his control.

Thus exteriority and interiority designate contrary things for Paul and Freud. But once we appreciate what each means, we have one more reason for exploring Freud's theories in terms of our present topic: "Freud wants the analyzand to take feelings and experiences that were alien to him and make them his own; to broaden the scope of consciousness; to live better and be a little freer; and to be a little happier insofar as that is possible. One of the first tributes paid to psychoanalysis regarded it as a 'cure for conscience.' The tribute is apt, insofar as psychoanalysis seeks to replace an instinctive, deceitful conscience dominated by an inner darkness with a reflecting consciousness that is guided by the reality principle." [10]

III. THE SOCIAL DIMENSION OF GRACE AND SIN

Throughout this chapter we have analyzed grace as a dynamism that liberates man. It takes as its starting point the human condition, which tends to impose the inertia of its determinisms on man and to sidetrack his projects for self-realization. Thus man appears to be a divided being, enticed on the one hand by determinisms that lead toward alienation and on the other hand by a liberty that urges him to fashion his own personal being.

Now it would be an error to conceive these dehumanizing determinisms solely in psychological and individual terms. To be sure, it is the determinisms of our psychobiological instincts that we experience most directly. So when Paul talks about the law of our bodily members fighting against our inner mind, we immediately think of the countless psychological forms our egotism takes to vitiate love. When we say that man is a divided being, we spontaneously advert to our own painful experience of bad faith, to those times when we know to some extent that we are not really carrying out the project we had envisioned initially.

But sin is not exhausted when we admit the determinisms that affect us as individuals. Nor is grace exclusively a liberative dynamism that allows us to gradually gain control over the inertia of our individual nature. If grace and sin were restricted in this way, then we would necessarily hit upon erroneous solutions with regard to the social and political realm. We would be inclined to say, as some Catholics do indeed say: "If we change individuals, then society itself would be transformed automatically." Such a statement is based on an erroneous conception of man. It does not appreciate the fact that the individual can be truly liberated only in terms of his total human condition: i.e., within his *social context*.

To what extent does this social context broaden the horizons of sin and grace, of enslavement and liberation? What determinisms, distinct from psychobiological ones, approach man by way of his social dimension, posing a new problem to the liberating dynamism of grace?

In order to answer this question, we must begin by clearing up an ambiguity in the term "social dimension." The social realm, at first glance, would appear to be essentially liberative. Suppose, for example, we have an individual whose whole life is centered around himself. He is enslaved within the narrow circle of his own selfish interests and concerns. Suddenly he breaks through this vicious circle and opens up to others, to self-giving and gratuitousness. Doesn't this opening up to the social dimension represent the triumph of grace over sin, of liberty over slavery? It does indeed! But the point is that here we are not interested in the moral connotation embodied in the contrast between individualistic outlook and social outlook. We are referring to something more fundamental when we talk about the "social dimension" here. We are referring to the fact that society is not the end result of juxtaposing already constituted individuals, that from the very start it is a system of human reactions and interrelationships that constitute the individual and form part of his total human condition. Thus we cannot talk about two types of conscience or human awareness: i.e., an individual conscience and then a social conscience that is added to it. There is one and only one conscience: The conscience of an "I" that is and must be fashioned within us in such a way that when we say "I," even from a highly individualistic viewpoint, this "I" is already inhabited by others (Fichte).

In saying this we are simply reaffirming a basic outlook that has been won by contemporary thought. This outlook is highly important for our problem here, especially further on when we seek to find out what is the scope of this "we" and what others we are referring to when we say that our "I" is already inhabited by others.

When we talk about *us* and *others,* these words take in society as a whole. From the very beginning of a man's life, even within the private and affective relations of the nuclear family, a culture is being transmitted to him. He encounters the norms, values, and behavior patterns that form the basis of a consensus which makes societal life possible and orderly. From the very beginning of man's life, he is being brought into relationship with all of society—in a way that is no less real for being indirect.

The social sphere, viewed as a dimension constitutive of man rather than as the content of conscience, confronts man with a new source of determinisms. And these determinisms are all the more dangerous in that they are normally lived inadvertently. What is transmitted to the individual and assimilated by him uncritically is the result of a cultural objectification. It is a readymade moral code which will hinder man's freedom to create values insofar as he does not take conscious note of it.

But there is more involved here. These norms, values, attitudes, and behavior patterns, which form the basic consensus of a given society, are an expression of the *way* in which the society's members conceive and experience their relationships with others—whether they realize it or not. And at the same time they are a *justification* of these relationships which are imposed and perpetuated by existing structures. In other words: the established moral code takes on the characteristics of an ideology justifying the situation.

To clarify this point, we must advert to some basic features of societal organization. Firstly there is the question that has preoccupied man throughout history: How are we to organize man's societal life? All societal systems, from the undifferentiated agrarian society of long ago to the complex industrial society of today, represent an attempt to answer that question. And there is no doubt that through these varied efforts man has been discovering new values and forms of coexistence. Here we are not interested in analyzing the mechanism and process of their evolution. But we are interested in pointing out certain other things. First of all any given social system, by its very existence, is a continuing expression of a specific way of conceiving interhuman relationships. In the great empires of antiquity we find small elites enjoying a high degree of culture at the expense of the masses, who are bound to servile work and slavery. Here we find expressed a conception of societal relationships that is centered around the notion of people being unequal, due to their race or family origins. In the Middle Ages we find society divided into closed estates composed of serfs and lords, whose place is dictated by birth. Here again we have a conception of societal life that accepts inequality as an intrinsic element of societal organization.

Secondly, we want to point out that any societal system tends to be embodied in institutions which perpetuate it. Owner-worker relationships, the regulation of economic transactions, and the situation of individuals vis-à-vis the means of production find expression in the economic structure. The mechanisms of control and authority, the relationships between different social classes, and participation in political decision-making find expression in the political structure. And these two structures generate a third structure, ideology, which is meant to justify the existing relations in a society. Without such ideological justification, it would be absolutely impossible for societies to endure for long periods of time when they in fact sanction flagrant inequities between human beings.

As we said before, the established morality (or the social conscience) is the complex of values and behavior patterns which a society communicates to its members. Now, in the light of all that has been said above, it acquires a new connotation. It is not just that it confronts the individual with a new fount of determinisms. These determinisms are also prejudiced in favor of vested interests within the society. They justify and perpetuate the existence of a dominant minority and a dominated majority. The established morality expresses the interests of a societal minority even though it may be shared by the whole society.

This may help the reader to understand better what we said earlier: That the individual can only be liberated within his total human condition, within his social context. It may also point up the significance of our question: To what extent does the social context amplify the horizons of grace and sin?

Man's liberation must necessarily involve his conscious realization of the unconscious determinisms that surround him. It takes concrete form when he shoulders the task of moving from an established morality that he did not choose to a creative morality involving the formulation of a new societal scheme, and then engages in action to transform the structures which are perpetuating his alienation. In short, it is concretized in ideological transformation and political action.

IV. IMAGES OF LIBERTY IN LITERATURE

It is not enough to attempt to work out a terminology. We must let the image bring something of its richness to the abstract concept. The image of liberty which finds expression in man's imaginative works contains hues and overtones that are useful to us here. One of the most essential connotations here is the frequently recurring tieup between liberty and risk. We shall try to bring out this connotation by discussing two literary "parables" which are separated both in terms of time and the situation of their authors.

We shall start with the more recent one, which is characterized by a radical atheism and which presents a noteworthy re-creation of the hu-

man situation we are talking about. In his work, *The Flies,* Jean Paul
Sartre makes a vigorous protest against a system which he regards as one
that oppresses man and destroys truly human values. He also stresses the
inescapable values of real human liberty. Such liberty, to be real, must
call into question human security when the latter is hollow and devoid
of subjective commitment and decision-making. In *The Flies,* the character Orestes embodies a complex of characteristics that are the outright
negation of everything truly human. He has submitted to an existence
without roots, without guilt, without personal stands, without creation.
It seems that for Sartre these characteristics embody the direct opposite
of an authentic existence.

Orestes arrives at Argos as a young man. Up to this moment he has
not experienced in the flesh the tragedy of his family: Agamemnon as-
sassinated, Electra enslaved by her mother, Aegisthus the traitor. And suddenly he realizes how he has been robbed of his past. He is a man without
any baggage because he has been spared the work of truly living his life.
There is so much that could have been but never was. He was spared terrible sufferings. His companion, the tutor, tries to console him by calling
attention to all the knowledge he has gained by virtue of the fact that he
was not encumbered by his accursed family. Instead of living with his
accursed family, he has learned much about different cultures and peoples. The tutor urges Orestes to rejoice over his youth, his learning, and
his good fortune. He is "free of enslaving bonds and beliefs—without
family, homeland, religion, or duty." He is free of compromise and commitments, and he knows that he need never get entangled with them. In
short, he has no reason to complain because he is "a superior man who
can teach philosophy or architecture in some great city university." [11]

Now all this depends on the absence of commitment. Only in this
way will he be fashioned into a superior person. But Orestes does not see
it this way. Recognizing his privileged situation, he sees it as a hollow
thing and complains bitterly: "You leave me the liberty of those strands
which the winds tears away from a spider's web. They float away in the
air. I weigh no more than they, and I am floating like them in the air." [12]
It is a feeling of weightlessness that also seems to guarantee his uselessness.

A human being is worth something because his memories are his own.
They are the point of departure for new options, for new marks he can
imprint in the body of time. The exiled Orestes has nothing that is truly
his own. Everything he sees and smells and touches belongs to others, and
he could never turn them into his own.[13] The world of this family that
slaughters its own has slipped through his fingers. Nothing is left for him,
not even repentance, as it is for the others who committed or suffered
evil. He has been alienated from his past, and he laments the loss. Hor-
rible as it might have been, at least it would have been his. As it is now,
not even the heat that burns down on him is his own; it belongs to others.
He and the tutor are about to melt "in the heat of another." [14] Since
everything around him belongs to others, he envies them. He would like
to have had a part in their crime, for that would give him roots: "If only
there were some act that would give me citizenship rights among them.
If only, even at the cost of committing a crime, I could come into posses-

sion of their memories, fears, and hopes. If only I could fill the emptiness of my heart, even if it meant killing my own mother. . . !" [15]

He means this, even though the lives of these other people are inhuman and laden with crimes. Electra recalls it all when talking about the absurd practice of public confessions that is customary among the people of Argos. But Orestes has no guilt or fault. He will be a stranger even to his sister if he does not choose to commit a crime with her. He will have chosen the liberty of a stranger who grew up in an alien city that is not really his own. Such a liberty cannot make him what he should be; it cannot make him a real human being.

Electra now needs him to carry out a real human task. It is not something that can be carried out by an exile from life. She has no part with upright souls. What she needs is "an accomplice." [16] Here we have another feature of liberty that is truly human: it involves being implicated in the lives of others. It has nothing to do with the spotless isolation of souls that remain too unblemished because they do not participate in the drama of human life.

Now "to participate" means to "take part in." And to do this one must "take sides." Orestes asks himself: "Who am I and what am I to do?" [17] And he answers this question by considering how alienated he has been up to now from his native city and its inhabitants. Only by taking part in the tragic struggle going on between his kin can he reconcile himself with them once more: "I choose to be a man who takes sides." [18] This means nothing more or less than being "a man among men." [19] He will wrap the city around himself like a mantle,[20] he says, thus indicating clearly his desire to be a human being no matter what the cost. He chooses to confront the people who have fashioned the tragic fate of his family. Even more importantly, he chooses to confront the gods as mysterious and suprahuman forces. This latter obstacle is the greatest one to be overcome.

The gods represent superior myths about the unknown. They fashion a superworld that is capable of choking man with fear. The counterweight to this fact is the "sad secret of gods and kings: that human beings are free." [21] But human beings surrender to the dazzling radiance of these mysterious powers. They abdicate their own selves and surrender their human options in favor of some divine power. In the name of religion or order, they set up some law extrinsic to themselves as the criterion of their own actions. Heteronomy replaces autonomy. And this criterion is grounded on unknown external forces, on egotistical and whimsical anxieties that make order an end in itself. It becomes desirable as a refuge from the critical demands of real living and choosing. Aegisthus admits this to Jupiter because both are kings. They are colleagues in terms of power and the religious fear they instill. Aegisthus asks: "Who am I but the fear that other men have of me?" [22] Jupiter replies: "Once liberty has broken out in man's heart, the gods can do no more against him." [23]

Now the independence described so far could be the endpoint of it all. But basically it represents a negative impulse only. It is not just a matter of arriving at a certain degree of rebelliousness, at the point where one does not allow himself to be hemmed in even by the temptation to enslave others in turn. It does not end with Orestes' remark to Jupiter:

"I am neither master nor slave; I am my liberty!" [24] One must begin a long and sometimes painful process of detaching oneself from all that is most dear to man. Man must detach himself from that which fashions him, which surrounds him with a mantle of warmth and security akin to his mother's womb, and which thus hinders him from growing according to his own law. If man is to be truly man, he must break away from Nature (with a capital N) to the point where his feelings of being enveloped and well-rooted are replaced by feelings of being alone: "I am a stranger to myself, I know. Outside of nature, in opposition to nature, with only my own inner resources. But I shall not submit to your law again. I am condemned to have no other law but my own . . . I can only follow my own road. For I am a human being, Jupiter, and every human being must invent his own road. Nature is horrified by man; and so are you, Jupiter, sovereign lord of the gods." [25]

And so Orestes makes his ultimate decisions on that basis. When he takes upon himself the sins and remorse of his own people, then he will have fashioned his own road. It will involve tragedy, of course, for he will commit matricide in accord with the ancient Greek myth. But the point here is the lesson underlying the literary symbolism: Only by breaking away from enslaving bonds and committing himself to action can man achieve authentic humanization. He must take the risk of enmeshing himself in time, of plunging into earthly realities. He must take the risk of turning himself into an absolute, of losing himself in liberty.

To be sure, much remains to be thought out in Sartre's image here, insofar as the goals of this adventure are concerned. Indeed it is the task of theology to interpret a revelation that gives meaning to this work of "inventing one's path." For revelation talks about love, hope, and interpersonal rather than reifying relationships. And it gives us glimpses of some personal being who, unlike Jupiter, does not alienate man but rather summons him to be free. Even though Sartre did not perceive this, his witness is valuable nonetheless.

Alongside this relatively lengthy exposition of Sartre's image, we can examine more briefly a parable by Rodó: *The Farewell of Gorgias.*

Gorgias is about to die by taking a cup of hemlock. One of his disciples, Lucius, proposes that all his disciples swear an oath of absolute fidelity to each and every word of their master, even to "what is only implicitly contained in them." [26] In short, he proposes unconditional, paralyzing submissiveness. Gorgias responds by telling them about a dream his mother had, the interpretation of it, and the effect this had on his own life.

In the dream Gorgias' mother was greatly attached to her baby boy's innocence. She yearned for him to remain an innocent child forever, lovingly devoted to her alone. So she obtained magic potions from a sorceress that would ensure his continuing innocence. They worked for many years, and his mother kept going back to the sorceress for a fresh supply. Then one day the supply ran out. She returned home empty-handed to find herself confronted with a bitter old man. He reproached her fiercely: "Your savage egotism has robbed me of my life, offering me instead a demeaning bliss . . . You have robbed me of ennobling action, illuminating thought, and fruitful love . . . Give me back what you have taken away!" [27] But now it was too late. It was time for him to die. All he could do was to despise and curse his mother.

Here the dream of his mother ended. Now she no longer mourned the fleeting nature of an innocence that crumbled before the involvement and commitment of real life. Gorgias then offered this final counsel to his disciples: "My philosophy has been mother to your mind and conscience. It does not close the circle of your own thinking . . . Seek new love, new truth. And do not be upset if it leads you to be unfaithful to something you have heard from my lips . . ." [28] And so a toast is offered to challenge the waning twilight of Gorgias' life. His disciples will survive him and go on thinking, thus moving beyond the thought of their master which provided the first impetus.

Undoubtedly this literary passage offers a variation on the theme of liberty and its riskiness which is no less valid and relevant today. Man's life is lost not gained if it is simply preserved in a state of woeful innocence. And parallel to this is the fate of human thought when it is shackled in formulas for its self-preservation, instead of being brought into contact with reality and new problems so that it may be corrected.

Both realities, life and thought, are inextricably linked. And both call for constant risk if they are not to end up in an impersonal vacuum: hoary masks for a life that never was lived.

V. LIBERTY, RISK, AND FEAR

Here we are not going to stress the undeniable fact that liberty is associated with fear. The literary passages cited above make that abundantly clear.

On the other hand, the initial section of this chapter should make it equally clear that we must put an end to such an association if we are to be fully Christian. For liberty is the gift of God himself, the presence of divine life within us. We could say that liberty, viewed in Christian terms, entails no danger at all. On the contrary, the danger lies in the fact that our free will can renounce liberty. The danger for man lies in the possibility of reification. Man can turn his liberty into just another thing: dominated, alienated, predictable, echoing alien thoughts, and passively submitting to the impact of society.

Let us try to probe into this paradox which is one of the most profoundly Christian paradoxes of all: the terrible thing is not liberty but its opposite. Only by moving in this direction can Christianity recover its power as a revolutionary ferment within the human race.

Let us begin our search with the example suggested by Rodó. In it the child's mother is uneasy over the possibility that her son may freely choose evil. So she suppresses this possibility by suppressing liberty itself and prolonging his infancy until the very end of his life. The son, by contrast, enjoys a few brief moments of adulthood at the very end of his life. And in them he curses the egotism of his mother for having deprived him of a free, adult life. Here we have a central problem of all education for adulthood. It is faced by government rulers in their relationship with the masses, by the ecclesial hierarchy in its relationship with the faithful.

But what lies beneath the alleged egotism of the boy's mother and the curse uttered, justifiably or unjustifiably, by the dying son? Why would maturity "with evil" be preferable to a childish innocence prolonged indefinitely? One conception of liberty is operative in the protective action of the mother. Another conception of liberty is operative in the curse uttered by her son.

For the mother, liberty is merely the capacity to choose between two things. It is not a good, a value, in itself. What one chooses is good or bad. Liberty then is the possibility of choosing for oneself the value or anti-value that inheres in the actions which free will chooses between. What is more, the possibility of evil is not a part of nature; it is due solely to the existence of human liberty. So the boy's mother decides to suppress it. In this conception, the mere fact that evil is offered to man as a possibility is not compensated for by anything. Good deeds, those which entail good and positive value, can be carried out equally well with or without free will. Why? Because the value lies in the action that is chosen. If we start from the initial assumption that man's liberty is a balance scale in which good and evil are weighed, everything else follows logically from this.

For the son, who curses this maternal logic, there is only one way of refuting it. He must value *liberty itself* above the value or anti-value of the objects proposed to it. What the son says comes down to this: Whatever the end result of my choice may be, the value of me myself choosing my own destiny is always greater. I prefer to choose, whatever evil may arise from the choice made.

In other words, liberty in this view is not simply the possibility of deciding between one project and another, both of which are already endowed with some positive or negative value beforehand. Instead liberty is a value in itself, and this more than compensates for the evil that may result from the act of choice. To be free, or to become free once again, is worth the trouble it may entail.

We could say that this problem, posed on the level of what man knows when he does not have an explicit knowledge of divine revelation, is less susceptible of a solution on the one hand and easier to solve on the other hand.

What does man risk by not being free, or to put it better, by renouncing his liberty? The man on the street may not know with certainty what is involved. Or perhaps we should say that he does intuit what is involved but cannot express it exactly. A man without freedom would not be a human person. Whatever that may mean in the long run, everybody is aware that there is a certain realm open to human beings only insofar as they exercise their personality. And everybody feels in some vague way that entry into this realm and perduring residence there represents a value greater than any other.

Psychologists offer a pertinent example here. Take two people who are truly and deeply in love. It is not merely a question of an erotic attraction. After spending a certain amount of time in which they show off their "good points," there comes a point when each person ceases to present himself or herself as an object of value and to offer themselves *as they are:* as subjects who are capable of great illusions and failures. Why this change? Because each individual wishes to be chosen freely as a person, not *purchased* for their natural value. "I married you, not your virtues," is a phrase that aptly expresses the realm in which a human being seeks and risks the most precious part of his existence.

Not to risk, then, is to close oneself off from this realm in a definitive way. Risking oneself obviously entails trouble. And while we cannot be completely sure about it, it would seem that being free and being a person is worth the trouble whatever the end result may be.

Now what does Christian revelation add to this basic position? [29] On the one hand, it underlines and certifies the solution glimpsed above. It conveys the *yes* that comes from God to man's question and yearning. Every person is worth the trouble of being loved, because in every person treated as such there is an absolute value. And this absolute is not subject to any provisos. Self-giving is *always* constructive and constructive *forever*. From this viewpoint there is no greater sin than not accepting this trouble, which is real, and this risk, which is only a seeming risk from the viewpoint of faith and its certainty. Finally, there is no greater crime than that of trying to preclude the possibility that another being may be able to fully live out his capacity for liberty and personhood.

Now all this may seem perfectly clear while at the same time Christianity may inexplicably seem to represent something quite the opposite. In history Christianity may seem to have become one of the most effective elements for arousing man's panic with regard to liberty. And since it operated in this way, it was accepted and defended as one of the most powerful antidotes to the disintegration of the existing social order.

Whence this "Christian" fear of liberty? On the one hand the Christian message would seem to be designed to enhance immeasurably the value of liberty. On the other hand it would seem to have done even more to increase its riskiness.

As we know from experience in making a human decision, even when it involves the being most intimately united with us, we never put our *whole* life on the line. We may physically risk our life, but we never risk its whole value in an historical option. In this respect we risk more in terms of intimacy than we do in terms of death. But not even a decision with regard to intimacy embodies the totality of value. There is a common expression that sums this up in rather rigorous mathematical terms; we call our spouse our "better *half*." In reality no human decision closes off all the roads open to us or exhausts all possible elements of interest and value—even though at the moment it may seem to do so.

Now it would seem that Christianity seeks to claim that, in and through these incomplete, inadequate, and mixed options, man puts the *totality* on the line—we know not how or when exactly. So the question arises: Is it really possible that man's concrete, situation-bound use of liberty can result in the definitive loss of all value?

It is worth noting that Dante, for all his dogmatic orthodoxy, was still able to paint a hell where love and human dignity exist even in the midst of torment. Even leaving him aside, there are countless popular expressions which indicate that man rebels against the idea that total loss of value can result from a decision in which some value, however base and impure, is sought after. A recent pop tune had this line in it: "We will go to hell *together*." [30] It is not a senseless piece of bravado at all. The notion of being together, associated with the image of hell, contains a powerful and moving human claim for vindication. Man claims his victory over fear, choosing to retain his right to exercise his liberty. *For liberty is worth the trouble and pain.*

Christianity confronts no small problem here. It must exorcise hell of its power to destroy the value of human liberty. For, as we have already seen, the starting point where grace finds us and rescues us is not a state of innocence but a state of nonliberty. If we are to entrust ourselves to this saving dynamism, then we must begin by realizing that hell is not ahead of us but behind us with respect to liberty.

In saying this we are not referring to something "behind" us or "ahead" of us *in time.* We are referring to the two extreme poles within which the dynamism of grace operates. In making us free through love, grace leads us toward the pole which, in its full totality, is God himself. In freely rejecting this dynamism and denying liberty through egotism, man moves in the opposite direction. He moves toward the pole which in its fullness—or better, in its total emptiness—is hell. Hell is the absolute destruction of all *personal* work and relationship; the *gehenna* which consumes implacably (*cf.* Matt. 18:9); the total separation from all persons, be they God or men (i.e., the exterior darkness mentioned in Matt. 8:12).

These two poles, and only they, give meaning and sense to Christian existence. But they only give meaning and sense to an existence endowed with liberty. Understood in this way, the pole of hell is as inseparable from Christian dogma as the other pole: God. Dante's error, if we can call it that, was to situate hell halfway along the road; to place real human beings in it. Insofar as they were still humans, they retained a lofty remnant of personality and liberty even amid their desperation and torment.[31]

VI. PELAGIANISM IN CHRISTIAN HISTORY

Hopefully the reader can now see that it makes no sense to ask whether Christian living is the triumph of our own effort or the triumph of grace. But the question was raised in Christian history, as we have already pointed out. The fact is that in certain epochs, and particularly in certain currents of thought, Christian spirituality believed it should be centered around the efforts of the human will. It relegated the divine factor of God's grace to second place, affirming its existence but depriving it of any concrete import.

What is more, we must admit that the same tendency is evident today. It is not easy for a mass-oriented Christianity to avoid the either-or of human effort versus grace. And since there is an innate tendency to move toward that which is closest at hand, understandable, and manageable, it tends to stress the first alternative.

Here we feel it would be useful to discuss some of the important currents that have cropped up in the history of asceticism, and that indicate the presence of a perduring temptation toward voluntarism in the spiritual life.

1. The first protagonists of this tendency to overvalue human effort in the process of living a Christian life were the anchorites. They arose as the embodiment of a nonconformist attitude within a Christianity that was no longer plagued by persecutions, that transmitted the faith mainly

through the pressure of the environment, and that had consequently lost the element of tension and the initial impetus of an authentic personal conversion. Since the life of faith lacked these latter qualities, this mass-oriented Christianity was unable to eliminate the aura of frivolousness from a society in which it represented a majority force.

The anchorites appeared as a protest against the secularized way of life and Christian mediocrity. They proposed to live Christianity as intensely as it had been lived when people had to risk persecution. These malcontents underlined their detachment from a frivolous society by living in the desert, without a roof or home of their own. They distrusted any spontaneous impulse, regarding this as the root of the frivolousness they saw around them. And so they condemned any and all pleasures, even the most innocent ones.

The whole history of the anchorites seems to be summed up in one virtue alone: mortification. Reading their lives, we get the impression that their particular competence was to find the maximum of inconvenience and privation. The principles and methods they proposed for achieving heroic self-control recall those of Stoic philosophy. Thus within Church history the anchorites, in practice though not in theory, turned themselves into archetypes of human effort rather than into miraculous exemplars of grace at work.

2. The need to live together as Christians saw the anchorites succeeded by the monks. Isolation gave way to community. The beginnings of this new spiritual pathway were auspicious, despite the heritage bequeathed by the anchorites. But habituation to monastic life diluted the initial fervor.

Near the beginning of this chapter we saw the theological error into which Pelagius fell, in his commendable desire to restore the initial fervor of monasticism. We also saw that Saint Augustine became the great defender of grace in this controversy, and thus his arguments were approved by the magisterium. Thus the realm of theology was liberated from Pelagianism; but this liberation did not wholly succeed in the realm of asceticism. The thrust of Pelagius was continued by another monk, John Cassian, who was the abbot of the monastery of St. Victor in Marseilles.

Cassian opposed Augustine's doctrine because he saw it as a paralysis of virtue: "Augustine's doctrine of grace leads to laziness." Following the doctrine of the Bishop of Hippo, lazy monks could surrender to the quietist embrace of spiritual fatalism. In his famous *Collationes,* which have offered spiritual nourishment to asceticism for many centuries of Church history, Cassian sets forth his program for Christian living. As he sees it, Christian asceticism seeks to eliminate faults; and to this end it offers an interwoven complex of virtues, methods, and examinations. The objective of Christian asceticism is the same sought by the Greeks: to achieve *apathia.* But it differs from them in saying that this state is the means whereby one obtains the kingdom of God.[32]

Thus the success of asceticism depends on one's own will. Grace is given room only as an aid to a will that is "infirm" with regard to doing good. This supernatural aid is just a tonic, and it is not always necessary. What is more, it is not needed for the start of virtue. At one point (*Collatio* 13, Chapter 12) Cassian rails against those who attribute all the good in the saints to God. As he sees it, real liberty would not exist if a person could not will and do good independently of any and every aid.

Pelagius, as we saw, eulogized human nature and its capacity to lead a Christian life, relegating grace to the external plane of example. Now Cassian picks up this eulogy, a bit more timidly. He acknowledges grace and its necessity for eternal life; but he also espouses the victory of virtue by human effort—not totally but in large part. His theory came to be known as Semi-Pelagianism.[33]

The importance of Cassian in the later ascetical life of the Church is easy enough to verify. His methods perdured, and his ideas and comments took on great authority in subsequent ascetical literature.

3. In Salamanca, on January 20, 1582, Domingo Báñez, a Dominican, accused Luis de León of being a "Pelagian." The latter had intervened on the side of the Jesuits in the "de auxiliis"[34] dispute. As time went on and the famous dispute continued, the Dominicans reduced the epithet to "Semi-Pelagian" in their reference to the Jesuits. They wanted to indicate the kinship of their theological doctrine with that of John Cassian.

Once the furor of debate over "de auxiliis" had subsided, it became evident that the appellation did not fit the theology maintained by the Jesuits. Nevertheless people have continued to apply it in a vaguer way to the ascetical practice that is embodied in the methodology of Ignatius Loyola's *Spiritual Exercises*. Even today the *Spiritual Exercises* of Ignatius are highly praised as a masterpiece of psychology. For this reason, and with some foundation, people still distrust them. They feel that it is a spiritual methodology which puts too much stress on human effort or, at the very least, on a "human methodology of conversion."

Now the *Spiritual Exercises* have been the most widespread school of training in Christian living, as recent Pontiffs have pointed out. So the accusation is a serious one that deserves closer analysis. For it would suggest that the *Spiritual Exercises* have transmitted Semi-Pelagian monasticism to the many and diverse sectors of the Church that have been nourished by it: i.e., to priests, religious, and laity.

But one need only take a brief glance at the aim and methods of the *Spiritual Exercises* to realize that such is not the case. Only a mutilated or erroneous interpretation of them, quite at variance with the experience that Ignatius wove into them, could turn them into a purveyor of Pelagian spirituality. Some people approach them in a superficial or purely external way. And they are often put off by certain features: the initial postulate of *indifference,* the method of prayer, and the harsh language of a soldier who expressed his mystical experience as best he could. These features have prevented some people from making contact with the authentic dynamism of these Exercises.

The outline of the *Spiritual Exercises* is very simple. The person is to discover the personal plan of God who appeals to human liberty. And the means to arrive at this discovery is nothing other than the "discernment of spirits." The person is to penetrate into the dynamism of grace operative within, to recognize the mission to which God summons us from within history. In a word, it is a matter of seeking the face of a God who is present and who is trying to dialogue with man's heart.

There is a pedagogy involved in arriving at this encounter. One must renounce his own egotism in order to hear God's voice and see his face through the only pathway that leads to the Father: Christ. For Saint Ignatius, the first step is liberation from our alienations and enslavements. But this liberating indifference is not the *result* of our efforts. It is a grace we receive on our knees. We must plead for it insistently; for it alone can give us affective and effective union with the life of Christ, who gave everything including himself. Christ is the truly "free" man and our liberator.

Being a grace, this liberation cannot represent an inhuman *apathy* toward life, as it is often presented. It is a quest for deeper truth and authenticity in one's development as a person. To use the example of another author,[35] indifference here is akin to the transformation which takes place when a woman becomes a mother. Love for her children will cause her to look with "indifference" (i.e., liberty) on the things for which she had an inclination when she was single: parties, etc. It does not mean she will cease to have an interest in them. But her new love sets up an emotional distance which radically modifies her scale of interests without destroying them.

Understood thus, "indifference" is a grace that involves placing the supreme reality at the center of our interests and values. It is precisely the teaching of the gospel. In the *Spiritual Exercises,* indifference is put first as the theoretical "foundation and first principle"; it is then followed by meditations on Christ. But we must remember that this is merely a pedagogical necessity. The two things are inseparable, and Christ comes first in the existential order.

Contemplation on the life of Christ is an attempt to "feel with him." This is the one and only way to come face to face with the Father, since the Son is the transcription of the godhead within human limits. In the thought of Ignatius these meditations are existentially the fundamental ones. For in the process of thinking and feeling with Christ we journey through the mystery of death and resurrection that is a part of any redemptive (i.e., liberative) process.

In this effort to affiliate ourselves with the Son, as proposed by the *Spiritual Exercises,* we do not seek a universal pathway but our own personal vocation. Through this journey with the Son, the Spirit "moves" us, enabling us to discover the vocation incarnated in our dimensions as a person. And this vocation is presumably framed within our "feeling with the Church," that is, our social responsibility resulting from the encounter between our particular circumstances and the mission of the Church in a world evolving here and now.

The content and organization of the meditations in the *Spiritual Exercises* take second place to its fundamental element; they are purely pedagogical and instrumental in this sense. The fundamental element is the "discernment of spirits," or of the "Spirit" (with a capital S). Nothing could be further from voluntarism or closer to mystical experience (i.e., to sensitivity for the workings of grace). Indeed it is no accident that Ignatius was accused of being an "illuminist" soon after he published his *Spiritual Exercises.* The illuminist error is the direct opposite of Pelagian voluntarism; and it was attributed to the writings of this man who had tried to express the encounter he had with God over a number of years.

Different reasons explain why the *Spiritual Exercises* have been mis-construed and misused. The mass-directed approach of many missionaries set aside the "discernment of spirits" and replaced it with an emphasis on the meditations of the first week. In their moralizing zeal, missionaries turned these first-week considerations into awesome but alienating spec-taculars. On a mass scale fear proved to be more effective in converting peoples and communities on the spot to the practice of religion than in deepening people's faith. Thus the focus of the *Spiritual Exercises* was shifted, so that one could not longer recognize in them the mystical ex-perience of Ignatius that had spawned them.

Others reduced the *Spiritual Exercises* to a method of exercising psy-chological pressure and obtaining priestly or religious vocations. Or else they made them an instrument in cultivating a disembodied, aseptic Christian ideal. In an age lacking a theology that could give sound orien-tation to Christian life, psychologism gained sway over the *Exercises* to inculcate flight from the world and a strong dose of individualism.[36]

So we come back to our starting point: the relationship between hu-man effort and grace. Taking a panoramic view of the history of ecclesial asceticism, we see the preduring temptation to voluntarism. It continu-ally tries to undermine creative initiatives in Christian living, and it con-tinually hovers near the edge of the theology of grace. So long as wrong-headed notions of Greek philosophy perdure, so long as Christians live a schizophrenic existence by separating religion from life and nature from grace, then the temptation will persist. People will try to oppose human effort to grace in Christian living, and they will naturally tend to put too much value on the former.

VII. MASS-DIRECTED MEDIA AND THE WORK OF GRACE

Can mass-directed media[37] achieve the effects of grace? In trying to answer this question, let us begin by citing a few concrete examples. They may help us to frame the point of this question more precisely and to prove its present-day relevance. Alas, they may also show how widespread in the Church is the tendency we are going to criticize.

Up until a few years ago, a detestable system of advertising and pro-motion was used in Montevideo (Uruguay). It was called the "talking air-plane." Equipped with a high-power speaker and a tape recorder, the plane flew over the city, constantly repeating a brief announcement of some sort. It was first used for political propaganda during several elec-tion campaigns. Then it became a promotional tool for commercial firms, which used it to advertise their products and bargains.

Now this particular year the priest in charge of the "publicity" for Holy Week was on the verge of renting the plane. For an hour each day of Holy Week it would fly over the city, publicizing the slogan: "Go to communion on Easter Sunday." The idea had been favorably received by a commission of lay people who were to contribute the funds for imple-menting this brainstorm. And they would certainly have gone ahead with it, if a public-opinion expert had not voiced such a strong conviction against it that the priest could not go through with it.

Now to be perfectly frank, the priest gave up the idea because he was moved by the vehemence of the expert's criticism, not because he understood that there was something reprehensible in the project itself. For years he had resorted to similar techniques when Holy Week rolled around. For example: he had used "radio spots," so that people heard "Go to communion on Easter Sunday" between beer jingles and aspirin commercials. As he explained it: "Of course people should not go to communion because they hear it on the radio or from an airplane. But there are many lukewarm Catholics whose piety is not up to par, and we simply want to give them *a little push* now and then."

The same philosophy of the "little push" lay behind a recent advertisement which urged Catholics to contribute hard cash to the worldwide work of the missions: "Christ saved you. Help him to save millions and millions of pagans." *Help Christ to save: ergo,* Christ's saving grace needs the help of human beings—nay more, the help of man's money—to carry out the work of salvation.

Now one has every right to ask why we react unfavorably to these approaches. Is it simply because they shock our esthetic sensibilities as members of the Christian elite, because we are more cultured than the masses? That is what some people suggest reproachfully when we criticize these methods: "Of course they are not meant for educated Christians like you, but they do get through to the common people." Our criticism, they say, is the criticism of "Ph.D.'s" not of "pastors of souls." The latter know well enough that grace makes use of many instruments. What may be unnecessary or even shocking for some Christians can be good for the masses. So, leaving aside the esthetic aspect, can we offer a criticism of this tendency from a theological viewpoint?

1. Right away we must point out that the term "mass-directed media," as used here, is not to be equated with the common English term "mass media." We are not referring to the media of social communication as such (e.g., radio, television, the press, etc.). The term "mass media," as we ordinarily use it, refers to the numerical scope of these media, to the size of the audience. That is not what we are referring to here, for these same media can be used to "de-mass" the individual and turn him into a real person. This may not be their typical or most frequent use, but neither is it an impossibility. In any case our use of "mass-directed" here does not refer to the size of the audience reached. It refers to the level of human life and action to which they appeal: i.e., their appeal to the "mass" qualities and reactions of man.

Let us start with a basic definition of "mass" as it is used here. *Mass* refers to a complex of human beings who allow those around them to take charge of thinking, choosing, and acting in their place. Thus it is clearly not a specific social class but a line of conduct. Mass is defined here in terms of liberty, in terms of not thinking, in terms of allowing oneself to be led by others. Thus it is equivalent to inertia, passivity, nonliberty. And it should also be noted that there is always a "mass" element left in every man, however much his personality may be developed. There are zones and behavior patterns of nonliberty. In this context, mass-directed media refers to those which try to operate on the mass element in every man, on his determinisms and nonfree facets.

Publicity and advertising, for example, decidedly operate on the mass level because in this way they more quickly and effectively achieve the desired objective: to win a specific act from the consumer. Note well what we said: not a conviction, an act. Whether the individual is convinced or not is ultimately of secondary importance. The important thing is that he do what the advertiser wants. The brewery concern does not care what considered judgment the consumer may have about its beer, so long as he buys it.

If we want a person to purchase a given brand of beer, we hound him with advertisements urging him to buy it. We follow him everywhere: TV, radio, buses, subways, newspapers, magazines, etc. And so it goes until at some point he, without knowing how or why, asks for our brand the next time he goes into a store for beer. Why? Because it is the first brand that comes into his head. Or because he doesn't want to be regarded as an oddball.

In terms of what we might call its argumentative content, the advertising process appeals to the most primary aspects of the consumer: to his instincts and the satisfying of his elemental appetites. Not only do we appeal to his tastebuds, convincing him that the beer is delicious to drink. We also put the bottle in the hands of a luscious, half-naked girl, so that the image of the product is associated with sexual satisfaction. Appealing to the mass element in the consumer, we want him unconsciously to substitute the thought of drinking our beer for the thought of getting that girl. Or we may put our beer in the hands of someone driving a luxury automobile, knowing full well that the consumer would like to move in such high-class circles. Drinking our beer thus becomes a way of satisfying his frustrated social ambitions.

In short, advertising operates on the determinisms of the human person. And this means that it works on his egotisms, his desire for pleasure and individual well-being, his fear of being lonely, etc.

Ideological and political propaganda is also mass-directed insofar as it is irrational and emotional. One need only look at most of the slogans used during election campaigns by political parties and individual candidates. Take the slogan, "I like Ike," that was used during the Eisenhower campaigns. It was chanted repeatedly at rallies and in the media. Why the voter should like Ike was not discussed much at all. The hope was that endless repetition would lead the voter to convince himself that he too had this friendly emotional reaction toward Eisenhower. So when he got into the voting booth, he would pull the lever next to his name because he certainly did like Ike. What counted were the votes, not the reasons behind them.

So again we see mass-directed media at work. They seek to exert pressure on the determinisms of the individual. It is not that they directly violate or attack man's liberty; they simply sidestep it and overlook it.

2. Let us recall briefly some of the tendencies of the mass, as we understand the term here, remembering that it is present in every human being. The mass tends toward simplification and immediacy. If an idea is to penetrate the mass, it must be simplified to its most elementary expression and made immediate. On the mass level what counts is that which is immediately tangible, that which one can see and touch and taste and measure: e.g., the number of votes or sales. There is here a

peculiar materialism which demands that effectiveness be able to be measured in numerical terms, even when it is a question of attitudes that call
for a different type of valuation. What cannot be counted simply does
not count.

Now do we not find the same viewpoint in the idea of publicizing
Easter with the slogan mentioned earlier? Is not the aim to get a large
number of communicants at Easter? We must recognize the strong tendency we have to measure our Christian life and its effectiveness in terms
that can be added up numerically: "conversions," baptisms, communions,
etc. And in the absence of such measurable results we tend to regard
Christian practice as nonoperative. We conceive the triumph of grace as
being dependent more on our quantifiable human efforts than on grace
itself.

We need only consider the census figures we use to deceive ourselves.
Consider a country like Uruguay, which is clearly pluralistic and has a
long laicist tradition. The ecclesiastical yearbooks still give figures which
would suggest that 97 percent of the total population is Catholic! It is not
difficult to figure out the criterion and outlook used by the compilers to
convince themselves that this figure is valid.

We Catholics often evince this dangerous tendency to religious materialism, to quantification. We do not notice how much we are deforming
and falsifying the true essence of the Church, and hence the notion of
grace itself. We readily fall into a mechanical, materialistic notion of
grace: e.g., when we base it on mere external practices such as going to
communion on the nine First Fridays. As Paul might put it, it is the flesh
on the prowl in our Christian way of life. So it is not surprising that
some Christians rack their brains, trying to figure out the most effective
tool for convincing everyone to go to Mass or to receive the sacraments
of the Church. Any means is valid and plausible so long as it "works."
One priest who went to visit the parish of John Vianney, the famous Curé
of Ars, was astounded by what he saw. The power of the Curé was so
great, he reported, that few people could resist the work of grace. Considerations of human respect were turned inside out, so that people "were
ashamed not to practice their religion." [38] As this visitor saw it, human
respect was an instrument in the service of "grace"; and he lauded the
fact that people practiced their religion simply because they were ashamed
not to.

When Christians regard grace in such a way, it is not surprising that
missionaries and preachers base their success on mass conversions and
mass baptisms without noticing the profound contradiction entailed in
this approach. They do not see that conversion and mass behavior are incompatible terms; that conversion only begins when human liberty manages to slip away from the weight of mass attitudes.

Herein lies the basic question: Are grace and mass elements compatible? Can they be? So far we have seen that grace is associated with spontaneity and authentic liberty as opposed to determinisms and rigidity.
Grace is the free communication of God which evokes a response in the
human person that is equally free by virtue of his liberty. And the very
existence of this liberty itself is already the fruit of grace. Grace and mass,
then, are opposing forces that operate in opposite directions. With a pro-

found intuition into Paul's dialectic, Simone Weil set grace over against the force of gravity. The former seeks to free man, to inspire him to the difficult venture of shouldering personal authenticity and liberty. The latter keeps him in bondage to the forces of inertia and the chains of determinisms.

It is a difficult venture, to be sure. Being a Christian and fully shouldering the life of grace involves a perduring obligation to seek authenticity, liberty, and truth. The mass element in us, by contrast, relates to what is simple, immediate, and easy—as we have seen from the examples cited above. So we must realize that the Christian ideal, as presented in revelation, is not an easy one. In John's Gospel, for example, there is a perduring opposition between the kingdom (i.e., grace) and the world. And this world that says no to Christ is precisely the inert mass elements: that which is rigid, nonfree, determined, and incapable of abnegation. To be of the world is to withdraw oneself from grace and to deny the liberty that grace gives and demands: the "liberty of the sons of God," so dear to Saint Paul. Perhaps now we can see the fallacy involved in the idea that we can "facilitate" the work of grace, that we can make it easy, that we can give it "a little push."

Paul knew from his own experience how difficult it was to shoulder this liberty, and so he told us that the flesh kept dogging our Christian way of life. And it continues to plague the Church in what one writer has aptly described as "the legacy of Constantine." Ever since the day when Constantine turned Christianity into the official religion of the Roman Empire, thus transforming it into Christendom, the Church has run the danger of being converted wholly into a mass Christianity. The high price of this legacy is seen in the tendency to confuse—and even identify—grace with quantity, when in fact the two notions are irreconcilable.

So there is more than just an esthetic reaction involved when we refuse to recognize "mass-directed" media as instruments of grace. People argue that their use is justified because they are good for mass man even if not for particular individuals. But we would regard this argument as the strongest one against their use. For the point is that man cannot heed and respond to grace so long as he continues to be part of the mass and its determinisms. With the help of grace itself, he must first begin to free himself from the mass elements to which he is subject.

3. We must not forget, however, that any conception of a liberty without determinisms is merely a utopian ideal. This should already be obvious from what was said earlier in this chapter.[39] Is it possible, then, to have Christian grace without mass procedures, insofar as the latter are equivalent, on the societal plane, to the determinisms that Paul called "the law of our bodily members?" Clearly no. That brings us to another question: How does the acceptable use of social determinisms differ from the attitude we have just criticized?

The "mass media" are not something new, even though their present organization on a global scale may well make them look like a new phenomenon. According to Freud, all education consists in substituting the reality principle for the pleasure principle. In other words, it involves

CHAPTER TWO

Height: Eternal Life, the New Earth

divine gift, heals our congenital tendency toward sin which,
is intertwined with impersonality. Not the impersonality that
a radical incapacity for personalization, as is the case in the
ld, but that which arises from the decision of our own egotism.
re is more. The human condition is nothing more than the
nt for this dynamism which pierces our existence and changes
oes this dynamism point to? *To what heights?*
ain we shall look for the answer on three levels, actually fol-
tages in which the formulation of the question was developed
thought.

Section I

in with John the Evangelist. The third chapter of his Gospel
ighly interesting scene in the life of Christ: his nocturnal
Nicodemus.
place of this scene in the structure of John's Gospel is the
interest. It is part of the section that exegetes have aptly
ok of new beginnings." And it is precisely here that Jesus
f the wind that is his Spirit: that comes from *on high,* takes
s on high as if we had been born to a new, higher existence.
well to focus for a moment on the image of Christ's inter-
emus is a great personage. He is one of the leaders of the
r of the Jewish Council that governs the strictly internal
ation (John 3:1; 7:50). Christ himself calls him a "teacher
h suggests his expertness in religious matters (John 3:10).
emus is a Pharisee (John 3:1). For us, who normally rely
spels and what happened later in this matter, this designa-
ive one. It certainly was not pejorative, at least to such a
t's own time. Here we have a clearcut example of how an
o into decline and suffer decay. Just as the term "bour-

inculcating certain lines of conduct that are useful to society and associating their performance with some sort of pleasure. This pleasure
differs from that involved in the immediate satisfaction of desires, but it
is sufficiently close at hand to exercise its power of attraction.

Now Christianity, too, certainly presupposes that its message will
come to a human being liberated from the immediate allure of the instinctive. Otherwise it would have no meaning for him.

So let us go back to our earlier examples. The fact that advertising
leads people unconsciously to choose a certain brand of beer when they
are thirsty, at least on more than one occasion, is not in itself a deperson-
alization, as some would have us believe. If a person saves time and psychic energy in selecting beer this way, this could be a liberating thing
provided that he uses the time and energy he has saved for something
with deeper significance and value. But if the same approach were used
in other areas where man's real destiny was at stake, then that would
indeed be depersonalizing. It has no place in the realm of moral conduct
or choosing a marriage partner, for example.

So now we can draw some conclusions about the use of mass proc-
esses in the right way, so that Christianity has real meaning and grace
can be truly efficacious. What holds true for the education of the child
holds true here as well. We must use them insofar as they are necessary
for man's liberation, insofar as they have a proper part to play in the
progress of civilization. But, by the same token, we have no right to
equate Christianity, faith, the sacraments, and sound moral attitudes with
the effect produced by such procedures. Nor is it right to prolong their
use beyond the "childhood stage." They are proper to the stage which
Paul described as one of tutorship, where custom, fear, and naive interest still play a forceful role.

The Church has not always been wise enough to make this essential
distinction. And there is no doubt that she has paid dearly in pastoral
terms for failing to do this.

NOTES

1. "What is certain is that all nature, which precedes liberty, offers resistance to the person's free and total disposability over himself. Thus the dividing
line between person and nature is vertical over against the horizontal line that
separates the spiritual from the sensible in man." Rahner, *Theological Investigations,* Vol. I, p. 396.

2. "The situation confronting language today involves this twofold possibility and summons: (1) to eliminate excrescences from our discourse and make
it more sober . . . (2) to use the most iconoclastic procedure so that fresh sig-
nifications may find expression. Thus, as I see it, hermeneutics (i.e., interpretation) is motivated by two reasons and goals: a desire to cast suspicion on things,
and a desire to listen . . . Today our situation as human beings is such that we
have not finished yet with our *idols* and have just begun to listen to *symbols*"
(Paul Ricoeur, *De l'Interpretation: Essai sur Freud,* Paris: Ed. du Seuil, 1965, p.

36; Engl. trans. *Freud and Philosophy,* New Haven: Yale University Press, 1969). The entire first section of this work is very relevant to the topic under discussion here.

3. *Ibid.,* p. 181.

4. *Ibid.,* p. 182. See CLARIFICATION III in this chapter.

5. See the previous note.

6. See Chapter III in this volume, part III of the main article.

7. Sigmund Freud, *The Ego and the Id* (New York: Norton, 1962), pp. 38–39.

8. Ricoeur, *op. cit.,* p. 187.

9. Cited by Ricoeur, *op. cit.,* p. 185.

10. *Ibid.,* p. 43.

11. Sartre, *The Flies,* Act I, Scene II.

12. *Ibid.*

13. *Ibid.*

14. *Ibid.*

15. *Ibid.*

16. *Ibid.,* Act II, Scene IV.

17. *Ibid.*

18. *Ibid.*

19. *Ibid.*

20. *Ibid.*

21. *Ibid.,* Act II, Tableau II, Scene V.

22. *Ibid.*

23. *Ibid.,* Scene VI.

24. *Ibid.,* Act III, Scene II.

25. *Ibid.*

26. *Motivos de Proteo,* CXXVII (Montevideo: Biblioteca Rodó), p. 308.

27. *Ibid.,* p. 310.

28. *Ibid.*

29. See Volume I of this series, Chapter III.

30. The song is a French tune by George Brassens, "Il suffit de passer le pont." In the original: "Et tant mieux si c'est une péché; nous irons en enfer ensemble." "So much the better if it is a sin, we will go to hell together." The phrase in its entirety puts even clear stress on the disproportion between that which is chosen and the result that arises from it.

31. We fully realize that we have not finished the task of exorcising fear from liberty, the fear that Christianity seems to associate with liberty. We have simply gone as far as this chapter allows us to go. One might well feel that we have dissociated fear from liberty only to attach it to free will. In reality it is ultimately free will which must decide whether man moves toward hell or God; i.e., whether he will accept or reject liberty. Chapter II and Chapter IV will give us new data we can use to judge whether the victory of grace is certain or not. See especially Chapter IV, CLARIFICATION IV.

32. PL (Migne) 49, 486.

33. Other features of Semi-Pelagianism, such as its theory about the preparatory steps to faith, were treated in Volume I, Chapter III.

34. It was called "de auxiliis" because it dealt with the way in which grace *aided* man's decision in choosing the good.

35. Piet Pennig de Vries, *Discernimiento: dinámica existencial de la doctrina y del espíritu de S. Ignacio de Loyola,* Spanish translation by Bojorge (Bilbao: Mensajero, 1967), p. 20.

36. We do not mean to suggest that a spirituality framed in a theology of the sixteenth century can *without modification* handle the needs of Christianity today. The fact that the *Spiritual Exercises* are not Pelagianist does not mean

that, as they stand, they can prepare today's (
signs of the times.

37. Translator's note. See below for a d
means in the present context.

38. François Trochu, *The Curé d'Ars* (

39. See also Section I, above.

Grace, the
at its roots
stems from
animal wor

But th
starting po
it. Where

Here a
lowing the
in Christian

We shall beg
presents a h
meeting with

The very
first point of
called "the b
speaks to us o
us, and leads

But we do
locutor. Nicod
Jews, a memb
affairs of the n
of Israel," whi
Finally, Nicod
only on the Go
tion is a pejora
degree, in Chri
institution can

geoisie" was once synonymous with active enthusiasm and a spirit of enterprise, so the Pharisee movement stood primarily for great religious enthusiasm, a detachment from everything that was not in tune with God, his law, and his service, and a heroic, radically religious outlook. But this religious movement fell prey to the decadent tendency which we examined in the preceding chapter. Instead of maintaining its interior thrust, it stagnated in purely external forms. The Pharisees were at the center of a Jewish movement which gradually lost its forward thrust. As Congar describes it:

> This movement was carried out in stages, its course of development involving progressive and successive realizations. But it could only reach its final goal provided that it did not come to a halt at one of the intermediary stages. But there is always the danger that a given stage already reached will refuse to allow itself to be surpassed; that the individuals or the group who bear the promise and *the seed* will allow themselves to be tied down to the forms in which the living idea has found expression so far, as if these forms were unalterable and definitive. The dynamism of the seed would have required that these forms be superceded. This precisely is the temptation of the synagogue.[1]

To get back to Nicodemus, we are surprised to find that he is an appealing person. Christ severely criticized the hypocrisy of those Pharisees who tied themselves down to external forms and thus checked the inner thrust that might have led them to faith. But such criticism does not apply to Nicodemus. Until Christ's death, of course, we do not see that he is part of the group composing Christ's disciples. But here we can be a bit anachronistic, operating from the viewpoint of grace; we shall picture him here with the traits that show up clearly only at a later point. What characterizes him then is his strong reaction against pretence, against an unjust and superficial judgment, against facile submission to majority opinion. When his colleagues condemn Christ, he comes to his defense openly, simply and sincerely: "Does our law . . . permit us to pass judgment on a man unless we have first given him a hearing and learned the facts?" (John 7:51). And later, when all Jerusalem turns against Jesus and he is sentenced to death and executed, Nicodemus, who had not figured in the triumph of a few days previous, appears on the scene to bear witness to the fact that he believes in Jesus' innocence.

In short, Nicodemus seems to be a man who to some extent has conquered man's penchant for taking the easy road and succumbing to inauthenticity. And if we attribute this quality to him on the night of his encounter with Jesus, it is not an unfounded assumption. For the Lord spoke with a knowledge of men's hearts, and he undoubtedly glimpsed this unmitigated sincerity in the heart of Nicodemus.

Nicodemus comes to see Jesus at night. Being prudent as well as sincere, he does not wish to compromise himself before knowing what he is getting into. He comes to the interview with his personal baggage: his power, his virtue, his knowledge. There is no false boasting, no false modesty, because he is not a hypocrite. He begins with an oblique question which makes clear his wisdom and his uprightness: "Rabbi . . . we know that you are a teacher sent by God; no one could perform these signs of yours unless God were with him" (John 3:2). It is an oblique question, stimulating Christ to speak about his doctrine of the "kingdom"; to spell out what he is adding to what people already know.

The reply of Jesus drops like a thunderbolt. John presents it in precise, incisive terms. Never before had Jesus presented entry into the kingdom in this form. On this occasion, addressing, by way of Nicodemus, those who are powerful, wise, virtuous, and even those who take God as their basic foundation (as is the case with us), he lays down an unheard of condition: "In truth, in very truth I tell you, unless a man has been born over again,[2] he cannot see the kingdom of God" (John 3:3). Nicodemus is astonished, but Jesus repeats his remark and spells it out a bit more: "In truth I tell you, no one can enter the kingdom of God without being born from water and spirit" (John 3:5).[3]

With these words Christ was clearly indicating that the kingdom of God he was proclaiming was situated on another plane. Hence the use of the phrase, "born over again." Nothing, absolutely nothing in this life, however good, just, or holy it may be, has a right to entry into this new life. One must be born again, *start over again,* on a higher plane: the plane to which we are introduced by grace, the gift of God, which is God himself, the Spirit.

Nicodemus, a wise, powerful, and just man, came and asked Jesus for an "added dose" of virtue, knowledge, and power. Christ lets him see that it is not a matter of getting an additional dose of what he already has but of beginning all over again.

Using a metaphor which is a bit incomprehensible for us today but which was well understood by the Jews of his day, Christ lets Nicodemus see that this change of levels is profound and necessary. "Flesh can give birth only to flesh; it is spirit that gives birth to spirit. You ought not to be astonished, then, when I tell you that you must be born over again" (John 3:6–7). What does "flesh" and "spirit" mean? In the Old Testament, whose images are often employed by Christ, "flesh" is the creature and "spirit" is God. When Isaiah wants to convince Israel not to put its trust in the Egyptians, for example, he tells them: "The Egyptians are men, not God; their horses are flesh, not spirit" (Isa. 31:3). The same point is made here. Christ's point comes down to this: Everything that comes from man, aided as every creature is by God, is in the last analysis something human, something that ever remains on the creaturely level. But there exists another plane: the divine plane. Only by transforming ourselves into God, so to speak, can we enter into it. Hence God himself must take us up, transform us, elevate us. Christ had already taught many human things: i.e., precepts of justice that hold true for what we would call the natural plane on which man normally seems to live. This is the first time that he expressly mentions this new plane which is above everything human and creaturely: i.e., the plane of heaven, of personal communion with God. So it is not surprising that Nicodemus should have difficulty in accepting this teaching: "If you disbelieve me when I talk to you about things on earth, how are you to believe if I should talk about the things of heaven?" (John 3:12).

This marvelous gospel dialogue[4] embodies a doctrine that is evident in the very first writings of the New Testament: the aim of Christianity is not obtained by any sort of human means but by a "new birth," a "new creation."

It is worth noting that Paul, right near the start of Christianity, had to fight hard against the all too human current to establish man's relationships with God on something tangible and suited to man's measure. God introduces us directly into the wondrous plane of the divine through Christ's death and resurrection. But we, poor human beings that we are, would prefer to have something human to hold on to in order to feel safe and secure. This is the meaning which the term "flesh" has in the writings of Paul. In the Old Testament this term had served to signify the lowliness and humility of the creature, who was obliged to avoid too close contact with the divine and the sacred. And now that God deigns to summon man to intimacy with him, man remains tied to the flesh, to human rites and human things, to the human plane; he does not dare to let himself be introduced totally into this new life.

An analogy with human relationships may help us to understand all this better. Quite often when an offer of friendship is made by someone who is on a much loftier economic, social, or authority level, the friendship is rejected. The other party prefers the proffer of specific services, fixed in advance and recompensed, over any such friendship. Paradoxically enough, in such a situation the intimate relationship of friendship appears as a danger and generates an unbearable fear; for it would require that the person constantly create unforeseen personal relationships in an unknown world, and there is a possibility that he might deeply wound someone upon whom he depends. Hence for Paul it is most important that we do not picture God in terms of such categories as power, authority, and nature (creator-creature). For man must not "fall back into fear." He must not tie himself to the law or to the Church—in a word, to the human—in order to defend himself from "sonship": i.e., from personal intimacy with God.

Paul also had to fight against the Judaizers, who tried to make eternal life conditional upon circumcision and the observance of the Jewish law with all its rites. Paul could have permitted these practices because they were not wrong. But he did not, because he wanted people to understand the Christian message in all its grandeur. Christians must abandon the "flesh" totally and entrust themselves totally to the "Spirit" of God. So he tells them: "Circumcision is nothing; uncircumcision is nothing; the only thing that counts is new creation" (Gal. 6:15). And by the latter he is referring to man born again on the plane of God himself.

Paul also had to pave the way for our Church, which today does not rely on any direct recollection of Christ's physical person but which does live wholly on his grace, on his Spirit. So Paul had to fight against those who claimed to be important because they had seen the Lord personally or had been part of his retinue. All these claims, too, were "flesh" and without value: "With us therefore worldly standards have ceased to count in our estimate of any man; even if once they counted in our understanding of Christ, they do so now no longer. When anyone is united to Christ, there is *a new world;* the old order has gone, and a new order has already begun" (2 Cor. 5:16–17).

In this way Paul echoes the doctrine of Christ. He was a passionate proponent of the *absolute newness* of Christianity. If we ever read through all his epistles once, we will be surprised to note the persistent contrast he sets up between "before" and "now."

So here we have the three fundamental terms which the New Testament uses to designate the gift of God from the viewpoint that concerns us here: new birth, new creation, spirit (in opposition to flesh). By virtue of its end goal, which is God himself (i.e., Spirit), the order in which grace places man is radically new—not because it begins in time, but because it does not proceed from man himself but from above.

Section II

What we have just said should make it clear that the Pelagian controversy also dealt with a second point. The doctrine of Pelagius left a second point obscure when it affirmed that man could, with the resources of his nature alone, do good and obtain eternal life. In effect, the virtues which the young virgin Demetriades was trying to acquire, and which she asked

Pelagius about, were nothing more and nothing less than the Christian virtues leading to salvation.

Now Pelagius affirmed that they were available to man's natural powers. In so doing, he not only overlooked the congenital infirmity of the human condition. He also overlooked man's radical incapacity for union with God: the absolute disproportion between all that is human, be it good or evil, and the divine that goes to make up eternal life.

To put it another way, grace not only heals but also elevates. The gift given to us not only humanizes us but also divinizes us. Hence the condemnation of Pelagius mentioned above recalls this twofold aspect. Already in the regional Council of Orange (529), this proposition was put forward: "If anyone claims that he can effectively ponder or choose anything good pertaining to the salvation of eternal life with the powers of nature alone . . . he falls into heresy" (Denz. 180). And the Council of Trent gives to this doctrine, already *de fide* by virtue of the ordinary magisterium of the Church, the weight of a dogmatic definition. In its definition, it touches upon the theme of the previous chapter as well: "If anyone should say that the grace which comes from Jesus Christ is given solely so that man can more easily live in righteousness and merit eternal life, as if free will were capable of these two things though perhaps with difficulty, let him be anathema" (Denz. 812).

For it is clear that we must consider the avoidance of sin and the fact of being elevated to God's level and eternal life as two distinct aspects of one and the same movement. In his first epistle, John is already uniting these two aspects: "A child of God [i.e., the new creature placed on the plane of eternal life] does not commit sin [i.e., also received from God the power that heals his fallen nature and permits him to avoid sin]" (1 John 3:9).

These two effects of the same movement, the movement that bears us up toward eternal life through Christ's grace, are united in the schema prepared for Vatican I which was to proclaim it as a *de fide* truth: "The Catholic Church professes that the grace given to us through the merits of Christ the Redeemer is such that it not only liberates us from enslavement to sin and the power of the devil but also enables us, renewed in our mind and spirit, to recover the righteousness and holiness which Adam lost for himself and us by sinning. For grace does not only repair the forces of mere nature so that, with its help, we can fully adapt our habits and actions to the standard of moral good. It also transforms us, above and beyond the bounds of nature, in accordance with the image of the heavenly man [i.e., Christ], and causes us to be born again to a new life." [5]

This specified an essential dimension of Christian existence: man is gratuitously summoned to the superhuman. And from this dimension there was born a word that would serve as the technical term to designate the realities of an existence now raised to a new level: *the supernatural.*

Nonetheless this idea of elevation above and beyond the possibilities —and consequently the exigencies—of man's nature to the divine was open to an oversimplification. Elevated, with respect to what? We would say: with respect to merely human possibilities and exigencies. But in the concrete, where are these possibilities and exigencies operative? In the world, in its development and construction, in the history of mankind. From there comes the temptation to oversimplify the matter. People would regard the supernatural as the celestial as opposed to the terrestrial, the eternal as opposed to the temporal, "God alone" as opposed to human concerns.[6]

Even the official prayer of the Church has not evaded this over-simplified dichotomy. This occurs only rarely, to be sure, but there were examples of it in the prayers of the liturgical year until the recent reform of the Roman Missal. In one we find a plea to God to convert our hearts, "so that we may be drawn from earthly desires to the joys of heaven." [7] To achieve this ideal, we ask God "to teach us to disdain the things of earth and to yearn for the things of heaven." [8] This Christian ideal operates by cutting our affective ties with the things of this world. With "our passions under control, and thus more easily attain the rewards of heaven." [9]

In other words, this form of expression conceives the elevation of grace, not as an elevation *of* the human, but as an elevation vis-à-vis the human. It was a relatively easy way of resolving the problem of knowing what use to make of liberty in the world. A morality based on licitness and illicitness resolved this problem in a purely surface way—on the crudest level, as it were.

In such a framework, every attempt to get beyond a mass-oriented morality was bound up with a spirituality based on *contemptus mundi:* i.e., contempt for the world. Indeed this is the subtitle of the *Imitation of Christ,* one of the most fundamental works of Christian spirituality since the Middle Ages. Closely tied up with this was the fact that monastic life and withdrawal from the world were presented as the model for the spiritual life of the laity. What is more, one of the deepest roots of the clericalism from which the Church has suffered in recent centuries lay precisely in the notion that the layman was a less earnest Christian who sought to serve two masters, while the cleric devoted all his time to the eternal.

This overall outlook, both in its Catholic and its Protestant versions, delayed recognition of the supernatural value of man's historical task. Viewing it in terms of its horizontal, human dimension, this outlook saw history as the domain of the unimportant standing over against the decisive, eternal domain that was embodied in man's vertical relationship to God.

In *The Secular City*, Harvey Cox presents three notions that served to impede the creation of a theology of history in the Christian world. Let us summarize them here: (1) whereas the kingdom of God is the work of God alone, the secular city is the result of human effort; (2) whereas the kingdom of God calls for renunciation and repentance, the secular city demands only competence and flexibility; (3) whereas the kingdom of God is above and beyond history, the secular city comes to term within this world.[10]

It is certain that this mode of thought and expression clashes with the formulas that Vatican II has familiarized us with. This is evident from the very first words of *Gaudium et spes*, which talks about the Church sharing the world's joys and sorrows. How could it say this with sincerity if the revelation of the supernatural order were in fact the revelation that some had been elevated above and beyond the vicissitudes and concerns of this world and human history?

Section III

Just as there was a third stage of dealing with the first dimension of Christian existence—i.e., healing grace (see Chapter I)—so there has been a third stage in dealing with the second dimension of grace: i.e., elevating grace. Here again there has been an effort in recent years to achieve a deeper, less simplistic synthesis on this matter. The unfolding of the whole human problematic, and of the concepts employed to express it, has made this new stage possible.

Above we noted that there was an overly facile solution to the problem of how to conceive this elevating grace, this grace that raises man to regions which he can enter only if he is "drawn by the Father" (John 6:44). This facile solution consisted in imagining that grace elevates, starting from the (already) human. In other words: while the human in general remained human, one part of it turned into the *supernatural*, the superhuman, by virtue of God's grace.

A whole system of realities was involved in this work of elevating one part of the human. It had its own proper instruments, habits, values, and hopes. And it was only a short step from this conception to another conception which saw *merely* human values and *merely* natural hopes as

being of second-rate importance and hence false when compared with
man's supernatural possibilities. One of the more salient features of recent church history in Uruguay exemplifies this. Once upon a time there
was sharp opposition between the Masons in the national government
and the ecclesiastical hierarchy represented by Bishop Vera and supported
by the Jesuits. The struggle ended with the Jesuits being expelled from
the territory of the nation. The immediate cause of this expulsion was a
sermon in which a Jesuit maintained that "Philanthrophy was the counterfeit of charity." Why counterfeit? Simply because it was *natural*. In the
context of a country with great Christian potential it was therefore opposed to the one and only love with overtones of eternity: supernatural
charity.

By comparison with this attitude, which sums up the common, orthodox position in the last century, Vatican II represents an important
change of mentality. And we are not referring to one or more specific
conciliar texts, but to the overall conciliar event.

Vatican II can be regarded as the Council of church-world dialogue.
At the same time it was centered around the concept of a Church in the
service of mankind. Both these notions really go to make up one and the
same thing. And both are based on a rejection of the notion that reality
is divided into separate levels, into systems with their own autonomous
instruments, values, and hopes. For it would be a fiction to claim that
one part of reality, the supernatural, could be in the service of another
part, the natural. A dialogue would have to be pretty indirect indeed, if
it were carried on between two parties moving on completely different
roads to different goals.

But there are other facts, outside of the doctrine of the Council,
which clearly indicate the radically different outlook of Vatican II. Certain theologians, known all over the world for having fought against the
oversimplified separations current in past centuries, were the very ones
which the Council restored to favor and heard most intently. One of them
was Henri de Lubac, for example. His well-known book, *Le Surnaturel*,
had been withdrawn from circulation at one point. Now it was officially
sanctioned once again and republished. Another theologian was Karl
Rahner, perhaps the theologian who was heeded most during the Council.
He created the clarifying notion of a "supernatural existential." It led
others to realize that in the one and only reality of history all men,
whether they know it or not, make all their decisions in terms of one
single vocation: the supernatural summons of God (*cf.* GS 22).

Now what about the approach of arguing against the *separation* of
the natural and the supernatural? Is that equivalent to denying the *dis-*

tinction between them? Or to suppressing the natural in the concrete? Certainly not, for that would be replacing one oversimplification with another. Let us consider this further.

Supernatural and *grace* are strictly synonyms, insofar as one is an adjective and the other is a noun. To put it better: supernatural adds nothing to the quality of gratuitousness which, as we saw earlier, is the determining feature and content of the concept of grace. If grace signifies something given *gratis,* a gift, then supernatural signifies exactly the same thing—nothing more and nothing less. For it signifies what is added as a gift to the natural, that which does not belong to me by virtue of any right inherent in my nature as man.

To say gift is to oppose it to that which belongs to a person by right, either because he possesses it already or has a right to it in justice. If a person talks about grace and gift, then by that very fact he introduces this unavoidable distinction.

Now where does the simplification come in here? It comes in when one applies the habitual schema of "before" and "after" to this essential notion of a proffered gift. The gift almost always comes after, when that which is not a gift is already constituted and operative. By comparing the before and the after, we recognize the gratuitous element and separate it from the natural.

To translate this into theological terms, it would seem that the before and after of the divine gift should be able to be found in the loftiest change we can visualize, conversion: i.e., the moment when, through faith and baptism, one comes to form a part of the Church, when one ceases to be simply a human being and is turned into a Christian human being.

But we live in a world where the majority of Christians have not passed through this moment. So clearly, in such a world, this before and after distinguishes not so much two chunks of our own personal existence as two categories of human beings separated by a hypothetical conversion: i.e., Christians and non-Christians.

So it would seem that one need only take an inventory of the experience of the non-Christian in order to be able to describe the content of man's *natural* existence. For example, it would be enough to take account of his more universal ideas in order to be able to talk about a "philosophy" accessible to the "natural light" of human reason. And we could simply ask the nonbeliever about his hopes in order to be able to talk about man's "natural end."

Thus this outlook, as Rahner points out, proposed to start from the anthropology of daily experience and from metaphysics. From them it felt it would be able to obtain a fully delineated concept of man's *nature.*

"The presumption is that the essence of man encountered in concrete experience is satisfactorily identifiable with his nature: i.e., with that which, in theology, is the counter-concept to the supernatural." [11]

But experience soon showed that there is an extraordinary similarity between believer and nonbeliever when we inquire into the deeper levels of their activities. Indeed the only thing that seems to be different for sure is their *intention*. When all real-life differences between philanthropy and charity have disappeared, the only distinguishing feature that remains is the motive: "For the love of God." Not surprisingly, then, the concern to place oneself on "the supernatural plane" became pretty much identified in Christian practice with the cultivation of intention. By virtue of one's intention a human, natural deed was elevated and placed on the road to eternal life. Not surprisingly, life eternal seemed to be the result of intentions which divested themselves of man's (natural) deeds at the moment of death to enter heaven by themselves. For heaven, in this outlook, was not the *end result* of human history but the reward for that which was performed in it for the love of God. Supernatural elevation (i.e., elevating grace) and the psychological elevation of intention were made synonymous for all practical purposes.

But another outlook is possible. Just because a gift is a gift (that is, something gratuitous) does not mean we must necessarily differentiate a before and after. It can accompany the whole existence of a person without thereby ceasing to be a gift. What is more, it can accompany the whole existence of *all* men. And it would not cease to be a gift just because it was so all-pervasive. If we realize this, we can appreciate the line of reasoning offered by Rahner and others.

But first let us look at a hypothetical example. Suppose someone were given the gift of a fortune even before he was born. That would certainly start to alter his life right from the moment of his birth, or even before. He would be born and raised differently. In short, everything would be changed—except his human nature, of course.

Now if this person later tried to locate this gift in his existence (as we are trying to do with grace here), he would not be able to resort to a comparison between before and after. For him the gift would be something that had always been there.

Another course would still remain open to him. He could try to locate the difference by comparing his life with the lives of those who did not receive a comparable gift and hence live by "purely human nature." But let us suppose that all the other human beings he knew were in the same situation as he. They knew from revelation that they had been given a gift, but they could not imagine concretely what their lives would have been without the gift they have indeed received. And they could not do so because the gift is not extrinsic (and God knows whether money is more extrinsic than grace!) to anything that has happened in their lives. It impregnates and transforms every bit of it. The other term of the comparison—what their life "would have been"—does not show up as an historical reality or even as a precise image. Yet the gift has not lost its essential nature as a gift, its gratuitousness.

Hence it is not necessary that we be able to separate grace from what "existed before" or what "exists in others," for grace to continue to be what it is: i.e., gratuitous. But it is necessary that we always distinguish it from the *concept* of the natural, which is what *would have been* the total reality if the gift had not always been there.[12]

In other words, the purely natural is a limit-concept: i.e., a possibility which must be kept in mind always to appreciate and remember that the gift is a gift. But it is not a concept that has real, historical content: i.e., a concept that points to something which can possibly be found or imagined concretely within our history.

What it comes down to—and this is a major point relating to the whole topic of divine grace—is that we are not accustomed to gifts like this one. For us the very idea of gift entails the notion of *scarcity*. In our minds the natural is associated with that which abounds; it is what everyone has. In our ranks, gifts always constitute privileged moments. So we set about looking for grace, convinced that if it is a gift, it must be missing at some point in our own lives or the lives of others. And by comparing presence and absence we hope to find the line of separation where pure nature lies on one side and the supernatural on the other.

But reality does not lend itself to such a separation. As Rahner puts it: "Experience alone cannot determine exactly in every case—at least not without the aid of theology—whether that which is found in man belongs to his nature as such . . . or to his historical nature inasmuch as the latter—ever in an empirical way but conditioned by the fact of a vocation to a supernatural end—possesses within itself traits that it would not have if such a vocation did not exist." [13]

Even before this gift effectively transforms our whole existence and opens the gates of eternal life to it, it is present in germ in what we called a *vocation,* a call. And this call is to something above and beyond man; it is a supernatural vocation. Every man who awakens to the call of conscience finds alongside himself the hand and voice of God, elevating him toward that place where eternal life already appears on the horizon. And the product of that vocation is *man,* all the concrete human beings we know: that is, man dwelling in history and acting it out.

"From the very circumstance of his origin, man is already invited to

converse with God" (GS 19). Hence he cannot separate the exigency of
that vocation from himself, yet it ever remains gratuitous and hence a
gift. The most necessary thing is also gratuitous.[14]

> Couldn't one say quite rightly that the essence of personal being consists pre-
> cisely in being ordered by (concrete) nature toward personal communion
> with God in love and having to receive this same love as a free gift? But
> doesn't the same thing happen in earthly love? It is the reality toward
> which the person who loves and is loved feels himself or herself clearly
> ordered. And in such a way that they would be wretched and forlorn if they
> did not receive this love. Nevertheless they receive it as a "miracle," as an
> unexpected gift of freely proffered love: i.e., of love not owed to them.
> Might not one ask: Couldn't the essence of the personal spirit consist pre-
> cisely in this, in this and nothing more—in having to receive personal love
> as something undeserved if one does not want to lose its meaning . . . ?[15]

After what we have said in the previous chapter, we can only answer yes
to this question.

And here we come to the knot that ties these two chapters together.
In the previous chapter, grace seemed to be moving in a horizontal direction: from the human condition, which showed us man rising from the
prehuman and falling back into it, toward hominization. In this chapter,
the movement of grace seemed to change direction and become vertical.
And yet there has been no change of direction, and the proof is plain to
see. When grace healed us, was it not precisely to make us capable of
gratuitous relationships, to make us free and creative? And when grace
elevates us, whereto does it elevate us if not to the divine plane of gratuitousness, to the realm where the divine reality is free and creative?

To put it another way: Turning ourselves into *persons,* in the fullest
sense of the term, was the end goal of hominization. And turning ourselves into *persons* also seems to be the end goal of our elevation, our
divinization.

Grace, then, is that which enables us to journey forward as human
beings—without interruption but through the effect of an essential gift—
from the natural human condition to the creative liberty of the sons of
God (Rom. 8:21).

Within the context of our present theme, this also transforms the idea
we must entertain about the goal toward which God's gift elevates us:
eternal life.

1. A recent French novel contains two brief passages that can help us
to appreciate the point here. Indeed its very title, *The Wind Blows Where
It Wills,* alludes to the theme of grace.

One passage is part of a letter which the wife of the main character
sends to him. He is a prisoner in a concentration camp. "My love, on

Christmas Eve when the priest who baptizes you speaks to you of eternal *life* . . . I do not know what eternal life is, but I know for sure that it is simply life: this life that I love, your life, the lives of our children, our life." [16]

And so it is. No one knows what eternal life is except by starting from what life itself is. There is in man a deep and justified opposition to the idea of conceiving *another* life as a reward to be received when this one ceases. The opposition is not something new in our day. Paul himself expresses it clearly: "We yearn to have our heavenly habitation put on over this one . . . We groan indeed, we who are enclosed within this earthly frame; we are oppressed because we do not want to have the old body stripped off. Rather our desire is to have the new body put on over it, so that our mortal part may be absorbed into life immortal" (2 Cor. 5:2–4). "This perishable being must be clothed with the imperishable, and what is mortal must be clothed with immortality" (1 Cor. 15:53).

The first conclusion, then, is that the Christian image of eternal life can only be fashioned with the materials, that is, the values of this one.

2. Furthermore, if the mission of grace were to console us with the appearance of another life for the disappearance of this life, then it would be a total failure. Because, thank God, no hope in *something else* consoles us when something like death separates us from the beings we love and the little we were able to create here on earth. Only the return of all that can slake our thirst.

This brings us to the second passage in Lesort's novel. Two characters are discussing the advantage of being a Christian, and one notes that it offers hope in a heaven. The other person reacts strongly: "Heaven! Christ himself, who had risen and returned to his Father, still came back to earth again to see his friends. He went all over, from house to house and from roadway to inn, as if he could not resolve to leave them. And in fact he left them his spirit, his *alter ego* . . . So what about a poor creature who is not God, who cannot say: 'This day you shall be with me'? How can he leave a tattered human race and a tattered Church? No, dying does not solve anything. So I do not see what good it is to be a believer!" His interlocutor replies: "You are right. It serves no good at all." [17]

If indeed serving any good means replacing the problem with a solution, then believing in eternal life serves no good. It would be the worst turn one could do for a human being.

Christian hope in eternal life is a disinterested hope, if we understand disinterest in the proper way. It does not signify a lack of interest. It signifies the absence of any interest other than the *result* we seek with the gift of our lives. A person who builds wills this building with a passion, but he has no selfish interest.

Thus what we have said so far leads us to conclude the same thing that Johannes Metz did: "From the viewpoint of theology we must reunite two notions that have long been separated in theological consciousness, i.e., transcendence and the future." [18] To put it in other words, we must reunite eternal life and the construction of history. Eternal life is *the new earth*.

To picture and construct eternal life with the materials of this life alone is not a new idea. It is a basic datum in the Bible. And we are not referring to the Old Testament solely, where the panorama of a life beyond death is absent until a time near the coming of Christ. We are also referring to the New Testament even though, or precisely because, it is more dominated by the idea of resurrection.

One of the New Testament images of eternal life is the heavenly banquet. There is a beautiful commentary on it in a book by Father Pierre Charles (*Prayer of All Things*):

> Lord, today in your gospel I came across the surprising phrase which you use to describe heaven, the reality which we all look forward to and which our mind tries to comprehend here and now. . . . It turns out that you have told us that heaven is a great banquet-table at which we all will sit with you to drink our Father's wine and to converse as friends.
>
> The family table! I need not dwell on it very long to call up my most beautiful memories . . . The image allows me to get a foretaste of the joy in paradise. There you will not sit on a distant throne. What sense would there be to such solitary grandeur amid those whom you yourself have chosen? Even at the Eucharistic banquet here, are you not within the reach of all and practically at our mercy? And is it not, as you yourself said, the prelude to the festive table of heaven?
>
> Well then, we are in agreement. This is the way I choose to see you. Your heaven is not a big entertainment hall, it is a cozy dining room. In an entertainment hall, the person next to you does not count at all; empty seats do not bother anyone; and conversation is frowned upon. At the dinner table, by contrast, glances pass back and forth, jokes are shared, and the joy of each and all is shared mutually. Your heaven is a place of hospitality, a fiesta. And if we cannot express this mystery of divine simplicity in philosophic formulas—patience! [19]

And if this is the case, it is so because in the New Testament eternal life and the new earth are truly synonymous, as the Apocalypse says (21:1).

Now what does this adjective "new" mean precisely. It is worth pointing out that while there are two Greek words to designate "new" (*neos* and *kainos*), the term used almost invariably to designate the new reality to which we are elevated by grace is *kainos,* not *neos*. And exegetical studies indicate that while *neos* signifies that which is new in time and hence *another* of something (e.g., a new year), *kainos* designates that which is new in quality and hence that which is renewed or transformed. A new man is the same man transformed. *Kainos* is also the term used to signify the results of transformations effected by God: i.e., renovations which come from above.

Hence the use of one single term joins the two meanings with the Greek word *anothen,* which can also mean one of two things: anew or from on high (see note 2 in this chapter).

Hence it is the *earth* that we are looking forward to and that is identical with eternal life. It is our earth and our history and our effort transformed by the gift of God's grace. Through this gift our transient and mortal earth acquires perduring incorruptibility and immortality, the qualities that come from on high. Grace elevates man's earth and man's history.

Vatican II tells us this in three essential texts that describe the content of the "new earth." "By his incarnation the Son of God has united Himself in some fashion with every man. He worked with human hands, He thought with a human mind, acted by human choice, and loved with a human heart" (GS 22). "For after we have obeyed the Lord, and in His Spirit nurtured on earth the values of human dignity, brotherhood, and freedom, and indeed all the good fruits of our nature and enterprise, we will find them again, but freed of stain, burnished, and transfigured" (GS 39). "Then, with death overcome, the sons of God will be raised up In Christ. What was sown in weakness and corruption will be clothed with incorruptibility. While charity and its fruits endure, all that creation which God made on man's account will be unchained from the bondage of vanity" (GS 39).

4. As Paul tells us, we Christians who possess these hopes are framed between two epiphanies (i.e., manifestations): the manifestation of grace and the manifestation of glory (Titus 2:11–13). This means that we human beings, who have already in a certain sense been resurrected with Christ and elevated by him through grace, already see dawning over our horizon the end goal of our history. We see our full measure and adulthood: eternal life, the new earth.

It also means that we must work out two indivisible realities: our construction of human history in Christ and our concrete, joyous acceptance of his gratuitous gift. Work and gift are two facets of the same reality, like day and night. And we often forget the meaning of night. We are too rigid in our demands and our work to appreciate why God has given us night. We need the calm hopefulness of a few quiet hours. As Péguy puts it, God does not want human beings who "do not sleep, who burn with fever and impatience in their beds." [20]

Hence the elevation of grace should be translated into an attitude that respects both poles. It should arouse in us a passionate interest in the history of man and an openness to a gift that surpasses our hopes.

The risen Christ was new and distinct and glorious in the eyes of his friends. Even his closest associates were slow to recognize him. Yet he was the same person. Two disciples were on their way to Emmaus (Luke 24:29–31) when they met him. His lucid explanations of Scripture dazzled them and they did not recognize him. He pretended that he was travelling farther, but they persuaded him to dine with them. And they recognized him at dinner, for he broke bread in his customary way.

On another occasion the disciples went out fishing (John 21:4–13). They spent the whole night out and returned to shore with empty nets. He was waiting for them on shore, bent over a fish-fry. He could have invited them to a "heavenly" meal, but instead he shared the fruit of a regular day's labor: fish and bread.

On another occasion he appeared suddenly in their midst, and they were so amazed and terrified that they thought he was a ghost (Luke 24:36–43). But it was truly he, and they recognized him, not because of any familiar ideas or words he used, but because he sat down to eat with them as usual. In short, he shared the ordinary necessities of life, which form a secret but powerful bond between all human beings and their labors.

Again when Thomas had doubts about his identity because his reappearance went beyond all expectations, the resurrected Jesus did not appeal to his newly won glory. He showed Thomas the very same wounds he had received in his passion and death here on earth. They were the perduring bond between his divinity and his humanity. Thus through the resurrection of Christ, who is "the firstfruits of the harvest of the dead" (1 Cor. 15:20), we glimpse eternal life and its relationship with our life here: the start of the new earth.

NOTES TO CHAPTER TWO

1. *Vraie et fausse réforme dans l'Eglise,* 2nd ed. (Paris: Ed. du Cerf, 1968), pp. 141 ff.

2. The phrase can also mean "unless a man has been born from on high." This in fact is the sense that Jesus is going to explicate. But, in accordance with a usual method in John's Gospel, the audience takes off from the more "earthly" meaning, if we may use that term. Hence Nicodemus understands it as being "born again." He is not mistaken, even though Jesus' teaching goes even further.

3. Following the opinion of many exegetes, Ignace de la Potterie points

out that the inclusion of water alongside Holy Spirit is due more to the reminiscence of a Church which is already practicing baptism than to the development of the dialogue itself. In the latter it is the categories of spirit, heaven, and on high that enable Jesus to present his "evangel" for the first time in the Johannine account. See Ignace de la Potterie and Stanislas Lyonnet, *La vie selon l'Esprit*.

4. This treatment here does not exhaust the wealth of allusions in this passage by any means. On the Spirit, in particular, see the work of De la Potterie and Lyonnet cited in the preceding note.

5. *Cf.* Emile Mersch, *La Théologie du Corps Mystique* (Paris: Desclé 1946), II, 337. Engl. trans., *Theology of the Mystical Body* (St. Louis: B. Herder, 1951), p. 596.

6. Here we stress the temptation to oversimplification arising out of the very task of communicating the Christian message to a mass of people who sought to find a facile principle of election. But one must not minimize the historical background either, which contributed some important elements. To be sure, Christianity offered a truly new idea in its notion of an elevation conferred by grace. But the originality of this element was not immediately perceived as such, since it was immersed in a large-scale religious current that swept both Occident and Orient around this time and dominated religious life in cultural centers for almost two millennia. This current put an interpretation on Christianity and added it on as an appendage, as it were. In the first millennium after Christ one of the major phenomena in the history of world religions was the emergence of a religious attitude involving *rejection of the world*. This current evaluated both man and the world in extremely negative terms, and it exalted religion as a unique reality which alone had value. And it survived and dominated the civilized world for almost two thousand years. All this is treated in an article by Robert N. Bellah, "Religious Evolution," *American Sociological Review*, 1964, 29:358–374. In support of his view, Bellah cites postexilic biblical currents, Greek religious philosophy especially Platonism, Buddhism in India, Chinese Taoism, etc. While the first two factors mentioned may indeed have lent support to nascent Christianity, they also interpreted it and vitiated it in their own ways. This is attested to by John, Paul, and the controversies of the early Church.

7. Prayer over the Gifts for the twenty-fourth Sunday after Pentecost.

8. Prayer after Communion for the second Sunday of Advent.

9. Entrance Prayer for Thursday of the fourth week in Lent.

10. Harvey Cox, *The Secular City*, 6th ed. (New York: Macmillan, 1965), p. 110.

11. Karl Rahner, "Concerning the Relationship between Nature and Grace," in *Theological Investigations*, I, p. 299. See note 4 at the end of the main article in Chapter I of this volume.

12. "We can resort to a transcendental deduction to spell out the irrevocable essence of man. That is, we can consider as the purely natural essence of man that which results from the very formulation of the question. But in using this approach we would never know if we had put too little into this notion of man; or if, on the other hand, in the very asking of the question itself there was already operating, de facto and inevitably always in the questioner, a supernatural element that could never be put in parentheses and that consequently prevented us from apprehending purely the natural essence of man in the concept" (Rahner, *ibid.*, p. 301.)

13. *Ibid.*, pp. 298–299, note 1.

14. So we come to the definitive image that we spoke about in note 2 of the main section of Chapter I. Far from being an addition to nature, grace is something which establishes the sense, value, and destiny of the "natural." For grace is liberty, interiority, and personality that lives in and by love.

"If God gives man a supernatural end, and this is the first in the order of intention, then the world and man by that very fact are distinct, in all their parts and in their intrinsic structure, from what they would have been if they did not possess this end, even before they have attained it. . . . And it is thoroughly legitimate to start from this perspective to outline the one and only concrete 'essence' of man (if not indeed his nature as a counter-concept to grace)." Rahner, *ibid,* pp. 302–303.

15. *Ibid.,* p. 310.

16. Lesort, *Le vent souffle où il veut* (Paris: Plon, 1954), p. 271.

17. *Ibid.,* p. 273.

18. Declaration of Johannes Metz at the Marxist-Christian Dialogue meeting in Salzburg, April 29–May 2, 1965.

19. Perhaps the best way to express this transformation of our lives into eternal life is through poetry: e.g., Francisco Luis Bernárdez, *Poem to St. Francis.*

20. Charles Péguy, "Le porche du mystère de la deuxième vertu" *Cahiers de la Quinzaine,* Oct. 22, 1911.

CLARIFICATIONS

I. THE GREAT ANTAGONISTS IN THE BIBLE: "FLESH" VERSUS "SPIRIT"; THE "WORLD" VERSUS THE "HOUR"

The whole discussion of these first two chapters would remain opaque and strange-sounding to dedicated readers of the Bible, if it did not point up the special meaning of certain biblical terms. The meaning is both metaphorical and profoundly theological, and it is found above all in the New Testament. The first two terms of key importance, which stand over against each other as antagonists, are *flesh* and *spirit*. The second set of antagonistic terms are the *world* and Christ's *hour*.

1. Let us begin by considering Paul's use of the term *flesh*. Any assiduous reader of the New Testament will have noted the heightened pejorative connotation that Paul gives to this word, to the point where he uses it to designate the anti-Christian attitude *par excellence*. The assiduous reader will also have noted that this pejorative note has little or nothing to do with the sexual overtones that the term acquired in later inspirational literature, where it is presented in the triad: the world, the flesh, and the devil.

What exactly does this term signify for Paul, and why does it acquire a pejorative connotation? To answer this question we must go back to the Old Testament.

In its oldest sense *flesh*, like *bones*, is used metaphorically to signify a great affective unity.[1] Flesh and bones are precisely the most perceptible and characteristic feature of each human being. To be part of the flesh and bones of someone, or simply to be part of his flesh, means to be deeply united with that person. When the Yahwist writer says that husband and wife "shall be two in one flesh," he undoubtedly was not referring to the sexual act but to the formation of an affective unity that was stronger and more bedrock for them than their unity with their own original families: "That is why a man leaves his father and mother and is united to his wife, and the two become one flesh" (Gen. 2:24).[2]

Thus the notion of being flesh of another, in its metaphorical use, will take in every deep union, since flesh in Hebrew literature is the seat of one's sensibility and affective life. The flesh of a human being, then, is everything that surrounds him with ties of emotion and affection; it is the world of his family, kin, and tribe with which he is identified.

Much later on, at the time of the Babylonian captivity, the Hebrews would discover the significance of God's transcendence as creator of the

77

universe. This would lead them to look for a single term which they could apply to all beings which are not masters of their own existence and which owe it rather to their Maker. They did not choose a term as logical as our term *creature*. Instead they expressed the same notion in a metaphorical way, using the term *all flesh*.[3]

The experience which led them to choose the same word "flesh" for this different notion was itself different from the first one. In reality it was the experience of death. In death the flesh remains, seemingly intact and the same. But the person no longer exists, and the unequivocal sign of this fact is the fact that the flesh no longer breathes. It lacks the vital puff of breath. This puff of breath or wind is what is signified primarily by a term that has been greatly "spiritualized" today: *spirit*. The latter term does not refer to some disembodied region of the human being but to the puff of breath that makes him a living being. Thus the Yahwist writer describes creation in terms of a direct contrast with the phenomenon of death: Yahweh, as it were, fashions a being of clay and then breathes into its nostrils, thereby transmitting to inert flesh his own life, his spirit. Hence the term *all flesh* is a figurative way of designating the ensemble of beings who receive existence and conservation in it from Yahweh.

We now have two metaphorical uses of the word *flesh*. It signifies the sensibility and affective life of man on the one hand, creature on the other hand. There was nothing to stop the two meanings from being combined, so in the latter eras of the Old Testament the term *flesh* metaphorically signifies the *sensibility* of the *creature,* his religious sensibility: i.e., the sensible, affective reaction of man to the activity or proximity of the Spirit of Yahweh.

Confronted with the power and solidity of the Spirit, it is only natural and proper for the flesh to feel absolutely perishable, fleeting, and fragile. It is only natural for it to feel its absolute contingency both in philosophical and moral terms. And hence it is only natural for it to feel a deep thirst for the Creator and his Temple and his Law, while at the same time experiencing profound terror over his proximity and knowing that it cannot endure this proximity without dying.

In other words, the religion of Israel was converted into a religion of the flesh: i.e., into an attitude toward God based on the creature's keen awareness and sensibility of his own nature as such.

This is precisely the positive connotation of the word "flesh" that Paul received from the Old Testament. Far from being a negative element or an animal zone in the person, it signified the creature's vital recognition of his relation to a transcendent God and the religious attitude proceeding from this recognition.

How is it then that Paul comes to turn "flesh" into the anti-Christian element *par excellence,* without ever indicating that he is giving it a meaning different from what it had in the numerous Old Testament passages he cites? The fact is that right from his earliest letters on, such as that to the Galatians, the fleshly outlook shows up in the religious realm as something that empties the Christian message of all meaning.

What has happened is that the message and the very reality of Christ have ushered in different relations between human beings and God than those which obtained between creature and Creator in the Old Testament. Let us try to sum up these changes briefly, as they are seen by Paul.

Firstly, if God in the Old Testament summoned man to a relationship centered around the difference in *natures* between creature and Creator, he did so because man had not yet reached his adulthood. Only in his childhood state was man ruled by the nature of things and his own nature. Christ fulfilled and proclaimed the full maturity and adulthood of man as a son of God. With the arrival of man's adulthood, things ceased to be over him and now are put at his disposition. And things here means everything in the universe: the sacred and the profane, the things of earth and the things of heaven. Man is no longer under the law, or at least he should not be. If he chooses to remain under it, it is because he is still fleshly, because he does not choose to assume the maturity of his new personal and creative relationship with God. So we can see why the fleshly outlook nullifies Christ. The whole transformation he ushered into human existence centers around this transition from a determining nature to a nature determined by liberty.

Secondly, as we noted earlier, the law of least effort causes man's personal projects to be dominated by the very instruments with which he proposes to carry them out. And in the catalogue of these instruments we must give first place, according to Paul, to religious instruments: to the moral law which reveals sin to man, and to the ecclesial structure and its sacraments and personnel which reveal redemption and liberation. On the all too ready road to inauthenticity, the Christian allows himself to be led to convert these means into mechanical, deterministic conditions. For example, he tries to invest his righteousness in works that allow him to "put an obligation" on God; or he tries to tie up his salvation with rites whose sacred efficacity must be evaluated carefully. He can even convert Christian liberty itself into a licentiousness which allows him to retain the name of Christian while becoming once again the slave of his own desires.

Thirdly, all this indicates the ambiguity of everything that is fleshly. On the one hand it is the inevitable starting point, the place where grace and revelation pick us up. In this respect it corresponds to an "age" of man that is not the mature measure of Christ. On the other hand it is something that Christ must take on, in everything save sin, if he is to unite himself with man and thereby redeem him: i.e., liberate him and allow him to move from flesh to spirit. For Christ to take on flesh does not mean to live according to the the flesh, i.e., to sin; it means to live *in* the flesh. Living according to the flesh means allowing oneself to be dominated by it.

Finally, in the view of Paul the spirit is not something new in the sense that it is a region apart where man can live sheltered from the flesh and its mechanisms. It is a new way of operating with the flesh itself. It is a way of orienting the religious, in whose absence the religious itself is enslaving and anti-Christian. It is a way of orienting the law, in whose absence morality is infantile and practically sinful. It is a way of reading the gospel, in whose absence the good news itself becomes a dead letter that deals death not life.

Thus everything that man can accumulate in the realm of flesh is incapable of obtaining the most minimal spiritual result. The spirit comes from another world; but it does not operate in another world, it operates in the world of the flesh. There is difference but also continuity, exactly paralleling the situation between life in time and life in eternity.

2. John's use of the term *world* is easier to understand to a certain degree. Its origin is probably more Greek than Hebrew, hence its religious history is less complicated. We would say that it was more laicized when John adopted it for his theology. Moreover, its different connotations are already clear to a certain degree on the basis of what we have already said about "flesh."

The term *world* is sometimes synonymous with *humanity* and sometimes with *creation* in general. And right off we can see that the same thing happens to it in John's writings as happens to "flesh" in Paul's writings. It acquires a pejorative connotation.

This is already evident in the Prologue of the Fourth Gospel, where all three meanings appear: The Word came into the world (i.e., the ensemble of mankind), the world (i.e., the entire universe) was made by him, but the world did not recognize him. What does *world* mean in the last phrase? Is it once again the ensemble of mankind? Not exactly, because a subsequent verse mentions those within the world who are "his own" and who acknowledge him to a certain extent. So in the third case *world* does not refer to all mankind but to the majority of human beings.

So now the question is: Why does this majority, rather than the small minority, deserve to be called the "world" without restriction? Why not simply say "one part" or "the greater part" of the world rejected him? Whatever the answer may be, it is obvious enough that the term *world* has acquired a pejorative connotation. Those who deny the Word, and only they, are "the world." One can say that the whole Gospel of John does nothing else but depict a battle between Jesus and this "world." Jesus certainly emerges victorious, but that does not finish off the "world." As Jesus himself foresees, the world will continue to operate on those who will carry on his message and attitudes.

If those who reject the Word, and only they, are considered "world," then in John's eyes there must evidently exist an analogy between what the word *world* commonly signifies and the attitude that denies Jesus. In some way those who are opposed to Jesus give in to the force that constitutes the world. What is the why and wherefor of this?

To begin with: What sort of force is it? Both in his Gospel and his first epistle John characterizes it for us in terms of a *nature,* a systematized determinism, a structure that ignores liberty.

The fact is that everything which the world possesses and values is something that comes from this same world. Within this vicious circle, which feeds upon itself, it seems impossible to introduce newness, light, truth. For the world is a system of desires which are sparked and snuffed out within itself, a system of thoughts wherein one listens only to what he already knows, and a social system wherein one loves only what he has always loved already.

Thus within this system it is not just the liberty to create that is impossible. Equally impossible is the humble liberty to receive, to listen, to comprehend; even this liberty must come from above and provoke a *crisis*.

This precisely is the mission, the salvific mission of Jesus: To provoke this crisis, the root meaning of which is *judgment* in Greek. He has come to shed the light of truth and authenticity on the system of slavery which the world constitutes. And his disciples are to continue this mission. But there will always be something terribly explosive about fashioning truth within a system which is founded on a lie and which alienates man and destroys his humanity.

The fated lot of the truthful, free human being moves toward this explosion, toward the terrible confrontation between love-liberty and an enslaving world. It is the *hour* toward which Jesus moves, the *hour* toward which his followers will also move later. Only free human beings, only those who do not derive what they must say and do from the world, have such an hour: i.e., a personal destiny. The world, closed up in its own vicious circle, does not show variation or creative power; it is engaged in endless repetition. The only thing that disturbs it, and that sometimes permits some people to free themselves of it, is the breaking in of the light of truth that condemns it.

Those enclosed in the world urge Jesus to get acquainted with it. They want him to subject himself to its system of values. But Jesus replies that he cannot because he has his *hour*. For the world, by contrast, every moment of time is the same.

Here again, then, we find the same opposition that was signified by the term *flesh*. On the one side we find true liberty which, when its hour comes, radically opposes the world and thus feels the full weight of its tragic defense mechanisms. Only a love that goes all the way can pass through and survive these defenses, like a light of searching appeal and judgment. On the other side we find the world, which is to say the force opposed to liberty and hence to Christ the liberator. It is the force of a natural world that has already been neatly systematized; in it hate and love are already fashioned once and for all, knowledge and prestige are handed out readymade, and desire is sated as soon as it is expressed.

But let us note once again that there is an element of ambiguity in the pejorative term. Even though liberty bursts into the world from outside the vicious circle of the world, the only place where it can work itself out is the world. The *hour* in which liberty and persevering love find fulfillment must take place in the world. For the world is nothing else but the community of mankind, and it also constitutes the very object of liberty. To give in to the world and its mechanisms is to oppose Christ; but by the same token, to love the world and give one's life for it is to follow the pathway of God himself. "God loved the world so much that he gave his only Son" to save it from itself by injecting a higher liberty into its mechanistic routine.

To repeat once more: None of the great themes of Christianity can be understood without reference to liberty, to that liberty which, like eternal life, comes from on high but is at the same time breakthrough and continuity, crisis and incarnation, life in the world and eschatology.

II. TEILHARD DE CHARDIN AND THE VALUE
OF HUMAN ACTIVITY

Teilhard de Chardin offers his own witness to the problem of human activity and its value. The divine value of our activity in history has always been an important problem for spiritual writers. The classic outlook maintained that its value depended on the rightness of our intention. Teilhard de Chardin offers a somewhat crude caricature of this position in *The Divine Milieu,* when he puts the following words on the lips of a spiritual director:

> You are anxious, my friend, to restore the value of your human endeavour which seems to you to be depreciated by the Christian vision and Christian asceticism. Very well then, pour over it the marvellous substance of good will. Purify your intention, and the least of your actions will be filled with God. No doubt the material side of your actions has no ultimate value. . . . But what *will* count, up there, what *will* always endure, is this: that you have acted in all things *conformably* to the will of God. . . . Try to grasp this: the things which are given to you on earth are given you purely as an exercise. . . . You are on trial. So that it matters very little what becomes of the fruits of the earth or what they are worth. . . . You should not, therefore, cling to the coarse outer-covering of human activities: these are but inflammable straw or brittle clay. But try to realise that into each of these humble vessels you can pour, like a sap or a precious liquid, the spirit of obedience and of union with God.[4]

This problem of Christian spirituality is one chapter of a larger story that must be framed within a dualistic current of Manichaeism and Catharism, the overall current being much vaster than the heresies which go by those names. Within the history of the Church, particularly at the time of the Renaissance, it found expression in an outlook where the world and God, science and faith, seemed to have taken different pathways. Man's religious outlook was divorced from real life in Christian thinking.

As man continues to expand and deepen his research and technological dominion, he takes more notice of the magnitude of nature and of his own capacity to intervene in the futher shaping of the world. Thus there was born in modern man a keener sense of responsibility toward history, and the cult of earth and man's mission on it gave rise to a new humanism. It is not by accident that modern philosophy focused its attention on the theme of liberty. The construction of a better world is in the hands of man. The allure of modern atheism is rooted in its effort to give man Promethean control over his own existence.

This presentation of the issue and its accompanying polemics created a false problem. After all, was it not true that the novel feature of Christianity was its identification of the religious outlook with man's responsibility toward history? As one author puts it: "The first thing that strikes the attention of the historian of religions when he reads the Bible attentively is its identification of man's religious task with his creative commitment and effort." [5] Right near the beginning of Genesis we find that man is like God by virtue of his creative task vis-à-vis the cosmos. It is both his vocation in history and his religious aspect.

But this fundamental truth of Christian revelation was forgotten. Indeed it was forgotten to such an extent that people felt they must avoid commitment to worldly realities of all sorts if they were to integrate themselves properly into the reality of the Christian religion. Vatican II put things in order once again. Despite some ambiguities in the text, *Gaudium et spes* is clearly the best indication of this. For it points to the divine vocation of the Christian in the work of history, labelling the divorce between religion and life as the most pernicious error for today's believers (GS 43).

Gaudium et spes marks the start of a new chapter in the attitude of Christians toward the world. To ascertain this, one need only look at what has happened since: the changed orientation of various Christian movements; the declarations and positions taken by them and the hierarchy itself with respect to the critical problems facing humanity; the rapprochement with all men of good will who seek more real and universal justice among men; and the mistrust of the attitude held by those who enjoy the status quo and still yearn to keep a dualistic brand of Christianity, to maintain an inoffensive "religious" Christianity aloof from human realities.

The road leading to the statement of the issue found in *Gaudium et spes* has been long and rocky. But no one doubts that Teilhard de Chardin was one of the pioneer standard-bearers of this new outlook, his thought breaking upon Christians with forceful impact at the start of the Council. The "phenomenon of Teilhard" expresses and embodies the quest of most Christians to consciously resolve the spiritual schizophrenia in which their existence was framed.

Teilhard felt this spiritual schizophrenia from an early age, and he engaged in a "pathetic effort to reconcile my attraction for Nature with the evangelism of the *Imitation* that nourished my morning prayers." [6] In 1918, soon after his ordination, he states what he desires to be the mission of his life. He wants to be the apostle of "the relationships of continuity that make the cosmos in which we move a divinizing milieu." He wants to show that "the work of human beings is sacred," and that "human development is demanded by Christ."

Near the end of his life he affirmed that this union had been achieved and discovered that his personal synthesis provided the solution to the great spiritual problem of the present day. He writes:

> The original aspect of my belief consists in the fact that it has its roots in two realms of life that had usually been considered antagonistic to each other. By education and intellectual formation I belong to the "children of heaven." But by temperament and professional training I am a "child of earth." Thus my life has been set in the heart of two worlds whose theories, languages, and sentiments are familiar and well known to me. I have never erected an interior wall between them. I have instead allowed these two seemingly contradictory influences to operate upon each other with full freedom inside me. Now, after trying to forge an interior unity for thirty years,

I have the impression that a synthesis has been effected naturally between these two currents. The one has not killed the other. Today I believe in God, probably more than ever before; and I believe in the world just as much. Do we not have here, on an individual scale and in outline at least, the specific solution to the great spiritual problem that confronts humanity in its forward advance today? [7]

What was this synthesis that took shape within Teilhard de Chardin? On the one hand the "child of earth" became convinced that the history of the world is in a process of gestation that is not ruled by chance. The process of "cosmogenesis" has been, is, and will be coherent. In view of this coherence and without leaving the empirical level, Teilhard postulates a center of convergence which he calls the Omega Point.

As a "child of heaven" Teilhard compares these conclusions with the Word of God. The result of this comparison between human history and salvation history leads to a clear and evident conclusion: the Omega Point is Christ.

> We may dig things over as much as we please, but the universe cannot have two heads—it cannot be "bicephalic." However supernatural, therefore, the synthesising operation attributed by dogma to the Incarnate Word may ultimately be, it cannot be effected in a divergence from the natural convergence of the world as defined above. The universal Christic centre, determined by theology, and the universal cosmic centre postulated by anthropogenesis: these two focal points ultimately coincide (or at least overlap) in the historical setting in which we are contained. Christ would not be the sole Mover, the sole Issue, of the universe if it were possible for the universe in any way to integrate itself, even to a lesser degree, apart from Christ. And even more certainly, Christ, it would seem, would have been physically incapable of supernaturally centering the universe upon himself if it had not provided the Incarnation with a specially favoured point at which, in virtue of their natural structure, all the strands of the cosmos tend to meet together. It is therefore towards Christ, in fact, that we turn our eyes when, however approximate our concept of it may be, we look ahead towards a higher pole of humanisation and personalisation. In position and function, Christ, here and now, fills for us the place of Omega Point.[8]

This is the intuition that is at the base of Teilhard's thought. Anthropogenesis is followed by Christogenesis, not in temporal order nor at a separate stage, but in the very interior of the human phenomenon. "Supernatural" does not mean that the gift comes from *outside*. If the Christ of revelation and the Omega Point coincide, then in fact there is no room for Manichaeism. Why? Because the effort to build a better world is nothing else in fact than the effort of Christification. Just as the effort of the People of Israel was a slow and progressive effort making possible the Incarnation of the Word, so the effort that is required for the progress of the cosmos is nurturing the recapitulation of all things in Christ.

Once upon a time, notes Teilhard, it seemed that there were only two geometrically opposed attitudes for man. He must either love heaven or love the earth. Now a new dimension was opened up, and a third approach appears on the scene: man can go to heaven through the earth. There is a real communion between God and the world. "In a universe in whose bosom everything works together for the gradual formation of the spirit that God elevates to filial union, the tangible reality of every effort acquires the worth and significance of holiness and divine communion." [9]

In *The Divine Milieu* Teilhard censures those who are carried away by a disembodied idealism and who rest content with right intention alone. More than anyone else the Christian "knows" what the Christification of the world signifies. More than anyone else he knows that the definitive body of the Risen One is fashioned through human actions. So he, more than anyone, should show greater lucidity and responsibility in his activities.[10] "Without getting sidetracked into naturalism or Pelagianism, the believer sees that he, far more than the unbeliever, can and should be more passionately committed to the progress of the earth that is required for the full consummation of the kingdom of God." [11] In today's world it is the Christian alone who is capable of confronting the complexities of nature and grace and performing an act of total synthesis which unites "the spirit of detachment and the spirit of conquest, the spirit of tradition and the spirit of search, the spirit of earth and the spirit of God." [12] Our faith in Christ does not signify a weakening or limiting of our human effort by any means; it represents the greatest stimulus possible to bettering the world (GS 39).

Yet it would appear that many people would like to see the Church stay in the sacristy and not get involved in the problems of mankind. That is what the defenders of the status quo would like. But the same result is also desired by those who propose to freeze the possibilities of dialogue for theological reasons precisely because remnants of a dualistic outlook remain in them. Teilhard de Chardin felt that this dualistic outlook posed the greatest threat of schism in the Church: "Christian and human tend to drift apart. Here we have the great schism that threatens the Church." [13]

Vatican II prevented this schism from turning into a reality. Today we can no longer voice the question that Teilhard asked only two years before his death: "How is it possible that nine out of ten believing Christians are skeptics in human terms? This is the great scandal to the gentiles." [14] But neither can we fail to see that there still remains a Manichaean movement which yearns for the past.

If *Gaudium et spes* is the response to the spiritual problem we were posing, then Teilhard de Chardin has been the prophet and witness of this new Christian attitude toward man's daily task. With his fundamental vision of the coincidence of anthropogenesis and Christogenesis, he was able to lay hold of the supreme value of man's transforming activity in creation. And he did so with all his passion as a Christian, and in a theological language that is more precise than many people think. To cite just one example, here is a brief passage near the end of *The Divine Milieu* which is devoted precisely to an explanation of the spiritual problem we have been discussing here:

We have gone deeply into these new perspectives: the progress of the universe, and in particular of the human universe, does not take place in competition with God, nor does it squander energies that we rightly owe to him. The greater man becomes, the more humanity becomes united, with consciousness of, and mastery of, its potentialities, the more beautiful creation will be, the more perfect adoration will become, and the more Christ will find, for mystical extensions, a body worthy of resurrection. The world can no more have two summits than a circumference can have two centres. The star for which the world is waiting, without yet being able to give it a name, or rightly appreciate its true transcendence, or even recognize the most spiritual and divine of its rays, is, necessarily, Christ himself, in whom we hope. To desire the Parousia, all we have to do is to let the very heart of the earth, as we Christianize it, beat within us. . . . Her enchantments can no longer do me harm, since she has become for me, over and above herself, the body of him who is and of him who is coming.[15]

III. HOLINESS FOR A CHURCH IN DIALOGUE

In CLARIFICATION III of the next chapter we shall have occasion to show that for centuries the Church moved and operated without a theology of history.[16] That was only logical because those times lacked an historical perspective on our planet and even elementary data on the origin, multiplicity, and disappearance of human culture.

Moreover, in one sense it is false to assert that the Church lacked a theology of history. She certainly possessed what we could call a theology of history relating to her "inner precincts." And to the extent that it looked at "universal" history, the latter entered the picture as a preparation for the city of God or as its antagonist.

In reality the situation reached the point where the world seemed to have been subsumed almost totally by the Church. The stage of preparation was relegated to a distant past while her enemies were relegated to relatively far-off borders that were defended militarily.

So the question is: How was holiness lived within this fairly a-historical context? How was it pictured? And finally, how will this perspective change with the discovery, in relatively recent times, of a universal history into which the Church herself is inserted?

Now a Church which sees itself as including practically the totality of the world is a community which, for the moment, has replaced preoccupation for *what is to come* with a qualitative preoccupation for *what ought to be*. While the mass contents itself with the bare minimum required to maintain itself as Christian, a minority looks in the Gospel for "counsels" to live Christianity to its "perfection."

The classical, and a-historical, distinction between *commandments* and *counsels* in the Gospel does not correspond precisely, in its broadest sense, to the distinction between the lay state and the religious state. It is certain that every religious is presumed to be in a state that tends toward the perfection mentioned above. But since there does not seem to be any other perfection, lay holiness—which always existed—is frequently conceived and formulated as "living like a religious in the world."

The *Imitation of Christ and Contempt for the World,* the full title of the famous work by Thomas à Kempis, is perhaps the clearest example of this tendency. Monkish in essence, over the centuries it was converted into the manual of Christian perfection for both religious and lay people. People of our own generation have undoubtedly read it at one time or another. And one of the most suggestive indications of the transformation that is now taking place in the Church would be derived from rereading it now in the light of the image of the Church presented in a document like *Gaudium et spes.*

1. In the *Imitation,* the notion of "world" is central. It is with good reason that it appears in the complete title of the book. De facto holiness is to be found in adopting toward the world the theoretical valuations and practical attitudes that are consistent with the Christian counsels relating to perfection.

Now the first thing that strikes our attention about the "world" of the *Imitation* is that *it is not in a process of fulfilling itself.* It is already finished and readymade. Its values or pseudo-values are conceived as already ripe fruits hanging on a tree. They are there for man to take. All he can do is savor them or reject them.

Since it is not the raw material for creation, the world appears solely as the sum total of things that a person can *have* and *possess* (or leave alone), that arouse man's concupiscence and greed. "It is also laudable in a religious person seldom to go abroad, seldom to see others, and seldom to be seen by others. Why will you consider what it is not lawful for you to have? The world passes away with all its concupiscence and deceitful pleasures" (I, 20).

In effect what the world offers is essentially temporal in a negative sense. And here we are referring precisely to a time that does not create but attacks the consistency and flavor of the world's fruits: "The happiness of man does not depend on an abundance of worldly (or temporal) goods, because moderation is best. And truly, to live in this world is but misery" (I, 22).

Hence we get what may well be one of the most profoundly deprecatory remarks about the world ever written: "What may you see outside your chamber that you may not see within it? Look, within your chamber you can see heaven and earth and all the elements of which all earthly things are made" (I, 20). Besides insisting on a world already finished, this passage rules out any possibility of authentic newness. It is just as if someone were to say that the works of Shakespeare were merely infinite combinations of the twenty-six letters of the alphabet.

Since the world is thus and creativity cannot inject anything truly new into it, "how great a vanity it also is to desire a long life and to care little for a good life; to heed things of the present and not to provide for things that are to come; to love things that will shortly pass away and not *to haste* to where joy is everlasting" (I, 1).

So a choice must be made, according to the *Imitation,* and it involves a clean cutting. Reflection indicates to us that two attractions of a contrary sort exist: "There is a great difference between the creature and the Creator, between time and eternity . . ." (III, 34). Hence to delight

in the taste of God and divine things is quite different from delighting
in the taste of creatures and worldly things.

But how is it that two things so disproportionate as time and eternity,
Creator and creature, can be equal rivals for our decision-making choice?
The answer is that just as there are some people who are so tied to their
sense-faculties that they are interested only in the present, sensible world,
so there are some "who have their reason clearly illuminated by the light
of true understanding, and by it their affection is so purged and purified
from earthly things that they always desire heavenly things; so that it is
hard for them to hear of earthly things and a truly great pain to serve
the necessities of the body" (III, 4).

In other words, when a person tries to withdraw his heart from visible
things, he discovers that the eye is never satisfied with seeing nor the ear
with hearing (I, 1). Why? Because the visible, temporal world of sense
concentrates its attraction in a zone of the human person which the
Imitation calls "the flesh": "Thus, most wretched man, I fight within
myself and become burdensome to myself, while my spirit desires to soar
and my flesh is earthbound" (III, 48).

Despite the unequivocal allusion to Paul's text, *flesh* here acquires a
psychological sense that is very different from the theological sense it has
in Paul's text. For Paul there existed a fleshly way of seeking God, and
he talked about the inclination of the flesh to haughtiness, useless de-
bates, and so forth (see Chapter II, CLARIFICATION I). Here, by contrast,
man appears divided by his greater or lesser capacity to guide himself by
the perduring and invisible rather than by the immediate and visible.
Thus "the saints and devout followers of Christ gave no heed to what
pleased the flesh, or to what was pleasant in the sight of the world. They
fixed all their intention and desire on things invisible" (I, 22).

2. Now how is this principle of holiness to be converted into real life?
By cutting cleanly through the dualism we have just seen and converting it into complete, effective separation. What pertains to God and
eternal salvation is no longer to be one compartment of a person's life
and occupations. It is now to conquer a person's whole life, replacing all
the other sectors. "There are many things whose knowledge brings but
little profit and little fruit to the soul; he is most unwise who gives heed
to any other thing except what will profit him to the health of his soul"
(I, 2). "What peace and inward quiet should he have who would cut away
from himself all busyness of mind, and think only on heavenly things"
(I, 20).

The most real and effective division possible between these two opposed spheres of interest and things is to serve as the basis for fashioning
a way of life that will be identified with Christian perfection. "He who
seeks any other thing in religion than God alone and the salvation of his
soul will find nothing there but trouble and sorrow" (I, 17; see also I, 23,
etc.). And "trouble and sorrow" is not to be taken to mean mere inconvenience. It means the ruinous end of an existence made for the love
of God. For "he who loves God despises all other love" (II, 5).

Consequently we find a recurring image in most of the passages that
present this line of thought. It is the image of the "pilgrim" who pays no
heed to things around him so that he may concentrate all his apprecia-

tion on the goal he hopes to reach at the end of his journey (cf. I, 17; I, 23; II, 1; III, 53). Again we run into a Pauline image, but here it is imbedded within an impoverished dualism that does not faithfully reflect Paul's rich and complex dialectic.

Taking due note of the attraction of the world and the power of its accomplice within us, the flesh, the *Imitation* concludes that good works themselves which presuppose dalliance with the world must be eyed with reservations during this time of pilgrimage. They all contain a human mechanism that must be controlled and turned to good use, hence it is best to subordinate them to a direct quest for God and salvation. "Flee the company of worldly-living persons as much as you can, for the treating of worldly matters greatly hinders the fervor of spirit, even though it be done with a good intention. . . . I would I had held my peace many times when I spoke and that I had not been so much among worldly company" (I, 10). There is no doubt, then, that human beings and their temporal needs form part of the realm which is not God and salvation. In the dualistic setup of creatures versus Creator, visible versus invisible, temporal versus eternal, human beings do not stand on the side of God but on the opposite side, the side that is to be replaced by a life "all for God."

The successful carrying out of the clean break entails various options. Let us consider them briefly here because they explicate and complete the fundamental option we have just seen.

The first option is to give decided primacy to intention over deed. In other words, it is the why and wherefore, not the what, that counts most in human activity. What is more, when these two motivating factors do not coincide, preoccupation with the end result is equivalent to a lack of concern for the underlying intention. The latter is demeaned by interest in what is being fashioned constructively. The only person who accords real primacy to intention is the one who is equally disposed to construct or destroy, to work harder or stop altogether.

It is interesting to see how his logic causes one to forget Jesus' own words (Matt. 25) in the name of God's judgment. Jesus told us that human beings would be judged on this basis: I was hungry and you gave me *food to eat*. According to the author of the *Imitation*, however, God "judges all things according to the intent of the doer, not according to the greatness or worthiness of the deed" (I, 15).

Secondly, a long and extensive effort is presupposed in purifying one's intention and bolstering its value above and beyond the motives that reside in the end result of one's actions. And by the very nature of the case, the primary aim in this process will be to divest oneself of any and all creative ambition centered around the result of the work itself. What one must do is reach the point of feeling that "it is a much surer way to stand in the state of obedience than in the state of authority" (I, 9). Obedience shows up as an attitude of indifference toward the end result of our activity, or at the very least as a pathway that leads us toward this indifference which is "sure" from the standpoint of salvation. In the long run persevering obedience will suppose and effect the purification of intention.

In such a framework where it is safer to obey than to command, to take advice than to give it (I, 9), it is also safer to put up with evils than to commit oneself to reforming or eradicating them. The constant presupposition is that God does not ask man to put the world in order but to detach himself from perishable things. "Such faults as we cannot amend in ourselves or in others we must patiently suffer until our Lord of his goodness will dispose otherwise" (I, 16). The fact is that only passivity vis-à-vis the world is compatible with the primacy accorded intention over deed.

Thirdly, insofar as indispensable things are concerned, we must choose between using them and desiring them. This is a difficult choice for the human psyche, which normally uses, and uses well, only those things that provide it with certain satisfaction—even when it may subordinate them to some higher satisfaction. In the logic of the *Imitation,* use without desire—even when it undermines the end results of our action—is indispensable for unifying and totally orienting our existence around an intention that becomes ever purer and more exclusively directed toward God and salvation.

From this comes the sense of poverty which finds expression in this word of advice: "If you inordinately covet these present goods, you will lose eternal goods. So, use goods properly, but yearn for eternal goods" (III, 16).

But even more than things and our appetite for them, it is in fact persons that introduce these relations between perishable things and desires into our lives. So a fourth thing is logically required of us in this context: We must separate ourselves affectively and effectively from human beings. If the best chance of salvation lies in opting for the Creator completely, then this famous lament of the *Imitation* is apt: "As often as I have been among worldly company, I have left it with less fervor of spirit than I had when I came" (I, 20). After all, to be a human being means to focus one's whole life on what is of absolute importance.

As one can readily see, it is a matter of carrying the option through to its ultimate conclusions. And this is the full import of chastity, which embraces not only the sexual realm but also the affections, including even friendship and family life: "Therefore, our Lord and his angels will draw near and abide with those who, for the love of virtue, withdraw themselves from their acquaintances and from their worldly friends. . . . It is also laudable in a religious person seldom to go abroad, seldom to see others" (I, 20).

3. Now if we follow the thread of these options, how are we to picture concretely the best way of life in terms of holiness?

First of all, it is a tranquil solitude: "What peace and inward quiet should he have who would cut away from himself all busyness of mind, and think only on heavenly things" (I, 20); "I see well that no man is more at rest in this world than he who always has his mind and his whole intention directed upward to God, and desires nothing from the world" (III, 31).

This purity of intention, centered solely on God, liberates man from the flesh-spirit dualism within him. But the liberation comes, not from an integration, but from a cutting away: i.e., from suppressing the value of the fleshly and the temporal: "Learn also to despise now all worldly things so that you may then go freely to Christ" (I, 23).

Liberty is thus conceived as the empire of reason on a quest for the absolute; not being able to construct it with relative, perishable materials, it moves away from them so as not to be contaminated by their relativity: "It is the work of a perfect man never to isolate his mind from a consideration of heavenly things, and to carry on among many cares as if he were without care, not in the manner of an idle or a dissolute person, but by the special prerogative of a free mind always busy in God's service, not clinging to any creature by inordinate affection" (III, 26; cf. III, 5).

This liberation, which as we have seen involves a clean cutting away within one's personal psychology, requires our attention to be directed inward. It must be centered on the real battlefront, the realm of intention. Freeing oneself presupposes concentration on the inner self: "Where are you when you are not present to yourself? And when you have been all about, and have considered other men's works, what has been your profit in it if you have forgotten yourself? So, if you will have peace in your soul, and be perfectly united to God in blessed love, set aside all other men's deeds, and set yourself and your own deeds only before the eye of your soul" (II, 5; cf. II, 6; III, 53).

This looking at oneself is not narcissism. It is preparing for the true reality when man will be alone before the searching eye of God, his judge: "You do not answer for another man's deeds, but you must make answer for your own" (III, 24). However alien and opposed to the language of the Gospel this may seem, this inward-directed attention is justified by the *Imitation* as the purification of one's intention which, liberated by the exclusion process, will direct itself to total love of God. The devout man makes this plea: "Make me one with you in a sure bond of heavenly love, for you alone are sufficient to your lover, and without you all things are vain and of no substance" (III, 23).

There is a new shading in this phrase, "for you alone are sufficient." The time of the holy soul is no longer the time of history but the time of the sacred and religious: "Moreover, at the time of principal feasts, we ought . . . to dispose ourselves precisely as if we were then about to be taken out of this world and brought to the everlasting feast of heaven" (I, 19).

Here we see that the good works of love do not show up as the one and only authentic fulfillment of this divine love but rather as only the means to fill up the time which a person, however perfect he may be, must spend away from pure interior and cultic love of God: "For as long as you bear this body of death, you must feel some tediousness and grief of heart. . . . For you cannot, because of the corruption of your body, persevere in spiritual studies and in heavenly contemplation as you would. Then it is good for you to flee to humble, bodily labor, and to exercise yourself in good outward works" (III, 51).

In the *Imitation* as in Christian tradition as a whole, holiness, in formal terms, shows up as consisting of love of God. But in the *Imitation* there is an absolute chasm, devoid of any point of similarity, between love of God and love of God's children: "It behooves him, therefore, who would perfectly forsake himself and behold you, to rise above all creatures and himself also, and through elevation of mind to see and behold that you, Maker of all things, have nothing like to yourself among all creatures.

Unless a man is clearly delivered from all love of creatures, he cannot fully attend to his Creator" (III, 31).

It is precisely here that Christ's saying ("insofar as you did this to one of the least of these brothers of mine, you did it to me") seems to be erased in favor of an exclusivist, interior, solipsistic love. It is the *Imitation*'s notion of God that is at work in its notion of sanctity: "Your Beloved is of such nature that he will not admit any other love, for he *alone* will have the love of your heart. . . . You will find that all trust is, in a way, lost, which is put elsewhere save in Jesus" (II, 7).

4. The first observation that merits mention here is that this schema of perfection was never put into practice in fact. Or if it was, then at least it was not in the saints that have represented the ideal of sanctity for the Church. The doctrinal elaboration is one thing, the logic of the saints as lived under the impulses of the Spirit is something else again.

On the other hand, it would be equally erroneous to minimize the burdensome weight of a schema which provided orientation to the Church for whole centuries in seeking and defining holiness—at least on the level of explicit, undisputed teaching.[17]

In this context it might well be useful to reflect on the fact that this schema conditioned to a large extent even the possibilities of "canonizing" a Christian. In other words, the possibility of proposing a Christian to the Church as a model of life was conditioned in large measure by his separation from historical involvement. Apparently "heroic virtue" could only be perceived, if not measured, as a great thing independent of, and separate from, all human interest—as an egoistic thing basking in a situation of aloofness. Every human creation of an intense, passionate sort showed itself to be ambiguous, both with respect to its intention and to its end results.

In reality the canonization of saints was a normal procedure when the Church, failing to confront world history as we have already seen, did not accord to the laity its "principal" role in the work of the Church as it does today. Canonized sanctity was an a-historical sanctity because the very possibilities of canonizing it were linked to this a-historicity.

We need only recall here what Vatican II said in our day about lay people and their efforts to lead a holier life: "The faithful, therefore, must learn the deepest meaning and the value of all creation, and how to relate it to the praise of God. They must assist one another to live holier lives even in their daily occupations. In this way the world is permeated by the spirit of Christ and more effectively achieves its purpose in justice, charity and peace. The laity have the principal role in the universal fulfillment of this purpose" (LG 36).

Now we can see why it is both explicable and inconsistent for the Church to continue in its practice of canonizing cases that are "exceptional" in terms of her principal task. These cases are the martyrs for the faith (generally the victims of a lack of dialogue between Church and world), and religious who are frequently the founders of religious orders and congregations.

The practice is inconsistent because it does not give to the Church the public image of sanctity she needs to accord with her mission in the world and in history. Indeed this mission is recognized to be central by the Church's extraordinary magisterium itself. But the practice is explicable because the principles used to uphold this image are tied up with a different type of life that is equated with the quest for perfection: i.e., the religious state.

So we confront a paradoxical situation. While the Church is canonizing religious almost exclusively, religious find themselves in a wholehearted search for the tieup between their three vows (poverty, chastity, and obedience) and ecclesial sanctity in its more universal dimensions.

At present we believe that the quest is orientated in two principal directions. In one case people are trying to see, in the three vows and in the state grounded on them, a sign of the whole Church that is lived in a specialized form, as it were, by a part of the Church. The difficulty with this interpretation is evident in what we have already seen. Does this eschatology fit in suitably with the *whole* Church, or is this the sign of eschatology that the Church needs for her task? Furthermore, in the practical order, it would be difficult to define a religious vocation in terms of a desire to be an eschatological sign.

The second approach looks for justification of the religious life in the gathering together, the stable community, of a group of Christians for the sake of some special task that the Church has need of. Here the range of possibilities opens up, as indeed is happening in the Church, into a much broader spectrum than the three vows. These vows—or one or more of them—will find their justification depending on the particular task that the community undertakes.[18] This orientation, which is less canonical, appears to be more realistic and more related to vocations in history—whether it be those of individuals or of the congregations themselves.

Finally, we may make a comment on the whole matter of canonization as it relates to martyrdom suffered out of hatred of the faith (*odium fidei*). The maturation of the Church's dialogue with the world is making clear to the Church that we rarely find, at least in modern times, any "martyrdom" in the pure sense. In reality no one is inclined to see a threat to his own faith in the simple faith of another. Only disembodied abstractionism enabled the Church to be blind to the "political" values that were at work in almost all the martyrs—starting with those martyrdoms which were instigated by the arrival of missionaries (and seldom them alone) in "mission territories."

Indeed the Church is realizing this more and more. In one of the most public and passionate issues of recent decades, the Spanish Civil War, it seems that the Church was unable to decide whether there was any authentic martyr for the faith among the Catholics who died in that conflict. This marked a considerable step forward for the Church, and its consequences are not fully evident to us even now.

In reality all sanctity in a Church in dialogue with world history is so only within a context of commitment that can always be debated on both sides. It is there—in the total giving of self within a concrete, contingent option and a situation of mixed values and open-ended possibilities—that all Christian sanctity plays out its role.

Perhaps one of the most serious factors in Latin American Catholicism is the radical disproportion between the real-life tasks of the Church and the type of sanctity that the faithful venerate. And possibly something of this has been felt when popular sentiment has tried to canonize, or at least tie up with Christ and the saints, people like Eva Perón, Che Guevara, and Camilo Torres. To many it has seemed that total self-giving to the cause of the poor had a very close affinity with Christian sanctity.

The fact that one can disagree with the political options they have chosen is not precisely that which removes them from "canonization," i.e., from establishing them as models of Christian commitment. What we must clearly recognize is that what excluded these people from the possibility of being models of holiness for a Christian was objectively and externally less than the isolation of a Rose of Lima, for example, or the clerical occupations of a Toribio de Mogrovejo—just to mention two of the rare examples of people canonized on the Latin American continent. But here and now how can we understand a Christian heroism that does not passionately seek more justice and love in and through the obscurities of all real commitment?

It may well be that a community which claims to be wholly in dialogue with the world and its history must renounce the tack of delegating to *saints* its task of being saintly as a whole in the multiple, concrete, and fallible commitments of its members that are motivated by love.[19]

IV. THE DISTINCTION BETWEEN NATURAL AND SUPERNATURAL IN CATECHESIS

The distinction between "natural" and "supernatural" values has exerted great influence in educating and training people in faith.[20] What is more, different uses of the supernatural have been made in catechesis. Some of these uses have been highly ambiguous, not to say downright harmful.

1. To begin with, people have had recourse to the supernatural as a means of avoiding bothersome explanations. To take one example, when someone asks about the meaning of sin and the ensuing explanations prove to be poor and unconvincing, then one appeals to the term "supernatural" and says: "This cannot be understood on the natural plane; it can only be understood from a supernatural point of view." Thus the supernatural is converted into a panacea for catechetical difficulties. Under this light it shows up as a form of magic, blocking off all confrontation with reality and hence making all dialogue with nonbelievers impossible. It even rules out dialogue with those believers who are a little more clear-eyed and demanding, and who are therefore censured for lacking a "spirit of faith."

2. A second way of using the supernatural was a corollary of the first. It consisted in an ascetic effort to go beyond natural values to supernatural ones. "One must supernaturalize work and the social struggle." [21] And the mechanics of this supernaturalization is rooted in intention. One supernaturalizes what one does by thinking about God, salvation, and eternity.

We are not going to stress this point here since the reader will find pertinent comments in the preceding CLARIFICATION. We would simply like to point out that in this formulation the supernatural seems to be situated in a different realm from the one where human projects meet success or failure. The two realms appear to be juxtaposed and nothing more, so that one must jump from the human realm of daily activities and results to another realm above and beyond our present life.

This conception of the supernatural and the natural, which has controlled and guided catechesis in more or less explicit form,[22] is one of the principal causes of the dichotomy between belief and daily life that is denounced by Vatican II.

3. Thus today we must rediscover the unity that had been lost in earlier catechesis. When the Sixth International Convention on Catechesis was held in Medellín (August 1968), it published a document entitled "Urgent Guidelines for Catechesis." Section 12 of that document says:

> In each case catechesis has its fundamental message, which consists in the unity between two aspects of the total reality. This unity is complete, differentiated, and dynamic. On the one hand it rules out any and all dichotomy, separation, dualism; on the other hand it rules out simplistic, monistic identification. It is a unity between human values and man's relationship to God; between a human project and God's salvific design that is achieved in Christ; between the human community and the Church; between human history and salvation history; between man's experience and God's revelatory activity; between the progressive realization of Christianity within time and its eschatological fulfillment. Hence catechesis lives in a permanent tension between continuity and discontinuous breakthrough.

Here we have another formulation which is different from the ones cited in points one and two above, and which specifically seeks to overcome the dualism present in them.[23]

The Medellín Declaration points out that "we must avoid total confusion or monistic identification," as if one could infer the ultimate "supernatural" destiny of man from an analysis of human experience alone. Without the revelation that tells us of God's gift, man on his own cannot arrive at complete awareness of the truth. So we must try to get beyond dualism without falling into monism, without trying to suggest that the truth derives from our personal experience or some human criterion. It is not a question of suppressing the supernatural or confusing it with the natural. It is a matter of re-expressing it in a way that is more evangelical and more coherent at the same time. In this regard the supernatural vision teaches us about the ultimate profundity of our existence; it does not transport us to some other existence.

The supernatural viewpoint, then, does not draw us away from our daily task nor deprive it of importance. On the contrary, it offers us a new interpretation of man and his destiny as God's gratuitous gift in Christ. "Salvation-history" is not some history different from human history; it is history as interpreted by the message which enables us to comprehend its profundity and destiny.

In the light of this biblical vision of the faith, all catechesis takes on a very different import and educative force. Section 11 of the Medellín document alludes to this fact:

In line with a more satisfactory theology of revelation, present-day catechesis recognizes in historical situations and in authentically human aspirations the primary signs that must be heeded in order to discover God's plan for today's human beings. Hence these situations form an indispensable part of the content of catechesis. One of the essential tasks of the Church's prophetic mission is to progressively discover the overall import and definitive orientation of these aspirations and tensions as they are fleshed out in each moment of the historical process. In order to lay hold of the total meaning of these human realities, it is necessary for us to live life fully with the men of our time. In this way human realities will be able to be interpreted progressively and seriously within the real-life context of a given historical moment—in the light of the real-life experiences of the People of Israel, the man Christ, and the sacramental Church community in which the spirit of the risen Christ continues to live and operate. Thus an understanding of man helps us to explore the message more deeply, and deeper exploration of the latter helps us to understand man better.

So when we perceive that the elevation of grace is the most profound dimension of human history itself, this does not mean that catechesis becomes an effort to lead man to live a different life from the one he is living here and now. Instead catechesis teaches man to live the same reality he is living now with a different, fuller plenitude.

NOTES

1. *Cf.*, P. Dhorme, *L'Emploi métaphorique des noms des parties du corps en Hébreu et en Akkadien* (Paris: Lecoffre, 1923), pp. 9 ff.

2. "Oneness in the flesh" is applied in Genesis twice to matrimonial community, once to kinship between uncle and nephew, and once to the community between brothers of the same father. We find it again the Second Book of Samuel applied to the affective unity between David and his people, between David and the forefathers of Israel, and between David and Amasai.

3. The schema does not vary, at least for centuries, with respect to animals (Eccles. 3:19–21). The imagined schema of resurrection will be identical (Ezek. 37:7–9). In prophets like Isaiah, the opposition between flesh and spirit is applied to the moral plane, always with the same connotation: flesh is everything that man does on his own, spirit is that which God alone can do (Isa. 31:1–3).

4. Teilhard de Chardin, *The Divine Milieu*, Eng. trans. (New York: Harper & Row, 1960), pp. 21–22.

5. José M. González-Ruiz, *El Cristianismo no es un humanismo* (Madrid: Ed. Península, 1966), p. 69.

6. *Le Coeur de la Matière*, 1950.

7. *Comment je crois* (1934), in *Christianity and Evolution* (New York: Harcourt, 1971) pp. 96–132.

8. "Super-Humanity, Super-Christ, Super-Charity," in *Science and Christ* (New York: Harper & Row, 1968), p. 165.

9. *La Mystique de la Science,* 1939.

10. For this reason, and not because one must dissociate oneself affectively from it, there is no conceptual identity between human progress that is comprehensible to all and the progress of the kingdom (GS 39). On the other side of the coin, the progress of the kingdom adds a new unknown value to world progress.

11. *Note sur la notion de perfection chrétienne*, 1942.

12. *La Parole attendue*, 1940.

13. *Note pour servir à l'évangélisation des temps nouveaux*, 1919.

14. Letter of 10 January 1953. Cited by Cuénot, *Teilhard de Chardin: Les grandes étapes de son évolution* (Paris: Plon, 1958), p. 482.

15. *The Divine Milieu, op. cit.*, pp. 137–138.

16. To be sure, between the time of the *Imitation of Christ* and *Gaudium et spes*, the Church took part in several attempts to relate sanctity more directly to history. One of these moments, which was undoubtedly premature, was the foundation of the Society of Jesus with its marked differences from the beginning as compared with the classical structure of religious life. The perduring motif of Ignatius' spirituality was *"seeking and finding* the will of God," *sensing* and knowing his wi.l. To foster greater openness to what the Spirit might inspire in the Church, the classical notion of transmitting what one had contemplated was converted into the notion of "contemplatives *in action*," which presupposed contemplation of a God operating through signs in human encounters. The isolation of the novitiate was given up. All defined times for prayer were suppressed, along with every other particular which restricted the possibility of acting in accordance with the demands of a given concrete situation. But all these measures ran up against the irremediable lack of a theology of history that had not yet been elaborated. In the absence of such a theology, to guide this new project, the classic older concept took hold of the nascent community once again, especially through the personality of Saint Francis Borgia. He even criticized Ignatius for not knowing what to respond when candidates asked him how many hours were to be taken up in contemplation, whereas any street-vendor was well informed about these spiritual requisites. When Borgia later became the Superior General of the Order, he turned it back from the openings it had made to history and the imprecise but real steps forward it had taken. The Society of Jesus was creative precisely when it faced up to a developing history within the limits of Christendom: e.g., Ricci in China, Nobili in India, the Reductions in Paraguay. In Europe, by contrast, it made an about-face and closed the doors of the conventicle, naturally leaving the world outside. *Cf.* Leturia, "La hora de meditación en la Compañía naciente," in *Archivum historicum societatis Jesu,* 1934, III, 55 and 63.

17. On a lesser scale, the morality of the faithful followed the same schema, although on a level reduced to binding precepts. The Church's failure to face up to history logically produced parallel orientations on every level. This is the judgment that Bernard Häring makes on the current moral theology when he explains why he was led to write his great work, *The Law of Christ.* "We must open the whole casuistic approach of the occasions of sin and complicity to a more constructive and positive vision of the activity of the Christian in the world" (Supplement to *La Vie Spirituelle,* No. 53 (1960), 115–131.

Any accentuation of the danger of occasions of sin and complicity in it comes down to sacrificing to one's own personal salvation the salvific presence of the Church as a leaven in society. At the beginning of this CLARIFICATION we said that "a Church which sees itself as including practically the totality of the world is a community which, for the moment, has replaced preoccupation for what is to come with a qualitative preoccupation for what ought to be." And as another author notes: "It has already been remarked that Christian ethics is primarily concerned not with the good but with the will of God; it aims at maturity, not at morality. . . . It follows from this shift of concern that Christian thinking

about ethics finds it beside the point to take up the question of the nature of
an act and of the relation between the nature of an act and the nature of the
good . . . The Christian character of behavior is defined not by the principal
parts of an act but by the functional significance of action in the context of the
divine economy and of the actuality of the new humanity" (Paul Lehmann,
Ethics in a Christian Context, New York: Harper & Row, 1963, pp. 121–122).

18. This seems to take place at the founding of the principal religious orders
and congregations. The need of the Church takes priority in intention over the
aim of participating in the "religious state." Frequently the vows in their totality, or one or more of them, are debated not in terms of perfection but in
terms of the ecclesial function they purport to carry out.

19. Canonization can be precisely one of the ways of "delegating" to a few
the obligations that the whole ecclesial community should accept and live. See
Darío Ubilla, "Las vicarías sucedáneos del miedo," in *Perspectivas de Diálogo*,
17–18 (September–October, 1967).

20. On the correct interpretation of this distinction see, in addition to this
section, Volume I, Chapter I, CLARIFICATION II.

21. One example among many: "A large number of active Christian vocations are made up more of natural generosity than of a supernatural spirit,"
Jacques Leclercq, *Vivre chrétiennement notre temps* (Paris: Castermann, 1958),
p. 87; Eng. trans. *Christianity in the World* (New York: Sheed & Ward, 1961),
p. 167.

22. So explicit in fact that an informed author on the configuration of Western culture like Herbert Marcuse has no inkling that there may be another
strain akin to his ideas in Christianity itself. He begins the second part of *Eros
and Civilization* with this quote from Sean O'Casey: "What time has been wasted
during man's destiny in the struggle to decide what man's next world will be
like! The keener the effort to find out, the less he knew about the present one
he lived in. The one lovely world he knew, lived in, that gave him all he had, was,
according to preacher and prelate, the one to be least in his thoughts. He was
recommended, ordered, from the day of his birth to bid goodbye to it" (Sean
O'Casey, *Sunset and Evening Star*, New York: Macmillan, 1954, pp. 269–270).

While we may not want to accept Marcuse's position, we might note what
he says about eternity as Nietzsche sees it: "Eternity, long since the ultimate
consolation of an alienated existence, has been made into an instrument of
repression by its relegation to a transcendental world—unreal reward for real suffering. Here eternity is reclaimed for the fair earth—as the eternal return of its
children, of the lily and the rose, of the sun on the mountains and lakes, of the
lover and the beloved, of the fear for their life, of pain and happiness. Death
is; it is conquered only if it is followed by the real rebirth of everything that
was before death here on earth—not as a mere repetition but as willed and
wanted re-creation" (Herbert Marcuse, *Eros and Civilization*, Boston: Beacon
Press, 1956, p. 123).

23. Nonetheless we can see in this purported *tension* between unity and distinction the effect of a theology that is tinged superficially by a two-edged recommendation of the Council itself. In a later section we will show that Vatican II
itself allowed room for a two-sided interpretation (see Chapter III, CLARIFICA-
TION V), undoubtedly because of the differing tendencies that still show through
its documents as they did during the Council. But at present efforts are being
made to see in this twofold recommendation—unity but distinction—an attempt
to provide a balanced stress. In other words, unity and distinction are seen to
be extremes that alternately get the upper hand in order to maintain equilibrium.

As we have already seen, the unity is real and has no limits. To avoid confusion of the two is not to gloss over the unity but to acknowledge its omnipresent
gratuitousness. There is only one vocation, and it is divine. So one must not

confuse this one real vocation with a destiny proceeding from the mere nature of man. But this does not constitute a tension, unless one understands by tension the fact, already noted here several times, that both this divine destiny and its consequences are known and lived by man in dependence on revelation, and that this obliges the Christian to synthesize two idioms. One idiom comes from his experience in common with all men. The other comes from a revelation once turned into a word between human beings and continually resonating anew through man's maturation in history. But this task would seem to be more like interpretation than like a tension.

CHAPTER THREE

Breadth: Humanity, the People of God

In our lives as Christians we discover the great divine force that carries us from the basic human condition to the heights of divine life and creative salvation. But this discovery brings us face to face with a straightforward question that is very familiar to us and very deeply felt. We do not know whether the person next to us—be he parent, relative or friend—is living the same reality or not.

But is it really true that we do not know? The first spontaneous response within the Christian milieu tends to be that we are dealing with a mystery known only to God. Vatican II itself, in a passage that is not very clear, seems to move in the same direction when it says that all men do indeed enjoy the possibility of being associated with the paschal mystery (i.e., with the transforming power of grace) in a manner "known only to God" (GS 22). Once again we are left face to face with the same painful enigma.

So painful is it in fact that it has led more than a few people to submerge themselves in the enigmatic destiny of the mass of mankind, to stand side by side with them and share their uncertainty. Consider the words of Simone Weil, for example: "Christianity is catholic (i.e., universal) by right but not in fact. So many things remain outside it! So many things that I love and do not want to abandon! So many things that God himself loves because they would not exist otherwise! The vast expanse of past centuries beyond the last twenty, all the countries inhabited by other races, the whole secular life of the countries inhabited by the white race, the variant traditions accused of heresy in the latter countries, such as those of the Manichaeans and Albigensians . . . That is . . . what keeps me from crossing the threshold of the Church. I am sticking close to the things which cannot enter her portals." [1]

Undoubtedly saying "we don't know" is itself a solid point of departure. It stands over against the cutting sureness of the person who, when faced with the problem of a Simone Weil, believed he knew perfectly well what to think of realities that were not connected with Christianity, at least as far as outward appearances were concerned. And what he thought about them was hardly flattering!

So this is our problem here. And once again we shall try to examine it on three levels, which correspond to three stages in the development of Christian thinking about it.

Section I

At the start the primitive Church appears to have felt most keenly the wondrousness of its new vocation. But in what we might call a second phase of retrospective reflection, it also appears to have had a desire that prior humanity, especially those nearest and dearest to its members, might have been able to participate somehow in the call to faith.

Take Paul, for example. His enthusiasm for what he called "grace," which he logically identified with his conversion, led him on numerous occasions to compare the *before* and *after* in himself and others: i.e., the situation of Jews and pagans on the one hand, and that of Christians on the other.

Thus addressing himself to the formerly pagan Christians of Ephesus, he reminds them of their prior situation: "Remember then your former condition, you, Gentiles as you are outwardly . . . were at that time separate from Christ, strangers to the community of Israel, outside God's covenants and the promise that goes with them. Your world was a world without hope and without God" (Eph. 2:11–12).

He will say the same thing to the Colossians (Col. 3:5–7), to the Philippians (Phil. 2:15), to the Corinthians (1 Cor. 1:18–21), and especially to the Romans (Rom. 1–3). And in the last two cases mentioned, the pejorative evaluation of their prior, pre-Christian situation is extended equally to that of the Jews (*cf.* Gal. 3:19 and 2 Cor. 3:7–11).

Psychologically and sociologically this fact is explained to a certain extent by the fact that conversion to Christianity did in fact represent, in their actual situation, a real, perceptible change in their moral and religious conduct. It is equally logical that a newly arisen community should "over-evaluate" this difference, which is both its distinctive feature and its most visible justification. Finally, it is also understandable that, in the realm of concrete deeds once again, the discovery of the good news of salvation would be associated with this significant change and at first would appear to be identified with it.

Yet despite all this, Paul himself comes to recognize that not all those who call themselves Christians have changed their moral and religious conduct so radically. This recognition applies to himself (Phil. 3:4–6) as well as to many upright pagans of Corinth who moved from that state into the Church (1 Cor. 6:9–11).

One of the underlying reasons is that this very recognition was able, as it should have been, to lead to further reflection on the pre-Christian situation (which then would become simply non-Christian) with respect to grace and salvation. Dissociating the latter to a certain extent from conversion to Christianity, one would be able to show what their authentic dimensions, their authentic *breadth,* were and should be.

Along this line of thought, which is as much that of Paul as the line of thought cited above, Paul asserts this in his Epistle to Timothy: "Such prayer is right, and approved by God our Saviour, whose will it is that all men should find salvation and come to know the truth. For there is one God, and also one mediator between God and men, Christ Jesus, himself man, who sacrificed himself to win freedom for all mankind" (1 Tim. 2:3–6). The fact is that practically our whole treatment in this chapter could be summed up in this passage with its wholly universal perspectives. God is savior. He wills that *all* human beings be saved. And the reason is to be found in the unity and oneness of everything: one God, one mediator (Christ), hence one humanity over against him. And the guarantee is to be found in the fact that, with the Incarnation, Christ united himself intimately and definitively with all, linking his divine destiny with the destiny of all his brothers, however lowly they might be (*cf.* Math. 25:40).

Adhering to this line of thought, which implies that God's salvific plan in Christ embraces everyone and everything, Paul writes: "As in Adam all men die, so in Christ all will be brought to life" (1 Cor. 15:22). And this will be so because his grace will conquer the cause of death, which is sin (1 Cor. 15:56). Quite logically, then, Paul can proclaim the following: "It follows, then, that as the issue of one misdeed was condemnation for all men, so the issue of one just act is acquittal and life for all men . . . where sin was thus multiplied, grace immeasurably exceeded it" (Rom. 5:18–20).

The Gospel of John also confirms the notion that all humanity is brought face to face with salvation. Speaking of his Father, Jesus says: "It is his will that I should not lose even one of all that he has given me, but raise them all up on the last day" (John 6:39). When Jesus talks about those whom the Father has given to him, he is referring to the whole (John 3:17), to both those who are and those who are not in the "sheepfold" of the Church (John 10:10, 16). When the Samaritans proclaim they know that "this is in truth the Saviour of the world" (John 4:42), and when John the Baptist points to Jesus as the Lamb of God "who takes away the sin of the world" (John 1:29), we see further proof that John the Evangelist understands "world" to be the whole world.

Thus one cannot deny that the early Church, even though it stressed and perhaps even exaggerated the peculiarly Christian tieup with grace, went far beyond any simplistic, one-to-one identification between membership in the ecclesial community and salvation.

At a meeting in Frankfurt Karl Rahner said this: "No longer is it possible for Christians, living in this present epoch of church history, to share the pessimistic ideas about the salvation of non-Christians that Saint Paul was capable of holding within the religious outlook of his day . . . In the thinking of Paul, human beings who do not reach baptism are lost. It is true that Paul did not enunciate any dogma on this point, but in practice it was self-evident for him." [2] Rahner is right in saying that a changed historical perspective enables us to better understand a Christian dogma and to correct a simplistic idea that could in fact be entertained by Christians of any epoch, including those who lived in the apostolic era. But we certainly do not agree with him when he says that it was in practice self-evident to Paul that only those who managed to be baptized in the newly founded Church were on the pathway to salvation. We think that we have already demonstrated this point, even though we shall go into it in greater detail.

Perhaps the most apt expression of what the primitive Church thought about this question is to be found in Paul's words to Timothy: "We have set our hope on the living God, who is the Saviour of all men—the Saviour, *above all*, of believers" (1 Tim. 4:10).

Section II

So it is a matter of two opposed but complementary stresses. On the one hand membership in the community of believers or the faithful (both words bespeaking a relationship to faith) is identified with the "now" of grace. On the other hand it is recognized that grace goes above and beyond the boundaries of the Church and in some way reaches humanity as a whole.

These opposed but complementary stresses will in fact continue to perdure throughout the succeeding epochs of the Church's history. And where the main stress is put will vary with different needs and situations.

Clearly enough the dialogue of the Church with Greco-Roman culture, which was promoted by her apologists, was destined to highlight grace as God's gift to humanity in its totality. Christianity could hardly enter into the cultural world of its time if its "good news" proclaimed that nothing so far around and existing had the least value with respect to salvation.

Consider, for example, the case of Saint Justin, a Christian apologist in the second century after Christ. He maintained that Christianity re-

presented the full plenitude of a truth which pagan philosophers had
already known in a fragmentary way. And their fragmentary knowledge
of it was explained by the activity of the Word present in every human
soul from the beginning of the world. Says Justin: "All the correct principles which philosophers and legislators have discovered, they have discovered insofar as they have contemplated the Word in a partial way." [3]

The interesting point for us here is that Justin applies this relationship to the Word not only to philosophers but also to legislators. After
all, we do not find it hard to accept the notion that someone like Plato
glimpsed features of the one, creative Word in his philosophic quest.
But Justin also includes the legislator, who obviously did not manage to
glimpse the God of Judeo-Christian revelation and who probably did not
even manage to glimpse the purified, spiritualized God of the philosophers. The average legislator was probaby an ingenuous worshipper of
Zeus, Apollo, Dionysius, or Venus. Why, then, should Justin attribute
contemplation of the Word to him also? Because in the legislator there
is another kind of value and merit. It is not speculative knowledge but
another manifestation of God, that which shows up in good conduct, in
an upright conscience, in the fight for justice, right, and goodness.

Thus political activity, which is such a typically *temperal* value, is
considered by Justin to belong to the order of grace and to be associated
with Christ the Savior. Translated into our realm, it would mean that
Justin is telling us that all those who are fighting for a more equitable
distribution of wealth, for the betterment of man, and for the construction of a more fraternal social order, are responding to the summons of
grace, are following the Word whom they *already* know. And this holds
true whether they are Christians or not.

Indeed the theology of grace entertained by this second-century
apologist is so universal and clearcut that it does not stop at embracing
educated philosophers and legislators. For Justin goes on to say: "Christ,
whom Socrates knew in a partial way because the Word is present everywhere, did not exert influence solely on philosophers and educated
people. He also influenced laborers and uneducated people in such a way
that they spurned the opinion of the crowd and laughed at fear and
death. For the Word is the power of the Father, not a product of human
reason." [4] Perhaps the most interesting thing about this text is the fact
that as the activity of the Word moves away from intellectual and cultured categories to embrace humanity as a whole, the activity of the Word
more clearly takes on the lineaments of liberty. People learn to "spurn"
the opinion of the crowd and to laugh at fear and death. The relationship
of their attitude to the dynamism we have been studying in the last two
chapters could not be more evident.

So the primitive Church did not rest content with saying that God saved pagans in some way known only to him. From the Lord it had received a clear notion that humanity formed a unity with him, so it did not succumb to an individualistic notion of grace that related salvation to merely internal intentions that were ultimately mysterious. Christ came to save all human beings, not only every individual but *all together*. He came to save humanity in its totality, the humanity that goes to make up his own totality. What Saint Paul says is repeated even more clearly by Saint Irenaeus: "There is only one God. There is only one Son who carries out the will of the Father. And there is only one human race in which God's mysterious designs are brought to fulfillment." [5] Cyril of Alexandria teaches that Jesus assumes humanity as a whole. And Gregory of Nyssa teaches that human nature and humanity as a whole serves as the body of Christ; he assumes it all, bears it to calvary, brings it to resurrection, and saves it.[6]

But a Church which, in the West at least, progressively took on the quantitative dimensions of the civilized world, would tend more and more to minimize the universal and "external" dimensions of grace and salvation while focusing her attention on problems of internal unity.

The appearance of schisms and heresies within her borders would lead her to stress the relationship between salvation and membership in the true Church (i.e., adherence to the *true faith*). And it was within this climate that there arose the famous phrase of Cyprian, bishop of Carthage, which was destined to become the most summary and classical expression of the Church's awareness that there was an intimate relationship, not to say identity, between *belief* and *salvation*: "No salvation outside the Church." Augustine too, whose Latin mentality was much more juridical than the Greek mentality of the Fathers cited above, helped greatly to lay excessive stress on this aspect of the primitive tradition.

It was in this same climate of successive internal crises that people elaborated the harshest formulations about what we could call the "narrow road" of grace. Grace was seen to be conditioned by orthodoxy, that is, by rigid adherence to the faith. The Council of Florence, for example, took advantage of the Turkish-Moslem threat and tried to mend the breaches opened in Church unity. It may well have gone much further in its affirmation of the conditioning of grace by orthodoxy: "The Catholic Church professes and proclaims that no one who is not inside the Catholic Church—not only pagans but also Jews, heretics, and schismatics —can be a sharer in eternal life. Instead he will enter eternal fire . . . unless he is united with her before his death" (Denz. 714).

But the words of Paul already cited never ceased to resound within the Church, along with these words of his to the Romans: "When Gen-

tiles who do not possess the law carry out its precepts by the light of
nature, then, although they have no law, they are their own law, for
they display the effect of the law inscribed on their hearts. Their conscience is called as witness, and their own thoughts argue the case on
either side, against them or even for them, on the day when God judges
the secrets of human hearts through Jesus Christ" (Rom. 2:14–16). The
messianic promise uttered by Jeremiah (Jer. 31:31–33), which proclaimed
that the law would be inscribed in the hearts of men rather than on
tablets of stone, finds its fulfillment in the people of the "new covenant."
And the surprising thing is that this people reaches to the outer limits
of humanity. As one writer aptly remarks: "Pagans will not be judged
by a law they do not know, that is, by the written law of the Jews. Instead
they will be judged by the law they possess within themselves, that is,
by what they could know of God's law through their own conscience.
Paul does not say that they will be judged by what they have explicitly
recognized as the law of God. He says that they will be judged by the law
of God as it has been made known to them by conscience. We can take
this to mean that they will be judged by the law they did possess." [7]

So we should not be surprised to find that our dogmatic formulas
always leave open a pathway for the fuller and ever mysterious amplitude
of grace. Thus, even though the Council of Trent affirms that no one is
ever accorded justification without faith (Denz. 799), it acknowledges that
it is given not only by baptism—the sacrament of faith—but also by the
desire for it (Denz. 796).

Baptism of desire[8] corresponds to a faith which has not been explicated but is real. And right up to our own day, other documents of
the Church have added new elements to it. But they have not managed to
erase in us the impression that while grace and salvation outside explicit
faith and the visible sacrament are indeed an open pathway, this approach constitutes a private and somewhat shameful backdoor into
heaven.

By way of example we can cite the notion of "invincible ignorance"
enunciated by Pius IX. In one of his allocutions (1854) he begins by stating
that he does not wish to "set limits on God's mercy which is infinite, nor
to pry into the secret counsels and judgments of God." After this pre-
amble he goes on to say: "We must maintain by faith that no one can be
saved outside the Roman, Apostolic, Catholic Church; that it is the one
and only ark of salvation; that anyone who has not entered it will perish
in the flood. Nevertheless we must also hold as certain that those who
suffer from ignorance of the true religion, if this ignorance is invincible,
are not guilty of any fault in the eyes of the Lord. And who would be
presumptuous enough to claim that he is able to define the limits of this

ignorance in terms of the nature and variety of peoples, regions, characters, and numerous other circumstances?"

This question would seem aimed at broadening the conception and the hope we entertain with regard to the activity of grace. However, it leads to greater restrictiveness: "Indeed when we are free from the fetters of the body and see God as he is, we will surely comprehend how closely and beautifully divine mercy and divine justice are linked. But while we find ourselves here on earth, encumbered by the weight of mortality that enervates the soul, we follow Catholic doctrine and most firmly maintain that there is only one God, one faith, one baptism. *It is illicit* to go further in our investigation" (Denz. 1646 ff.).

Perhaps that is why the words of Vatican II have such a profound impact on us, conveying a feeling of liberation to some and a feeling of anxiety to others. For after it has delineated the portrait of the Christian, the person living a life in accordance with grace, it declares simply and forthrightly: "All this holds true not only for Christians, but for all men of good will" (GS 22).

What has happened? There is no doubt that over the last century "invincible ignorance" was appraised in all its quantitative dimensions and even in what we might call its qualitative depths. The fact is that something else took place in the interval between the declaration of Pius IX and that of Vatican II. While Pius IX might have been able to glimpse this development, the Council of Trent certainly could not have. What took place was a series of events: study of the psychological process of faith, growing fissures in the situation of Christianity, the penetration of secularization into the various levels of human life.

In the absence of this historical context it was understandable that a different conception would prevail. This conception stressed the following points: (1) God does entertain a universal salvific will, giving to each person sufficient grace to obtain salvation; (2) Christ placed his salvation in the Church that he founded; (3) Therefore one must presume bad faith in those adults who have heard the message preached but remain outside the Church. One might say that these people, in the absence of proof to the contrary, should be presumed to be not saved.

Now we hear other comments. Karl Rahner points out this: "For no matter how great the tendency may be for us today to be wary once more of conceding a clear conscience, we will hardly be able to suppose, in view of the immense amount of external conditioning of the personal spiritual life of man by disposition, race, upbringing, level of culture, etc., that the unnumbered millions of people, who throughout the Christian period have not come to the Church, were prevented from doing so by their own fault." [9]

In his encyclical *Ecclesiam suam*, Paul VI goes more deeply into the
qualitative aspect when he explores the reasons that have led the modern
atheist into his atheism. "They are obviously many and complex, and
we must come to a prudent decision about them, and answer them
effectively. They sometimes spring from the demand for a more profound
and purer presentation of religious truth, and an objection to forms of
language and worship which somehow fall short of the ideal . . . We see
these men serving a demanding and often a noble cause, fired with enthusiasm and idealism . . . They are sometimes men of great breadth
of mind, impatient with the mediocrity and self-seeking which infects
so much of modern society. They are quick to make use of sentiments and
expressions found in our Gospel, referring to the brotherhood of man,
mutal aid, and human compassion" (ES 104).

But is that all? Is it just that we see the backdoor opening wider? Or is
it that the main door itself is opening wider? Is it that the wall is being
converted into a doorway as spacious as our Father's house, one capable
of receiving and housing the entire People of God?

Section III

To put it another way, we are asking whether the Church of today will
recognize in today's non-Christian *something more* than the quantitative
importance of those men of good will who do not accept the faith, and
the qualitative authenticity of the values they are seeking to realize. And
we are asking whether this *something more* does not in fact represent
the possibility of knowing much more about what we believe concerning
the action of grace and salvation in the rest of humanity.

But to answer this question, we must go back a bit. The Church does
not invent. Guided by the Spirit, the Church rediscovers the revelation
that she received from her original source.

1. The first "rediscovery" comes from a re-examination of Paul's
texts referring to the meaning of "pagan." The pagan is by definition—
extrinsic, if you will—one who belongs to the realm of *before,* who is
outside of God's positive revelation to the Jewish people. He is the
heterodox person *par excellence,* who is therefore incapable of an explicit
faith. He represents a crucial problem for reasons we have already seen.
Even though Paul refers to the vast majority of mankind in the ages
before Christ, his comments apply by extension to anyone who, after
Christ's coming, has not recognized God's salvation in him. In other
words, the pagan continues to represent the realm of before vis-à-vis the
Christian faith.

So the question is: What is the pagan's *theological* situation? And we ask this question because we have already had occasion to see that Paul, in offering a pejorative description of the time before, did not presume to condemn the de facto conduct of pagans. Indeed in them he often recognizes virtues, positive values, and fidelity to the inner law which is none other than the law of love. So we are not inquiring about what we might call the *historical* situation of the paganism known to Paul. We are inquiring about the theological content that Paul gave to the notion of "being pagan" as such. And it is his Epistle to the Romans, a community which he does not yet know firsthand but which he knows to be composed of ex-pagans and ex-Jews, that provides him with his opportunity—not to judge concrete individuals or groups but to theologically situate the two components of humanity as a whole in the religious realm (i.e., paganism and Judaism) with respect to Christ's grace.

As Paul sees it, what characterizes the pagan as such theologically is his idolatry. This situation is all the more serious in view of what Paul says right near the start of his epistle: "I am not ashamed of the Gospel. It is the saving power of God for everyone who has faith—the Jew first, but the Greek also" (Rom. 1:16). In other words, from the time of Christ at least there is a restricting condition on salvation: the pathway via faith. And the idolatry which characterizes the pagan is directly opposed to this faith.

Paul presents this idolatry as the fruit of a responsible decision, even though it is undergirded by a strong tendency deriving from the human condition. The God who reveals himself to the chosen people does not leave the rest of mankind in the dark. He manifests himself in his works, which include not only creation but also the inner world of man and the events of history. "For all that may be known of God by men lies plain before their eyes; indeed God himself has disclosed it to them. His invisible attributes, that is to say his everlasting power and deity, have been visible" (Rom. 1:19–20).

What, then, is the force in man that opposes rapprochement with God and rejects encounter with him? According to Paul, the pagans are not mistaken in their knowledge of him, but they pervert their relationships with him: "Knowing God [*note:* not having known him in some early past], they have refused to honour him as God, or to render him thanks" (Rom. 1:21).

Right away we must underline the fact that Paul's reference to not rendering thanks introduces into his condemnation of paganism as such the central category we are studying in this volume: i.e., gratuitousness, to which corresponds gratitude. In other words, idolatry shows up as a falsified relationship to the extent that it represents the disappearance of the gratuitous, the personal, the free.

Paul goes on to comment on the first charge in his condemnation: "They have refused to honour him as God." He says this: "They boast of their wisdom, but they have made fools of themselves, exchanging the splendour of immortal God for an image shaped like mortal man, even for images like birds, beasts, and creeping things" (Rom. 1:23). Once again it is not that they worship another God, it is that they give way to man's tendency to become alienated in his objectifications, to be incapable of maintaining himself in the realm of the personal, the free, and that which cannot be manipulated or turned into a mechanistic thing. They succumb to man's proclivity for the prehuman in his encounter with other persons.

What is involved here is a tendency of the human heart which does not deform solely or even primarily the divine. When grace does not heal man and usher him into the plane of gratuitousness, when man continues to follow his own proclivity, then we do indeed find idolatry. But this idolatry is just the most salient, absurd, and shameful aspect of man's refusal to be man, a refusal that is made real in countless ways when he deals with others. Paul, using a classic formula of the Old Testament to describe the internal dynamism of sin, says: "God has given them up to . . . " (Rom. 1:24, 26, 28).

This dynamism does indeed show up first as man's descent to the level of the prehuman (Rom. 1:24–28). From there it splinters into a multitude of sins against other people (Rom. 1:28–32). And the chief reason for all this is put at the head of the list: "Because they have not seen fit to acknowledge God . . . " (Rom. 1:28).

The condemnation of the pagan, then, is not the condemnation of someone who has denied the orthodox faith, the precondition for salvation. It is the condemnation of someone who has said no to the gratuitous, interpersonal outlook that Paul calls faith and that consists essentially in overcoming, with the help of grace, the tendency to turn other persons, be they divine or human, into things with which one can crush the risk posed by love.

Hence, much to our surprise, Paul turns abruptly to the Jews and frames them within the same condemnatory judgment: "You therefore have no defence—you who sit in judgment, whoever you may be—for in judging your fellow-man you condemn yourself, since you, the judge, are equally guilty . . . you who pass judgment on the guilty while committing the same crimes yourself" (Rom. 2:1–2).

Here again we do not regard "the same crimes" as a description of the de facto moral conduct of most Jews. Once again it is a theological judgment. In the face of grace and despite the truth of the divine revelation it has received, Judaism is identified with the idolatry of the pagan.

Certainly the idolatry for which Paul reproaches the Jews is more subtle and less openly shameful. It does not involve the objectification of God in creatures made by human hands. What it involves is the absolutizing of the works of the law, which seem to contain God even as the degraded images of the pagans do. But this form of idolatry is no less serious for being more subtle (*cf.* Rom. 2:2–6 and 17–24).

Here we are not interested in making a detailed analysis of the theological situation of the Jews with respect to grace and salvation. What we are interested in is pointing out the new content invested in the pagan-Jew diad: i.e., in humanity as a whole considered as the realm *before* the Christian vocation. What disappears in this context is the ethnic separation based on God's positive revelation: i.e., based on orthodoxy. What is left is an identity of *outlook* toward a divine salvation which is offered in terms of gratuitous relationships—with respect to God: faith; with respect to men: love.

Thus opposition to the salvation proclaimed by the Christian message is not really conditioned by the ethnic-religious situation of a human being: "For God has no favourites" (Rom. 2:11). Depending on their attitude and outlook, a Jew can be "theologically" a pagan despite his partial orthodoxy, and a pagan can be "theologically" a Jew despite his factual idolatry (*cf.* Rom. 2:25–29).

2. And this brings us to the most important consequence. A person may have listened to the message of Jesus and believed in it as a message coming from God—in other words, he may have *faith* in the sense of a bloc-commitment to the person and doctrine of the Word—and he may nevertheless not possess the faith which is identified with the salvific outlook that relates us to God. He can be materially a Christian without having comprehended his own religious alienation, the alienation which is denounced by Christianity and from which grace liberates us in the true outlook of faith.

The Galatians, to whom Paul writes, are "Christians." But they have fallen back into a relationship with God where the works of the law replace personal, filial, grateful ties with him. Theologically speaking, they are really "Jews" and hence idolaters as well. In terms of its authentic salvation-content, salvation has not yet reached them. Christ died in vain for them because they "have fallen out of the domain of God's grace" (Gal. 5:4).

The Corinthians, too, are Christians. But they are trying to turn the people, structures, and sacraments of the Church into realities with which they propose to lay hold of God. They seek to glorify themselves before him, substituting pride and personal vainglory for a thankful attitude toward the God who has given them everything (1 Cor. 3). They too are idolaters. Just as the pagans have exchanged "the splendour of immortal God for an image shaped like mortal man" (Rom. 1:23), so the Corinthians "make mere men a cause for pride" (1 Cor. 3:21). In other words, they propose to manipulate God through the personages and structures of Christ's own Church. In so doing, they too remain in the realm *before* grace, on the plane of mere flesh (1 Cor. 3:1–4). Christ is not effecting in them the liberation of faith because they stubbornly persist in the outlook of religious alienation from which faith in Christ's message proposes to free them.

To repeat it once more: what counts truly is not one's de facto religious situation. Nor is it faith, in the sense of orthodoxy, that shelters one from alienation and saves him. What counts in the last analysis is faith as a religious attitude which can be found, as we have seen, in any group whether "religious" or not; but which the Christian message united inextricably with its concept of salvation and its message of liberation.

There is a very obvious parallel between the Epistle to the Galatians and the First Epistle to the Corinthians on this point. It shows us that lack of faith, in its deepest sense, always consists in picturing man's relationships with God as being conditioned restrictively by something which really ought to be in man's service. In the case of the Galatians it concerns works commanded by the moral law. The Galatians are tempted to buy God with a way of acting which is guaranteed in advance to be meritorious of salvation. The elements in Paul's judgment of this outlook are quite clear. Firstly, in Abraham we find an unconditional divine promise of salvation. The law appears only much later, prescribing what man must do. So it is contradictory to assume that the law could be a restrictive condition on a promise made much earlier in unconditional form (Gal. 3:17–18). To think something like that is a way of thinking proper to the realm of before and the flesh, not to the realm of now and grace (Gal. 4:9–11 and 6:12–14).

Something exactly parallel occurs in the Church of Corinth. Christ came not to judge but to save (John 3:17). The new covenant inaugurated in him is the one which God promised through the prophet Jeremiah: a covenant which is gratuitously given by God and which cannot be broken by man because it is inscribed in his heart (Jer. 31–32). Christ came to offer us a new life, one that would be at least as ample, rich, and total as man's earlier life in sin had been (Rom. 5:12–21). On leaving this earth, Christ sent his Spirit to create his Church in conjunction with him. It is absurd to suppose that this Church, with its visible and limited structures, constitutes a restricting condition on this unconditional sal-

vation. To think so is a way of thinking proper to the fleshly realm of
before, not to the now realm of grace (1 Cor. 3:3).[10]

For Paul, the law is the revelation of sin, while the Church is the
revelation of salvation. Clearly these two revelations require an adherence
based on a faith that somehow separates one from the rest of humanity:
chosen people, church. But this separation is nothing more than a special-
ization, so to speak, designed to carry to the whole world the help that
this revelation represents for the liberating faith that God has already
placed in the hearts of men. In the case of the Church, knowledge of
the mystery must be conceived as the message which God sends to man in
order to liberate him from his alienation from God and to send him out
to fashion, out of love, a humanity with *one* end.

The two things go together. If a person does not have faith-based
relationships with God—i.e., relationships of gratuitousness, sonship, and
liberty—then he separates himself irreparably from human beings (1 Cor.
3:3). And in fact, in the history of humanity, alienated religion has been
the source of the most profound and indestructible human barriers (*cf.*
Eph. 2:14–16) because it has absolutized and sanctioned them with the
aura of divine authority. The Church's "faith" has justified separation,
manipulation, and hatred.

When Christianity is understood correctly from a truly faith-inspired
attitude, it teaches us to see humanity as a *whole,* a whole to be fashioned
by love: "If we are in union with Christ Jesus circumcision makes no
difference at all, nor does the want of it; the only thing that counts is
faith active in love" (Gal. 5:6).

3. A concrete illustration may be worth more than countless explanations. In his *Diary of a Country Priest,* Bernanos offers us one. The
main character is talking to a man who was in the Foreign Legion. The
latter is explaining why the soldiers curse God before they die, even
though they believe in him.

> We all believe in God, all, even the worst of us—the worst believe in him
> most, perhaps. I think we must be too proud to sin without taking risks; we
> have always one witness to face: God . . . We've plenty of priests out
> there. My colonel's orderly . . . he'd been a priest at Poitou, at one time
> . . . How did he die? . . . Well, I won't lie to you. At those times our boys
> like to swank. And their way of doing it consists of two or three formulas
> which closely resemble blasphemy from your point of view, and that's the
> truth. . . . There are blasphemies and blasphemies . . . In the mind of
> those blokes it's a method of cutting off your retreat, a way they have. It's
> stupid, I consider, but not foul. They're outlaws in the world, and they
> make themselves outlaws in the next. If God isn't going to save soldiers,
> all soldiers, just because they're soldiers, what's the good of trying? One

more blasphemy for the sake of good measure, running the same risk as the other lads, avoiding a "not-proven" verdict, that's the idea. . . .[11]

It is not without reason that our country priest, after reflecting on many similar cases, reaches a conclusion that could serve as a summary of this chapter: "Grace is everywhere." Grace indeed is in us to lead us to the totality in which, as Irenaeus said, "there is only one God, there is only one Son who carries out the will of the Father, and there is only one human race in which God's mysterious designs are brought to fulfillment."

To return to our example of the legionnaires. What else but grace is that faith of theirs, their supreme liberty in dealing with God (mistakenly conceived, to be sure) with absolute contempt for their own interests and fate, asking only that he unite them, for better or for worse, with their battle companions? In the harsh apprenticeship of war they come to know that they must be saved together. Paul said exactly the same thing in his Epistle to the Romans when he declared simply and forthrightly: "I could even pray to be outcast from Christ myself for the sake of my brothers, my natural kinsfolk" (Rom. 9:3).

The only thing is that the faith of Paul knew one thing of which the faith of those legionnaires was unaware. Paul knew that God, far from wanting to snatch them away from others in order to save them, saved them precisely through their desire for unity. Paul knew that it is God who creates this absolute disinterest in them, this faith which is active in love, and which launches man from his experience of divine fatherhood into the creative task of fashioning human brotherhood.

Thus faith, conceived in terms of the Christian message, is the foundation stone of authentic secularization. In reality it does not liberate man from his relationships with God. On the contrary it liberates these same religious relationships in gratuitousness so that man may be capable of finding, in his task of fashioning universal brotherhood in history, the absolute value which comes to it from a God who shared this task with us.

So this is the conclusion we should reach in this chapter on the breadth of grace. Not only does the dynamism of grace truly and effectively reach humanity as a whole. Through faith, which at first glance may seem to separate people, it also liberates man from religious alienation in order to launch him into the fashioning of the total body of Christ: the new humanity.

NOTES TO CHAPTER THREE

1. Simone Weil, *Attente de Dieu* (Paris: La Colombe, 1950), pp. 82 and 84. Engl. trans. *Waiting for God* (New York: Putnam, 1951).

2. *Mission et Grâce* (Tours: Mame, 1962), I, 214 ff. Eng. trans. *Mission and Grace*, I. See José M. González-Ruíz, *El Christianismo no es un humanismo* (Madrid: Ed. Península, 1966), pp. 125 ff.

3. *Apol.*, II, 10; 1–3; I, 46:2–5; II, 10:4–5. Cited by Jean Daniélou, *Holy Pagans of the Old Testament* (Baltimore: Helicon, 1957).

4. *Ibid.*

5. Cited by Michael Schmaus, *Katholische Dogmatik*, V.

6. Cited by Henri de Lubac, *Catholicisme* 5th ed. (Paris: Ed. Du Cerf, 1952), p. 16. Eng. trans. *Catholicism* (London: Burns, Oates & Washbourne, 1950).

7. Ives de Montcheuil, *Aspects de l'Église* (Paris: Ed. Du Cerf, 1948), pp. 142–143. Eng. trans. *Aspects of the Church* (Chicago: Fides, 1955).

8. See in this series, Volume I, Chapter II, main article.

9. Karl Rahner, *Theological Investigations*, II, 46; Eng. trans. (Baltimore: Helicon, 1963). In the article entitled "Membership of the Church According to the Teaching of Pius XII's Encyclical 'Mystici Corporis Christi,'" pp. 1–88.

10. Liberation from the law and religion as alienating elements must go together. As Ricoeur puts it: "For Freud, ethics and religion have a common root . . . It is the impulse of *fable-making* united with the impulse for *prohibition*" (*De l'Interpretation: Essai sur Freud,* Paris: Editions du Seuil, 1965, p. 229). Precisely in pointing this out, the Christian message, if not the "Christian sociological reality," deserves to be regarded as a new element that does not fit into the Freudian concept of religion.

11. Georges Bernanos, *The Diary of a Country Priest* (New York: Macmillan Paperbacks Edition, 1962), pp. 206–208.

CLARIFICATIONS

I. GRACE AND ITS "PATHWAYS"

When Georges Bernanos describes his worthy protagonist, the country priest, he presents us with someone who is a "subject of grace," an active subject indeed.[1] There radiates around him a luminous quality akin to the clear light of dawn. It transfigures him without in the least snatching him out of the dark obscurity of everyday life. Instead it plunges him more deeply into it, so that he becomes a full sharer in its contradictions and inconsistencies.

Paralyzed by a clearly visible shyness, this priest is a great nonconformist. He, far more than a restless "militant," is convinced of his human frailty and poverty. This conviction pervades the whole web of his tendencies, reactions, and evaluations of his surroundings. The world, as he sees it, has become accustomed to boredom; *ennui* is the true condition of people around him.

Buried in this deadened world that is totally lacking in freshness and novelty, the priest finds no support for his own vision. The people he runs into in his ordinary rounds either share his doubt, or have become impervious to love, or else do indeed speak the language of Christianity but in terms that are totally distinct from his own. It is the latter group, people who do not speak from within the structures of the Church, that impress him the most: an idealistic, anticlerical soldier of fortune (M. Olivier); an atheist doctor who loves life in its very absurdity (Dr. Laville); and a renegade priest who was once his classmate (Dufréty). The other people around him are prisoners of their own narrowness and their ghetto-mentality.

It is in talks with the soldier of fortune and the atheist doctor that our country priest discovers new panoramas that are much vaster than those of his parishioners and fellow priests. The soldier of fortune, talking about the courage of his fighting companions, makes him wonder about his routine as a "man of the sacraments." Would he have the courage to die as well as they do? And when the doctor informs him that he has cancer, our priest feels both a strange sense of liberation and a terrible love for life that brings tears to his eyes. Yet these very tears seem to signify a communion that goes far beyond his repetitious sacramental routine. He has been a poor creature too afraid to admit or express his love of life and the beauty of the world.

116

These separate encounters culminate in the circumstances surrounding his death. He will seek shelter and die in the house of his old seminary companion, the renegade priest, who is now bound in a trivial relationship to a woman he does not love and who is living a vain existence. It is precisely in these surroundings that our dying priest glimpses the fullness of life and its broad, converging pathways. When his renegade companion laments that he cannot provide him with the consolation of the last rites, our country priest whispers slowly and distinctly: "Does it matter? Grace is everywhere."

This sentiment echoes and sums up the realization that has slowly dawned on him in the course of his life. Grace can conquer any obstacle, even his selfish distrust of himself. He must open up to the broad, incalculable pathways of grace and learn to love himself and life with humility. The night of obscurity and darkness gradually gives way to the light of dawn and its hopefulness. And it is in the dawning hours of a new day that he dies contentedly.

The image of dawn and its tieup with hope occurs in another contemporary novel by a Uruguayan author, *Con las primeras luces*.[2] Its very title refers to the first light of day. The protagonist, Eugenio, spends the night bleeding his life away in a vestibule. His obscure life and death is the image of a personal and societal decadence. Yet, even though the author does not say so explicitly, his dying character does look forward to some salvation. In the new light that is dawning around him he hopes to put together and integrate his only half-lived past. His misspent life takes on more and more meaning as it moves forward toward the dawning day. Youth and freshness, which appear to have been lost, can always be found and salvaged in the history of a person or a community.

II. THE "NEWNESS" OF CHRIST

Several time we have indicated that Saint Paul perceives and formulates the notion of grace in terms of a key experience: his conversion. From the new perspective in which the revelation of Christ's mystery situates his life he perceives, perhaps more acutely than the rest of the New Testament, the newness that Christ contributes to the universe as a whole. This newness is given to humanity first of all. In it is effected the conquest of all its petty divisions. Humanity is transformed into the oneness of a "new man": "For he is himself our peace. Gentiles and Jews, he has made the two one, and in his own body of flesh and blood has broken down the enmity which stood like a dividing wall between them; for he annulled the law with its rules and regulations, so as to create out of the two a single new humanity in himself, thereby making peace" (Eph. 2:14–15). "You have discarded the old nature with its deeds and have put on the new nature, which is being constantly renewed in the image of its Creator and brought to know God. There is no question here of Greek and Jew, circumcised and uncircumcised, barbarian, Scythian, slave and freeman . . ." (Col. 3:10–11). "When anyone is united to Christ, there is a new world; the old order has gone, and a new order has already begun" (2 Cor. 5:17).

Secondly, the "everything" of which Paul speaks is something that transcends humanity, that goes on to include Christ's work of reconciling and unifying the entire universe: "For in him the complete being of God, by God's own choice, came to dwell. Through him God chose to reconcile the whole universe to himself, making peace through the shedding of his blood upon the cross—to reconcile all things, whether on earth or in heaven, through him alone" (Col. 1:19–20).

In Christ a new heaven and a new earth have emerged from the old (2 Peter 3:13; Rev. 21:1). And from the experience of his conversion Paul sees the newness of Christ as a rupture and breakthrough that empties the old of meaning and power.

This obliges us to spend a little time considering the notion of "newness." For if Christ inaugurates a new existence, a new man, a new heaven, and a new earth, through the realization of a new covenant in his blood, that would seem to suggest that the newness he brings is wholly different from what preceded it.

1. "New" in current language. An analysis of the adjective *new* (or the noun *newness*) will start us off in our investigation. "New" has a twofold connotation. On the one hand it can be used to signify something recent or modern, with a clear temporal note being involved. A person wears a new suit (i.e., one recently bought), or holds new ideas (i.e., ones he did not hold before). But "new" can also signify something qualitatively different, something unforeseen and unaccustomed which evokes surprise, admiration, and expectation. Thus when one says, "I feel like a new man," he is referring to some experience of personal transformation. He is really the same person as before, but he feels invigorated with new energies and new hopes.

There is no doubt that both connotations are intimately related to each other. When we talk about a "new year," we are giving a temporal connotation to the word "new." But on a deeper level we can also refer to the unforeseen hopes and expectations of a fresh start, a new beginning. In other words, the qualitative connotation of newness always refers to some before, but the stress is placed on something more profound. It is placed on the experience of something fresh and surprising, on a quality of unaccustomed newness.

Presumably as we apply the adjective "new" to more profound experiences, the temporal element tends to disappear. Consider a group of people who work together. At the start they scarcely know each other. But the fact of living together, working together, and sharing common problems gradually knits a growing bond of solidarity and unity between them. Something new has arisen among them: the mere juxtaposition of individuals has changed qualitatively into the unity of a work community. In the same manner, when love between two people follows its usual dynamism of growth, each step is experienced as something new: a new encounter, a fresh start. The experience of their first encounter signified a totally transformed vision of the whole universe. Now, in the light of further stages, it appears as something old that would destroy their love if, *per impossibile,* they should choose to merely replay the record.

Thus the current use of the word "new," our first level of analysis here, enables us to glimpse that we are in the presence of an existential category of great richness. It signifies a discontinuous breakthrough or rupture within a framework of continuity. In other words, something be-

gins or opens up to deeper levels of experience; but we can say that this
"new" something, which makes the previous situation "old," was possible thanks to the old even though the latter does not explain it. "Newness," then, is a category essential to the notion of history.   ·

2. *"New" in the Old Testament.* Moving to a second level of analysis
and keeping in mind what we have seen so far, we ascertain that "newness" is not a concept exclusive to the New Testament. What is more,
we cannot possibly acquire an in-depth comprehension of the New Testament expressions (new man, new creature, new name, new heavens, new
earth, new covenant) if we do not first analyze the notion of newness in the
Old Testament and the experiences to which it is linked.

We can begin by pointing out a basic difference in usage. In accordance with the classical vocabulary, both the Greek tradition of the
Septuagint and the New Testament employ the word *neos* to express the
temporal connotation of newness. And they reserve the word *kainos,*
which began to be used around the time of the major prophets, to refer
to the transformations that God effects in his people. *Neos* primarily
translates the Hebrew root *'abib* while *kainos* translates the Hebrew root
hadaṣh,

a) Newness and salvation-history. In our analysis we shall discover
that the concept of newness went through a process of interiorization
which was proper to the whole of Old Testament revelation and which
undoubtedly paralleled the cultural progress of the Israelite people. The
notion of sin, for example, became progressively interiorized, moving
from an exterior flaw to an interior culpability that tainted the inmost
being of man. The notion of law was interiorized in the same way. Exodus
urges the people "to make sure that the law of the Lord is always on your
lips" (Ex. 13:9). By contrast Jeremiah gives us these words of Yahweh:
"I will set my law within them and write it on their hearts" (Jer. 31:33).
In what sense, then, was the notion of "newness" interiorized in a parallel
way?

In the first place, newness was perceived in the rhythms of nature.
Spring is the time when everything is reborn and acquires renewed freshness. Every primitive people, including the Israelites, saw this season in
terms of liberation, of the triumph of life over death. In short: in terms
of salvation.

In Hebrew the month of *'abib* (the root cited earlier) expresses this
experience of the rebirth of life. The Greek text of the Septuagint translates *'abib* as "the month of new things" *(ton neon)* or of firstfruits. And
it is precisely in this month that God effects his work of liberating the
people from Egypt: "The Lord said to Moses and Aaron in Egypt, 'This
month *('abib)* is for you the first of months; you shall make it the first
month of the year'" (Exod. 12:1–2). "Remember this day, the day on
which you have come out of Egypt, the land of slavery . . . for today,
in the month of Abib, is the day of your exodus" (Exod. 13:3–4). So
Yahweh institutes the rite of lamb and unleavened bread (the Passover)
in the month of new things that comes to be the first month of the year.

Thus, through Yahweh's intervention, the liberation which spring had
represented in every natural religion acquired a new meaning: i.e.,
liberation from slavery in Egypt. In other words, cyclic time was con-

verted into history. The month of new things associated with the Exodus, both being perpetuated in the liturgy of Passover, would remain as the basic structure of the whole history of the God who saves. And it would also be the definitive point of reference for prophetic interpretation of God's liberative activity in the world. Let us consider the readings for the Passover vigil.

Every time that the Passover is celebrated, its significance as liberation would be spelled out. "When your children ask you, 'What is the meaning of this rite?' you shall say, 'It is the Lord's Passover, for he passed over the houses of the Israelites in Egypt when he struck the Egyptians but spared our houses' " (Exod. 12:26–27). "On that day you shall tell your son, 'This commemorates what the Lord did for me when I came out of Egypt' " (Exod. 13:8).

b) Sin, God's fidelity, and the experience of newness. A history which is liberative in two ways begins with the Exodus. It liberates the Hebrews from the fetters of cyclical time and from enslavement to the Egyptian pharaoh. But it continues on with a very peculiar structural element, embodied in the constant and growing tendency of the Israelite people to infidelity. In other words, they continually tend to shun the liberation they have received, and to return to the cultic practices of nature religions: e.g., the cult of Baal, the fertility cult, sacred prostitution, and even child sacrifice.

This generalized state of sin ultimately represents a rejection of dialogue with the personal God who founds and directs history. It is particularly rampant in the Book of Kings and it is denounced by the prophets. To it is attributed first the split into two kingdoms and then the destruction of the kingdom at the time of the Babylonian Exile.

When the King of Assyria conquers Samaria, the Bible explains why: "All this happened to the Israelites because they had sinned against the Lord their God who brought them up from Egypt . . . they paid homage to other gods and observed the laws and customs of the nations whom the Lord had dispossessed before them" (2 Kings 17:7–8).

Jeremiah, who lived through the tragic final end of the kingdom, speaks prophetically in the name of Yahweh: "But they did not listen; they paid no heed, and persisted in disobedience . . . from the day when your forefathers left Egypt until now. I took pains to send to them all my servants the prophets; they did not listen to me, they paid no heed, but were obstinate and proved even more wicked than their forefathers" (Jer. 7:24–26).

The consequence is punishment: "I will scatter them among nations whom neither they nor their forefathers have known; I will harry them with the sword until I have made an end of them " (Jer. 9:16).

However, this approach of regarding disgrace as a consequence of sin would undergo a sudden change. Precisely at the moment when the predicted evils reach their most painful stage, when the Israelite people are conquered and lose everything that is most precious to them, they paradoxically discover Yahweh's relationship with his people as a *fidelity that pardons*, as a covenant that cannot be vitiated by man's infidelity. This is the original feature of the Book of Consolation in Jeremiah (chapters 30–31), the acme of revelation in the Old Testament.

It is precisely in this context that the notion of newness appears in its fullest sense: i.e., as the formulation of the complicated and disconcerting experience which underlies their new way of conceiving God. According to this notion, the history of Israel is not just the result of one liberative action on God's part, who starts his faithful people off once during the exodus from Egypt. Nor is it the story of Israel's growing infidelity that frustrates God's design and brings on his chatisement. Instead it is the progressive manifestation of his mercy and fidelity, now perceived in terms of pardon and new creation.

Hence newness is a category of encounter, or even more of re-encounter. It is an expression of God's growing proximity to man despite, or rather, through man's infidelity. No wonder, then, that at the moment when Israel's comprehension of God acquires a depth never reached before, the experience is formulated in terms of a "new covenant." It is new, not in the sense that it differs[3] from the covenant effected by God at the start, but in the sense that it marks a further stage in God's closer approach to man to renew and transform his existence.

Jeremiah will see this new covenant as an interiorization of the law: "The time is coming, says the Lord, when I will make a new covenant with Israel and Judah . . . I will set my law within them and write it on their hearts; I will become their God and they shall become my people. No longer need they teach one another to know the Lord; all of them, high and low alike, shall know me, says the Lord, for I will forgive their wrongdoing and remember their sin no more" (Jer. 31:31–34).

For Ezekiel the transformation is even more profound. Yahweh will transform the very heart of man, and the covenant will be effected in a total intimacy by the gift of a new spirit, the spirit of Yahweh (cf. Ezek. 11:17–20; 36:25–29).

The process of personalizing the covenant will reach its culmination in the Suffering Servant of Deutero-Isaiah (Isa. 42:1–7), in whom the newness is extended to the whole universe. There will be new heavens and a new earth (Isa. 65:17–18). And a new name will be given to every human being (Isa. 62:2; 65:15) because the Suffering Servant, by shouldering suffering and history, will win a definitive victory over man's temptation to abolish both in myth.

3. The "new" testament. Deutero-Isaiah brings us to the threshold of the New Testament. In Christ is realized the fullness of the covenant (testament), the closest proximity of the "God-with-us" that was already revealed to Moses (Exod. 3:12), and the definitive manifestation of God's "grace and truth" (John 1:17). The experience which goes along with comprehending the Christ-event "when the time was ripe" (Gal. 4:4) is certainly in a line of continuity with the process already indicated. That is how the primitive Christian community comprehended it. In Christ they spontaneously saw the definitive realization of the covenant promise and the ultimate fulfillment of the message of the prophets.[4]

At the same time, however, this new stage in the process of God's closer approach to us shows God with us and "one with us." So it constitutes a discontinuous breakthrough, a rupture, of which the Christian community would grow progressively more aware—not without painful conflicts. And it would eventually show up in Paul's formulations of something absolutely new, over against which everything prior is old: "Circumcision is nothing; uncircumcision is nothing; the only thing that counts is *new creation!*" (Gal. 6:15)

Our analysis of "newness" in the light of current linguistic usage and the revelation of the Old Testament has led us to the conclusion that "newness" is an historical category which expresses the complex experience of love. Within the framework of revelation it is explicated as God's fidelity which transforms our "stiff-necked" sinfulness and our "hearts of stone" (Ezek. 36:25–29) into an openness to grace. When this divine fidelity reaches its full expression in Christ, history, which had been a long preparation of humanity for this crucial happening, acquires a new import. It becomes the slow, progressive unfolding of all that which, in germinal form, was definitively given to us in Christ.

Outside of revelation and in a more general way, newness is the category which expresses the transcendence of love. Its very dynamism requires it to keep growing, transforming mere time into history.

But in both cases newness is the result of God's unique action, which liberates man from the limitations in which he is imprisoned by the human condition.

III. A THEOLOGY OF HISTORY: OBSTACLES AND PERSPECTIVES

With the elements brought together so far, we can try to respond to a question that was hotly debated in the decade of the fifties. Is there a *theology* of history? Or, to put it in minimal terms: *Should* there be a theology of history? And here we mean history as a task, a line of progress and hope that groups human beings together.

The alternative, presumably, is that theology must limit itself to pointing out the ever identical relationship of each moment of history to an identical judgment of God.

Leopoldo Malevez poses the problem in more technical terms from a theological viewpoint: "Does human culture, viewed in terms of its results, prepare the supernatural from within and direct the human race, by a process of slow maturation, toward the realities of the kingdom?" [5] Translated into more concrete language, this comes down to asking: Is the kingdom of God progressing *qualitatively* by the very fact that we are now in the twentieth century rather than in, say, the fifteenth century after Christ? Or is it progressing only *quantitatively*, in the sense that each generation, by responding to the summons of God, adds to the number of those who have made a positive response and joined the number of the elect already provided for by God—a number that could have been attained just as well if humanity had remained indefinitely in an earlier stage of evolution?

It was not easy to answer this question for several weighty theological reasons. These reasons can be subsumed under what is often called the "eschatological" perspective. With our ready tendency to put labels on ideas, names were quickly found for the opposing outlooks here. Those who were opposed to a Christian theology of history were called eschatologists, while those who favored this possibility were given the equally uninformative name of incarnationists.[6]

1. The principal reasons behind the eschatological point of view were, and continue to be, the following:

a) With Christ the end of time has arrived. The culminating, decisive happening of history has already taken place. We do not look forward to any future event that will surpass in importance what has already taken place once for all time: the redemption of humanity, that is, Christ's victory over all the forces that are opposed to the communication of divine life to man. For this reason the New Testament repeatedly states that the fullness of time arrived with the Incarnation and Redemption and the accompanying divine Judgment.

In contrast to what the overall cast of Greek thinking on history appears to be, Christian thinking on it is not cyclic but linear. This means that history does not repeat itself but rather moves on toward something. And that something occurred with Christ. Certain conclusions follow from this.

Daniélou puts it this way: "Firstly, history is not an eternal progress, it has an end. It constitutes a defined, limited plan . . . Secondly, *Christianity is this end*. Christ presented himself as one coming at the end of time and ushering in *the definitive world*." [7] From this the author concludes that the history which fills the void between Christ and the end of time in its most material sense is not, strictly speaking, a history. In other words, it is not a process of construction but a judgment in which each human being presents himself before the tribunal. History is a condemned prisoner, as it were, waiting in the death house for execution.[8]

What is truly important has already come from above. What is more, it will continue to come from above in the form of summons and judgment: "If we do not show how the cosmic order is dominated by the cross of Christ and subjected to his sovereign action, there is a danger that sacred history will lose itself in natural history, that Christ will be dissolved in cosmic becoming. It is necessary to show that what is involved here is not an immanent evolution but the creative actions of the Word." [9] Verticality, then, is the law governing what happens in the world; for the Vertical in person touched our history and put an end to it, at least in terms of what is meaningful.

b) The definitive judgment has begun. It operates in the fact that each human being is confronted with the summons of grace in this "fullness of time" when history has already reached its pinnacle but has not yet terminated. Grace does indeed summon man to tasks within the time of history. He is summoned to love his fellow men and save them from every possible evil. But the end results are not transmitted here. The love which passes judgment on man is never given in finished form; on the contrary, it is the very object of his liberty. "*At each instant* man faces the Son of Man, and judgment takes place *now*." [10]

Thus no one can replace another person in the face of judgment. And this means that no history can give love or morality readymade to a succeeding generation. From this it would seem to follow that "the only vision of history which corresponds to a positive scrutiny of the facts is that of Burckhardt. His vision shows man struggling with different sociological situations and demonstrating his grandeur by overcoming them. But this grandeur was *the same* in the days of Pericles as it was in the

days of Napoleon. Empirical history does not manifest any progress in
the sense of an acquisition of human value." [11]

In other words, a chasm seems to be opened up between that which
accumulates in history (that which progresses) and that which constitutes
the value of each human being (that which passes judgment on him).
Thus the final, eschatological judgment has to do with the latter, even
though it is realized in time.

If this is true, then history does not even have to reach fulfillment;
man has no real task and love has no real obligations. It would seem to
follow that the "successes of history" should not be conceived by the
Christian as advances from which the new generation would benefit on
the decisive plane of judgment. A distinction, indeed a real separation, is
thus effected between any and every historical hope and eschatological
hope.

c) Finally, the Church must play an essential role in the decisive
dialogue that takes place between God and man in the fullness of time,
that is, in the *now* that follows Christ.

Now in the realm of human history considered as progress, the
Church can only appear to be a particular community. But in the Christian eschatological perspective, the Incarnate Word is going to effect the
recapitulation of the universe through his Church. One more reason, it
would seem, to separate out a history that does not lead toward this vision
and to look for the fulfillment of the promise in the final intervention of
a force that is already present but invisible: i.e., the force by which Christ
rose from the dead and conquered his enemies (Phil. 3:20–21).

After all, what other outlook is left to us? "Consider the fact that
Christ has already come, and then look at the situation. Humanity has
not submitted unanimously to him. After twenty centuries it seems impossible to reasonably picture any such total conversion. The grace of
the Gospel seems to serve the role of a separating sword rather than the
role of union. It separates two cities in the bosom of humanity: the
Church on the one hand, the city of those who do not believe in Christ
on the other hand." [12]

As one can see even though one may debate its ultimate conclusions,
the "eschatological" conception does offer undeniable conditions for the
possibility of a Christian theology of history. Such a theology can exist
only if one accepts the challenge of these conditions rooted in revelation
and can show that they are truly fulfilled in its way of conceiving human
history. In the light of what we have already said, we can sum up these
conditions in three words: *verticality, liberty,* and *ecclesiality.*

2. The portrait which the Church offers us of herself in *Gaudium et
spes* is that of a community related essentially and intrinsically to history.
The Church "goes forward together with humanity," and her very life
is meant to serve "as a leaven" for this society on the move (GS 40). Being
a prophetic community, she must interpret the signs of the times (GS 4,
11): not to derive benefit for herself alone but to "search for truth and
for the genuine solution to the numerous problems which arise in the
life of individuals and from social relationships" (GS 16).

Thus it is necessary that the conditions governing the possibility of
a theology of history integrate here and now the conception which the

Church has of her proper mission and that of each of her members who are summoned to this task.

Firstly, the Church acknowledges that with Christ's Incarnation and Redemption "the final age of the world has already come upon us" (LG 48). But she does not picture this happening as *terminated*. The fact that God has become man and has liberated us is not a finished reality that puts history into a shroud. We can and must say that Christ *is coming*, insofar as we are referring to the total Christ, the Head of the Body composed of the Church and the entire universe structured by history. "Christ, having been lifted up from the earth, is drawing all men to Himself . . . Rising from the dead . . . He sent His life-giving Spirit upon His disciples and through His Spirit has established *His body*, the Church . . . He is continually active in the world, leading men to the Church . . . Therefore, the promised restoration which we are awaiting has already begun in Christ, is carried forward in the mission of the Holy Spirit, and through Him continues in the Church" (GS 48). But the process has not ended: "The Church, to which we are all called in Christ Jesus, and in which we acquire sanctity through the grace of God, will attain her full perfection only in the glory of heaven. Then will come the time of the restoration of all things. Then the human race as well as the entire world, which is intimately related to man and achieves its purpose through him, will be perfectly re-established in Christ" (LG 48).

So it is incorrect to view history as a process which, after the occurrence of its culminating event in Christ's thirty-three years on earth, has degenerated into the succeeding passage of individual lives until all have passed before the divine Judge. On the other hand the Church does not deny the verticality of history, nor the unique and ultimately decisive importance of the Christ event, when it gives to him the cosmic dimensions that are appropriate to him and that includes history as a process of construction. And this it does do in the documents of Vatican II.

Secondly, there is no need to picture the unfolding development of history as a process wherein something done in the past discharges the liberty or personal responsibility of someone today, or determines it in some way—for better or for worse.

What accumulates in history is not man's goodness or badness. The human species does not *become more moral* with its progress, but it is progress nonetheless. What we can and ought to transmit are the conditioning factors that will allow love, which will ever continue to be the object of free choice and intense struggle, to unfold in all its possible dimensions. As the Council puts it: "One of the salient features of the modern world is the growing interdependence of men one on the other . . . Brotherly love among men does not reach its perfection on the level of technical progress, but on the deeper level of interpersonal relationships" (GS 23).

Fundamental to any theology of history is this distinction between what is cumulative (hence undeniably constitutes progress), and what will never accumulate, what will ever remain tied to the risk of each person's liberty in his interpersonal relationships.

From this springs the mutual service that the Church and history render to each other (GS 11). On the one hand "the promotion of unity

belongs to the innermost nature of the Church since she is . . . both a
sacramental sign and an instrument of intimate union with God, and
of the unity of all mankind" (GS 42). On the other hand "love for God
and neighbor is the first and greatest commandment . . . To men growing daily more dependent on one another, and to a world becoming more
unified every day, this truth proves to be of paramount importance" (GS
24).

To put it another way: If Christian love is authentic, it will express
itself in an ever growing interdependence and unity in the history of
human beings. This (cumulative) factor will not make it easier to choose
love over egotism. In the face of this option each generation will be
equally free. But the person who chooses, out of love, to give himself to
others will have at his disposal greater means and objective possibilities
for going further and probing more deeply. And this portion of love, in
turn, will be translated into ever greater interdependence and unity.

Egotism, too, will objectively possess more means to effect its ends if
a person should decide for that alternative. And its carrying out will always be translated into an effort to curb or derail this growing interdependence and unity.[13] Hence Schoonenberg is quite justified in saying:
"Sin, although standing in history because it derives from freedom, is
antihistorical." [14]

Thus, seen from a perspective we had occasion to consider in Volume
I of this series,[15] the *subjective* possibilities of each individual vis-à-vis
God's judgment do not vary with each new generation and hence with
historical progress. But one is not justified in concluding from this that
historical progress does not pave the way for the supernatural from
within. For the fact is that, due to historical progress, the *objective*
presence of Jesus and his love in the world encounters human beings, each
succeeding generation of whom is capacitated for a love with ever more
universal possibilities. The process of undergoing a mental cure, for
example, does not prejudge whether love or egotism will spring from the
person's newly regained liberty. Nevertheless, each stage reached in the
cure does mean that the dosage of love that does freely arise will be more
ample and mature.

We can see, then, that a theology of history does not result in some
kind of "supernatural determinism," which would be a contradiction in
terms. Maturity for the good grows at the same pace as "maturity" for
evildoing—even though the latter use of the term is contradictory because evildoing represents a freely chosen reversion to immaturity.

Thus from the gradual progress of history under the guidance and
impetus of grace, we can look forward "to mature manhood, measured by
nothing less than the full stature of Christ" (Eph. 4:13).

Thirdly and finally, we might well ask whether the Church does not,
for all practical purposes, disappear from the final scene in this conception. In reality the Church, without losing her character as a distinctive sign and instrument, can only appear in the eschatological perspective
as *one* of the elements of this history which is moving toward its recapitulation in Christ. She would not appear to be the entity that brings
it about.

In Volume I we had occasion to see that both the New Testament and

Church tradition, embodied in Vatican II, picture her at the end of time
as she is today: a particular community going through "the same earthly
lot which the world does" (GS 40) and experiencing alternately "the
persecutions of the world and the consolations of God" (LG 8). But we
also saw that the Church is not limited to her visible reality; that in
Scripture and its extensions in tradition and the magisterium, the Church
always shows up with dimensions equal to those of the universe. Where
Christ is, there is the Church: "Wherefore this People, while remaining
one and unique, is to be spread throughout the whole world and must
exist in all ages, so that the purposes of God's will may be fulfilled . . .
After his children were scattered, he decreed that they should at length
be unified again" (LG 13).

Within this overall ensemble which constitutes the People of God,
and hence the Church in its fullest form, the visible Church even now
recapitulates the overall reality of this scheme in seminal form. Not
only is this plan being effected in her, as in the rest of humanity; in her
it also acquires its maturity in principle by becoming a conscious thing.
And this is not designed to be a privilege for her members but to contribute, by way of dialogue, to the solutions demanded by this common
journey (GS 40).

Thus the progressive recapitulation of humanity in the Body of
Christ, despite all appearances, is not effected without the Church or
parallel to her. It is effected in the Church, not only when she loses her
boundary-limits but also when, within those limits, she takes cognizance
of what is being fulfilled in history and serves it.

In the light of what we have said so far, it is not true that the Church
of Vatican II decided in favor of the incarnationist line and against the
eschatological view. The fact is that the truth does not lie in one *or* the
other but in a rich and difficult synthesis of both. Only in this light can
we appreciate the following statement of Vatican II: "A hope related to
the end of time does not diminish the importance of intervening duties,
but rather undergirds the acquittal of them *with fresh incentives*" (GS
21).

IV. THE BREADTH OF GRACE AND PASTORAL INHIBITION

Consideration of the notion that grace is coextensive with humanity
itself, both in geographical and chronological terms, provoked a phenomenon of inhibition[16] in pastoral activity. The man of the Church was accustomed to work for the "salvation of souls." Now, considering that his
action is no longer definitory for salvation, he appears to have no in-
centive for his hard and difficult work. He would seem to be nothing
more than a wet blanket, dampening the spirits of people who are distracted by, or wholly content with, the temporal realm.

On the other side of the coin, the conviction that God is working in
the world through human realities has made it impossible for many
churchmen to be able to distinguish activities on behalf of human development from pastoral activities as such. Some have said that the work
of evangelization is identical with development work. This second outlook is totally different from the first; but it leads to the same pastoral
impasse insofar as one does not grasp the specific nature and value of

pastoral activity. One of the underlying roots of the present crisis in the priesthood stems from the "discomfort" provoked by the discovery of the breadth of grace.

Today we are faced with the necessity of resituating pastoral activity in a world where grace is ubiquitous. We must spell out the distinctive features of this activity in order to evaluate it correctly and to orientate it in terms of its deepest, most authentic meaning.

1. The first feature is to be found in the fact that pastoral activity calls for development work. Evangelization is deeply and intimately bound up with human development as such. One cannot picture the work of evangelization taking place at some far remove from development work,[17] as if it were a disembodied reality. If our message is to proclaim the good news of a God-made-man, of a God who liberates man, then it must be framed within a *context of development* related to that which man understands as liberation. Just as the God of liberation revealed and transmitted his word through his activity of freeing the Hebrew people from Egyptian imperialism, so evangelizing activity today is framed necessarily within a development context. If we failed to do this, then we would fall into the error of divorcing faith from real life. Going against the admonitions of Vatican II, we would be setting up a private "religious zone" on the distant outskirts of man's concrete life.

2. Our second observation counterbalances the first. While it is true that all pastoral activity must be framed within a movement on behalf of human development, it is also certain that pastoral activity cannot be simply equated with development work. The gospel-preacher is doing something that is specifically different from development work, which the Christian will usually carry out in conjunction with the nonbeliever.

It is not that the presence of the non-Christian inhibits it. The essential factor here is the specific nature of the revealed Word. It is a Word which we do not discover or possess in our own experience but which nevertheless discloses to us the ultimate meaning of human history.

This deeper meaning, which comes to us from revelation accepted in faith, orientates and gives impetus to our developmental work. When a Christian and a non-Christian work together for man's betterment and liberation, their activity does not differ with respect to its practical efficacy. The Christian as Christian does not possess readymade solutions to human problems, nor does the fact of being a Christian place one on a plane where such solutions do not appear or count. Instead the Christian, drawing on revelation, will try to relate human development to the absolute dimensions given to it by God's Incarnation in our history.

3. We find a third characteristic precisely in the fact that pastoral activity, today more than ever before, must be keenly attentive to the work of the Spirit in history: i.e., to the "signs of the times." Pastoral activity has never been able to carry out its work in an a-temporal form, disregarding the web of history in which men are woven together and the God-made-one-with-us shared. But today more than ever before, when we are beginning to discern the major lines of this history, pastoral activity must be integrated into the *major points* of man's contemporary history. It must discover the divine activity that guides this history. Starting from there and operating within this movement, it must preach the gospel. In other words, it must reveal the ultimate meaning of this history,

the dimensions of personal involvement to which every person today is called.

This feature of pastoral work enables us to discover the way in which it is dependent on dialogue with the world. Pastoral activity cannot be carried out by prescinding from man's history. The "pastor"—and every layman is a pastor to humanity by virtue of his baptism—is not someone who *simply* knows the Bible and certain "dogmas." He is someone who knows how to read the plan of God in our contemporary history. Our pastoral activity is pointed out to us in some way by a human history that is taken seriously as the theological locus, the authentic and unique locus, of man's encounter with God.

It is precisely the recognition of the "breadth of grace" that leads pastoral activity to respect the pathway of every individual and every human grouping. On the one hand, the universality of God's gift deepens our pastoral effort and makes it more patient. No longer are we to simply make conversions and baptize, for people would find that inimical. Sacramental work finds its authentic place after a slow and careful process of preaching the Word. On the other hand, this preaching will not be presented as something alien to the situation of a given human group but as situated within man's continuing quest. And this presupposes a long process of listening. In this way pastoral activity will be able to vary, as it should, with the concrete needs of a given group and its relationship to the faith.[18]

4. Another major characteristic of this pastoral activity is embodied in what we might call a "re-expression of the faith." If we regard contemporary man and his reality, and if we note the dizzying evolution of history, we realize that God's Word must be expressed today in signs, formulas, and expressions that would be different from those of a prior day. Hence the Word of God will continue to take on new features, extensions, and depths. We cannot know all these new features because both man and his experience in history will continue to grow and change.

When all is said and done, the features we have enumerated do not seem to fully satisfy the uncertainty and distress we mentioned at the start. Is it perhaps that the universality of grace does not inhibit pastoral activity because it shows us that the salvation of others does not depend decisively on our managing to get them into the Church? The answer is simply no, if it springs as it should from the mandate of the Lord rather than from our own anxieties and complexes, if it is rooted in the *urgent duty of service* that goes to fashion our Christian life. God's word has been given to us Christians so that we might pass it on. For in the last analysis it reveals the fullness of man, his infinite possibilities and ultimate obligations. We must preach the gospel, not because man will be condemned without our word but because man needs this revealed word to reach his full measure. He needs the proclamation of the Good News and a personal knowledge of it: "I have come that men may have life, and may have it in all its fullness" (John 10:10).

V. VATICAN II AND THE REDEMPTION OF THE WORLD

It is of the greatest importance for the Church's pastoral task to redefine theologically the *world* over against which Vatican II chose to situate itself. In reality, the concept of "world" is not univocal. The "world" of which Greek culture spoke is one thing, the world of which John spoke in his Gospel [19] is something else again—perhaps several things. The "world" of ascetical theology and canon law is one thing, the world which fascinated Teilhard de Chardin is something else.

Perhaps precisely because the "world" is a concept which is difficult to define theologically and one which has both positive and pejorative connotations, Vatican II only rarely dared to present the Church as she is in reality: i.e., as a part of the world. Instead the Council used an image which is demographically and sociologically inexact and spoke about "Church-world dialogue," as if the Church would engage in dialogue from some nonworld.

That is the first impression we get from section 2 of *Gaudium et spes,* when it says: "The Council focuses its attention on the world of men." But then it goes on to define this world in the following terms: ". . . the whole human family along with the sum of those realities in the midst of which that family lives . . . that world which is the theater of man's history, and carries the marks of his energies, his tragedies, and his triumphs; that world which the Christian sees as created and sustained by its Maker's love, fallen indeed into the bondage of sin, yet emancipated now by Christ. He was crucified and rose again to break the stranglehold of personified Evil, so that the world might be fashioned anew according to God's design and reach its fulfillment" (GS 2).

Something poses a problem here which is critical for the dialogue that is to be initiated. While the first words give the impression that we are in the presence of two interlocutors over against each other, the latter passage inclines us to see *one within the other* so to speak. For the Church herself is made up of those who had fallen into the bondage of sin and were emancipated by Christ.

To put the problem in other words: If the Church stands over against the world in this dialogue, must the world be conceived as a merely natural reality? Or, to be more precise, must the world be conceived to be in a state of nature that has fallen prey to original sin and is still subject to it? Does the world still need to find refuge in redemption or is it, like the Christian, already operating from within the framework of redemption?

In other words it is not clear from these words of *Gaudium et spes,* and it never does become clear in that document, whether we can say that concrete human beings in history are still capable of being born and living in a state of original sin, or whether this situation has concretely and in fact been abolished for all.

Depending on our answer to this question—whether it be a yes, a no, or a "don't know"—our manner of approaching non-Christians and dialoguing with them in our common history will differ.

It is our feeling that a careful reading of *Gaudium et spes* will show that there was not a sufficient consensus among the Council Fathers to decide unequivocally for one of these lines. It may do so in certain passages, only to revert in other passages to expressions that are more consistent with the opposite line of thought. We do not present this vacillation as a defect but rather as an indication of *our* task. For it is the life of the Church that will enable us to go on spelling out what is not yet sufficiently clear. Chenu reports what one bishop said in the course of a discussion, when the participants were debating the details of the exact terms to use: "Let us not waste too much time in discussing *minutiae;* what will ultimately decide the meaning of these words is their implementation in reality." Chenu agrees, noting that church "praxis will make clear the meaning of the pronouncements." [20]

What is more, despite the wavering on the point under discussion here, we believe we can deduce an unequivocal direction from the Council itself. Our intention here is to do just that.

1. Let us go back to the first passage we examined. The Church "focuses its attention" on the world, "fallen indeed into the bondage of sin, yet emancipated now by Christ." If we examine the theological sense of the latter clause, we must admit that we are accustomed to considering the action of sin (of all sin and especially original sin) as a physical reality which adheres willy-nilly to every person, whereas we picture redemption from said sin as a "juridical" possibility to which the individual has recourse or not as he chooses.

But according to Paul, redemption had an effect at least as universal as that of sin—not just in principle but also in its consequences and results (*cf.* Rom. 5:12–21). "Where sin was thus multiplied, grace immeasurably exceeded it" (Rom. 5:20–21). The use of an expression such as "original redemption" is not exact because redemption can never be as original as sin in the conceptual order; after all, redeeming someone presupposes his prior captivity. Nevertheless, in the temporal order, the phrase under consideration would seem to indicate that all human beings are not only confronted with *potential* redemption and liberation but actually *have been* liberated just as surely as they had been enslaved.[21]

In another section of *Gaudium et spes* we find something similar: "An outstanding cause of human dignity lies in man's call to communion with God" (GS 19). The first thing to note is that the text does not refer to Christians but to the totality of mankind. The second thing to note is that this possibility of dialoguing with God does not depend on the use of reason, nor on the momentum of baptism, nor on the historical existence of the Church. "From the very circumstance of his origin, man is already invited to converse with God" (GS 19). Now for theology, and for the Council Fathers as we shall see, this dialogue with God is a supernatural dialogue. It means that man, right from his birth, enters the plane of supernatural redemption where everything is turned into a yes or a no to this vocation of dialoguing with God.

Further on *Gaudium et spes* says: "The truth is that only in the mystery of the incarnate Word does the mystery of man take on light. For Adam, the first man, was a figure of Him who was to come, namely, Christ the Lord" (GS 22). These words echo Paul's parallel between sin and grace, Adam and Christ, in his Epistle to the Romans. Just as Adam was the real father of all men in sin, so Christ is even more the new Adam who effectively and universally transforms all humanity into a new creation. So one cannot say that redemption is a merely juridical reality whereas sinfulness was a de facto reality.

Quite logically, then, the Council goes on to say: "Christ, the final

Adam, by the revelation of the mystery of the Father and His love, fully
reveals man to man himself and makes his supreme calling clear" (GS
22). Thus he teaches man what *already is* the reality to which he belongs
and in which he and all his activity is inserted. Otherwise it would be
called a possibility for man rather than a mystery. "He who is 'the image
of the invisible God' is himself the perfect man. To the sons of Adam he
restores (the word is very clear) the divine likeness which had been dis-
figured from the first sin onward" (GS 22). It is not an offer made to
those who request it. Christ actually did restore the divine likeness to all
men, that is, to the descendants of Adam.

Yet over against these clear and logical statements we find another
series of statements which appear to have no relation to them, or which
at the very least are ambiguous in this respect. In section 3 we find this
statement: "This sacred Synod proclaims the highest destiny of man and
champions the godlike seed which has been sown in him. It offers to
mankind the honest assistance of the Church in fostering that brotherhood of all men which corresponds to this destiny of theirs" (GS 3).
Considering the fact that the vocation in question is in fact "one and
divine" (GS 22), it would seem that the Church offers her collaboration
because this fraternal brotherhood, insofar as it is the supernatural vocation of all men, is also the primordial function of the Church. But will
not collaboration in the work of universal brotherhood be merely a *side
effect* of the Church's mission, which is carried out on a different plane?

Section 40 says that "the Church has a saving and an eschatological
purpose" (GS 40). To be sure, these words do not in themselves rule out
the first hypothesis (see CLARIFICATION III in this chapter). But was it not
in the mind of the writers to say that world history does not have the
same finality that the central function of the Church has? Section 40
would appear to see universal brotherhood as a merely human thing to
which the Church lends her support despite that fact: "Pursuing the
saving purpose which is proper to her, the Church not only communicates divine life to men, but in some way casts the reflected light of that
life over the entire earth" (GS 40). As the reader can see, the ambiguity
on this point was not erased from the overall makeup of *Gaudium et spes.*

In section 11 we find this fundamental affirmation: "Faith throws a
new light on everything, manifests God's design for man's total vocation,
and thus directs the mind to solutions which are fully human" (GS 11).
The singular is used for man's total vocation because, as we have seen,
it is one and supernatural whether man knows it or not. Thus everything that man is doing, his whole effort at fashioning history, must be
connected directly, not merely tangentially, with Christ's work of redemption and reconciliation. The outcome of history and that of salvation cannot be divergent. Nor can they even be merely parallel because
one and only one reality is at work: man's total vocation. That is why
faith "directs the mind to solutions which are fully human." And the
Council proposes "to assess in this light those values which are most
highly prized today, and to relate them to their divine source" (GS 11).

With the last phrase we are confronted again with ambiguity. The
text has noted that there is only one human vocation and one history.
Have they ceased to be related to this source at some point? Is that pos-

sible in a humanity where redemption is an effective reality in all men? Obviously enough there are false values and evil actions in history—both inside and outside the Church. But have human values lost their real connection with redemption, or only their *explicit, mental* connection? If it is only the latter, then logically the aim of the Council should be simply to relate them more or consciously to it.

Oddly enough the Council, after using the terminology just discussed, moves off in the other direction again. It seems to indicate a real connection between human values and their source. And defects in this connection apparently can be purified and healed with the help of the Church, which explicitly relates the two, thanks to revelation: "Insofar as they stem from endowments conferred by God on man, these values are exceedingly good. Yet they are often wrenched from their rightful function by the taint in man's heart, and hence stand in need of purification" (GS 11). "Purification" does not suggest a rupture or the need to start from scratch in relating these values to their source. Even the attitudes of Christians require constant purification (LG 8), but the Council does not suggest that their values are not *related* to their divine source.

The same ambiguity shows up in section 36, when it speaks of the "autonomy of earthly affairs." And it expands in section 39, which describes our eschatological hope: "For after we have obeyed the Lord, and in His Spirit nurtured on earth the values of human dignity, brotherhood, and freedom, and indeed all the good fruits of our nature and enterprise, we will find them again, but freed of stain, burnished, and transfigured. This will be so when Christ hands over to the Father a kingdom eternal and universal . . . *On this earth that kingdom is already present in mystery.* When the Lord returns, it will be brought into full flower" (GS 39).

If this is true, then logically "the expectation of a new earth must not weaken but rather stimulate our concern for cultivating this one. For here grows the body of a new human family . . ." (GS 39). But this statement makes it difficult to explain one which follows almost immediately: "Earthly progress must be carefully distinguished from the growth of Christ's kingdom" (GS 39). Doesn't the Council define Christ's kingdom as one of justice, love, and peace? Could it be that the justice, love, and peace sought by non-Christians are merely natural? If not, then what else does man's effort in history seek but the same values of human brotherhood, dignity, and freedom that we shall find on the new earth? What, then, is the goal of human progress and why must we *carefully* distinguish earthly progress from the growth of Christ's kingdom which is already present in mystery? Is it that this presence is given solely in the visible Church?

2. What we have already said shows clearly and not surprisingly two tendencies at work in Vatican II. Despite the fact that *Gaudium et spes* undoubtedly represents the high point of Vatican II, or perhaps precisely because it does so, it is marked by two tendencies that intermingle and interrupt each other in the text. One tendency sees the world and its history as being disconnected in itself from redemption, which operates supernaturally within the Church and unites human values to their divine source through religion. The other tendency sees only one vocation,

one history, and one end result, even though the unity of the religious
and the nonreligious in Christ constitutes a datum of faith (*cf.* n. 40);
even though it does not provide readymade solutions to the problems of
history; and even though we do not know to what extent God wills to
transmit it effectively, in an explicit manner, to the concrete human
beings with whom we are engaged in dialogue. The texts of the Council
which are the most clear theologically accord with the second line of
thought, but the recurrence of other expressions that do not accord with
it shows us that a problem persists here.

Two very different pastoral approaches spring from these two different tendencies evident throughout *Gaudium et spes*. Today these two
pastoral approaches are in conflict with each other throughout the ecclesial environment of Latin America. And both to some extent can
justifiably claim to be "postconciliar."

Neither tendency denies the fundamental importance of dialogue
between the Church and the world. Neither tendency refuses to seek out
and interpret the "signs of the times" in the happenings of history. But
the conciliar passages take on a very different theoretical and practical
significance, depending on which line of thought is followed.

Let us consider the human values which motivate human history.
No one doubts that they form the material of church-world dialogue.
And section 22 of *Gaudium et spes* is very clear with respect to them and
the value which sums them up: "Since Christ died for all men, and since
the ultimate vocation of man is in fact one, and divine, we ought also
to believe that the Holy Spirit in a manner known only to God offers
to every man the possibility of being associated with this paschal mystery" (GS 22). Not only is the vocation of all men one, but the supernatural reality unites us to all to the degree we have good will: i.e., to
the degree that we dedicate ourselves to fashioning a history in which
justice and love reigns. And what holds true for Christians also holds
true "for all men of good will in whose hearts grace works in an unseen
way" (GS 22).

But if this is the case, why is the work of grace in nonbelievers performed "in a manner known only to God," and "in an unseen way"?
The first obvious answer we get is that nonbelievers, unlike believers,
receive grace without the intervention of sensible (sacramental) signs
which manifest grace even as they confer it. In an even broader figurative sense, the "invisibility" appears to allude to the absence of an *explicit*
faith which "illuminates for believers" that which takes place within and
among man.

But does not the Council mean to say that even we Christians do not
know how grace operates in our contemporaries who do not believe or
are not baptized? Here there is clearly an element of obscurity. It does
not relate so much to the invisibility of grace, which can be interpreted
in terms of the perception of the non-Christian. It relates to the phrase
which says that the operation of grace in men of good will occurs "in a
manner known to God," which would seem to exclude the Christian as
well. The vernacular translation unjustifiably erases this ambiguity by
adding an adverb and changing the above phrase to "in a manner known
only to God." It is certain that the official text of the Council does not

show any traces of this "only." But neither can one deny that the statement that *God* knows how grace operates would seem to exclude others from this knowledge, unless one understands it to mean that this same God imparted his knowledge through his revelation.

And in fact there are passages which indicate this. For example: "He Himself revealed to us that 'God is love.' At the same time He taught us that the new command of love was the basic law of human perfection and hence of the world's transformation" (GS 38).

In this context that which *only* God knows is to what extent—in both non-Christians and Christians—the external effort does or does not correspond to the internal subjective intention of loving. If we maintain the other hypothesis on the other hand, we are obliged to maintain that even though the Christian may know that love is the basic law of the world's transformation, he would not know what is love in the concrete for non-Christians.

Depending on which interpretation one chooses, one will conceive the pastoral task of church-world dialogue in a very different way.

In the one case the interpretation of the signs of the times will be made by a Christian who tries to find out whither the objective demands of love are carrying the world today, and who joins with other human beings, not to bring them the truth but to seek it out (GS 16) in every concrete problem where love between human beings is involved. This Christian will confidently expect this dialogue to succeed when God so wills it, and to the extent that these problems are resolved in the light of the gospel; for he knows that the latter was proclaimed to direct men's minds "to solutions which are fully human" (GS 11).[22]

In the other case, equally grounded in the texts of the Council, we get a pastoral approach of a different sort. It certainly respects the invisible pathways of grace, being sincerely convinced of its validity and its unsuspected amplitude and being sure that in so doing this approach is also respecting a mystery known to God. But the Christian, however, knows the pathway of grace insofar as it is lit up by objective markers: i.e., by faith and the sacraments. For him the signs of the times are the events which are capable of bringing men to formulate direct questions on the value of faith and the Christian signs. They are the point of departure from which the Church can begin its own proper work and its distinctive service to humanity.[23] Thus we get a pastoral approach which is surely supported by conciliar texts and hence free of fanaticism, but which continues to be a pastoral approach of conquest under other terms and procedures. What other formula fits, once one admits that we do not know the pathways of grace outside the boundaries of the Church? What better service could we perform than to usher people into a realm where we know we can provide them with certain aid? So one tries to present to other men the appealing and sincere face of the Church which invites them to rapprochement and religious questioning.

In logical terms, we may indeed appear to be offering service to the world when we claim that the revealed Word is at the service of the problems faced in history by Christians and non-Christians at any given moment. But in this view it is a service that goes too far and that has lost its supernatural orientation. Hence it is suggested that this type of service is a version of "naturalism"; but the accusation is not spelled out in clear terms because it would clash with the clear statements of *Gaudium et spes*.

Countless differences in the orientation of the Church's pastoral work spring from this initial divergence in outlook and interpretation. The precise importance of the laity, what is expected of it, and its relationship to hierarchy and parish depend upon it. So does the distribution of ecclesiastical personnel in general pastoral work and specialized activities, and the very justification of the territorial parish. So does the involvement of the Church with money and the powers that be in order to hold the Christian masses in line within her, even though this may entail the danger of not being able to serve the cause of community dialogue on the historical problems facing it. Here too we find the dilemma of catechesis when it takes man in the individual and social situation in which he lives. Is he to rest content in this situation? Or must he change this situation, not just or mainly so that he will eventually ask explicitly about the Church, but because the Good News should help the human race to grow to maturity in its progress through history?

3. At this point one may well be inclined to ask: What does Vatican II say after all? We have already pointed out that the Council did not propose to replace but to reactivate the life of the Church; that the Christian community, moving forward under the guidance of the Holy Spirit, will acquire an ever clearer and more precise notion of what the Council Fathers meant to say.

Nonetheless, and in connection with what precedes, there does exist in theology, and especially in exegesis, a principle that can and should be applied here. We know that the codices in which Scripture (as well as countless other documents) came down to us were copied by hand. Thus they present slightly differing versions. This is not surprising when we realize that the ancient copyists suffered the same distractions that modern linotype operators do. In copying something, it is very easy for someone to make the text say what he has in his own mind.

The principle mentioned above comes in here. Suppose we are faced with two texts of a given work that do not say quite the same thing. The principle says that, all other things being equal, one should prefer the more difficult reading, the *lectio difficilior*. In other words, one should prefer the reading that is less likely to be due to the distraction of the copyist, for the distracted person tends to simplify things and to repeat what is known and taken for granted.

Now we can apply this principle to Vatican II. In *transmitting* the Christian message, the Council could certainly have allowed certain things, hallowed by custom, to slip by without paying attention to them. But when we are clearly and obviously faced with a statement that rectifies what the Church had been saying and thinking habitually in recent times, then we can be sure that deep reflection and a clear intent is at work. If the reader is patient enough to go back and read the conciliar passages cited here, in the light of this classic and well-established principle of internal literary criticism, the future-oriented sense of Vatican II on the matter of our pastoral approach will surely stand out as quite clear and profoundly prophetic.[24]

NOTES

1. This discussion focuses primarily on Chapters 7 and 8 of the book: *The Diary of a Country Priest* (New York: Macmillan Paperbacks Edition, 1962).

2. Carlos Martínez Moreno, *Con las primeras luces* (Barcelona: Seix Barral, 1966).

3. We use the word "differs" here, but in reality it is ambiguous. We wish to remind the reader about the meaning of a qualitative difference that does not entail numerical otherness. The new does not become an additional number alongside the old.

4. See Volume I, Chapter I, CLARIFICATION III.

5. Leopoldo Malevez, "La vision chrétienne de l'histoire," *Nouvelle Revue Théologique* (March 1949), p. 268.

6. As readers of this series know, the terms "eschatology" and "eschatological" come from the Greek term *eschaton* which means "last thing." It refers to that which will come to pass at the end of time and history. Without any doubt the opposing of the Incarnation to this sense of *eschaton*, however unjustifiably, comes from the fact that God did not merely touch our history tangentially but deeply immersed himself in what was occurring in it on the "horizontal" plane. Jesus wept over the death of his friend Lazarus and over the impending destruction of Jerusalem. One could also point out that for some time the primitive Church did not know whether to wait idly for the second coming of the Lord or to go out and face the ambiguous world of civilized value (*cf.* 2 Thess.).

7. Jean Daniélou, *Essai sur le mystère de l'histoire*, p. 14. Eng. trans., *The Lord of History: Reflections on the Inner Meaning of History* (London: Longmans; and Chicago: Regnery, 1958).

8. *Ibid.*, p. 23.

9. *Ibid.*, p. 35.

10. *Supp. Dict. Bib.*, col. 1356 (article signed by same J. Daniélou).

11. Daniélou, *Essai . . .* , p. 103.

12. Dubarle, *Optimisme devant ce monde*, pp. 103–04. The author does not share this opinion. He puts these words in the mouth of someone whom he calls a "pessimist." By virtue of this pessimism, such a person belongs to the "eschatologists" here, even though we know for a fact that pessimism and eschatology in themselves have nothing to do with each other. See Volume I of this series, Chapter I.

13. We have no intention of fashioning a theology of history, however brief, in these pages here. Our question is whether we can speak of such a theology at all in terms of what we have seen in this volume, and under what conditions. We shall return to this theme in much greater detail in Volume V of this series: *Evolution and Guilt*.

14. Piet Schoonenberg, *De macht der zonde*, Eng. trans., *Man and Sin: A Theological View* (Notre Dame: University of Notre Dame Press, 1965), p. 23.

15. See Volume I, Chapter V.

16. As we already noted, this third chapter links the theme of grace with the ecclesial outlook studied in Volume I of this series. The desire to make each volume a work that can be read independently forces us to reiterate briefly some of the points already made in the first volume. This is particularly true of this CLARIFICATION. See Volume I, Chapter III, main article and CLARIFICATION III.

17. We do not at all mean to suggest here that human development programs should remain in the hands of the Church—either in the hands of the

hierarchy or some band of laymen. This should be clear from what follows. On this question one can also see Volume I, Chapter V, CLARIFICATION IV.

18. *Cf.* Roberto Viola, "Hacia una pastoral especializada," *Perspectivas de Diálogo*, No. 24 (June 1968), pp. 95–98.

19. *Cf.* Chapter II, CLARIFICATION I.

20. M. D. Chenu, "A vous de jouer," in *Lettre* (January 1966), pp. 1–2.

21. We shall discuss this theme in much greater detail in Volume V of this series: *Evolution and Guilt.*

22. "Today, I believe, the main work of the manifest Church, certainly in terms of sheer numbers, is probably to make it possible for men and women to be met by Christ *where they are* . . . If so, then it must, for the greater part of its work, be prepared to *respect* rather than remove (which is its instinctive urge) the incognitos under which the parable of the Sheep and the Goats alone shows it possible for the Christ to meet and to judge the mass of men" J. A. T. Robinson, *The New Reformation?* (Philadelphia: Westminster Press, 1965, pp. 49–50).

23. To cite on example: According to a document of the Secretariat for Non-Believers, promulgated October 1, 1968, dialogue with nonbelievers is designed "to investigate jointly the truth in different realms, or to collaborate in solving the great problems confronting humanity today." But it is not to be confused with "apostolic" dialogue, through which "the Church carries out her primary mission of proclaiming the gospel."

24. A happy confirmation, not only of these last statements but also of Chenu's words on the praxis of the Church moving toward greater dogmatic precision, is the documentation issued by the Latin American bishops at Medellín. In their statement, and in the conclusions of the chief commissions, many of the themes of *Gaudium et spes* are reconsidered with abundant citations. The fact is that both the contents of the documents and the citations always follow one, univocal line: i.e., the one which we have described as the *lectio difficilior* of Vatican II.

CHAPTER FOUR

Depth: Love, the Definitive Power

Let us take one more step demanded by logic. We have already pointed out that between the *human condition* (the theme of Chapter I and *eternal life* (the theme of Chapter II) there operates a dynamic force: the great wind which blows and carries us with it. And in saying "carries *us*" we have already introduced into the pronoun the truly universal breadth of this dynamism (the theme of Chapter III). "Us" means humanity as a whole, all human beings. It does not mean a privileged few or some chosen elite, because the Spirit blows everywhere.

But is it certain that we are in movement? Is our life truly a gradual transition, however full of obstacles and backsliding, from our initial human condition to the new earth? Do we leave our point of departure or are we still in it?

In other words, difficult as it is to admit, we do not have the impression that our initial situation changes radically over the years. It does not seem that we move from egotism, facile mechanicalism, and inner bureaucracy toward youthful openness and an inner disposability to love, liberty, and personalism.

What, if anything, really does change because of grace? To what *depth* of our being does the transformation penetrate?

Section I

As in the preceding chapters, the first level of reflection here is provided by elements which inspired and marked the thinking of the Church as far back as the New Testament.

Let us recall the text of Paul in which he describes what we call the point of departure for the action of grace: "We know that the law is spiritual [i.e., the work of grace], but I am not. I am unspiritual [i.e., subject to the human condition], the purchased slave of sin. I do not even acknowledge my own actions as mine, for what I do is not what I want to do but what I detest . . . For I know that nothing good lodges in me—in my unspiritual nature, I mean—for though the will to do good is there, the deed is not . . . In my inmost self I delight in the law of God, but I perceive that there is in my bodily members a different law [i.e., that of the outer man], fighting against the law that my reason approves and making me a prisoner under the law that is in my members, the law of sin. Miserable creature that I am . . ." (Rom. 7:14–24).

Now about whom exactly is Paul saying this? To what span or period of his life is he referring? Does it apply to the pagan period? Or is Paul the Christian, too, subject to this conditioning? It is evident that the description, as far as we take it, alludes explicitly to a *before:* i.e., to a prior situation for which there is a corresponding and different *now.* The now is described a bit later: "There is no condemnation for those who are united with Christ Jesus, because in Christ Jesus the life-giving law of the Spirit has set you free from the law of sin and death [i.e., the human condition]" (Rom. 8:1–2).

What, then, is the work, the gift, the grace of Christ? It is "that the commandment of the law may find fulfillment in us, whose conduct, no longer under the control of our lower nature [i.e., the human condition], is directed by the Spirit [i.e., grace]" (Rom. 8:4). This is so because he has given strength and power to our inner being (*cf.* Eph. 3:16), which formerly willed to do good but was incapable of doing it.

Thus Paul sees God's gift as a transformation, as a *before-after* situation. And even though it is not identified with the transition from paganism to Christianity, it does indeed designate two different ways of behaving with their corresponding relationships to eternal life.

Various passages in the Gospel, more simple in form, converge toward the same outlook. To cite two examples: "Unless you show yourselves far better men than the Pharisees and the doctors of the law, you can never enter the kingdom of Heaven" (Matt. 5:20); "If you wish to enter into life, keep the commandments" (Matt. 19:17). Thus fulfillment of God's commands is both possible and necessary. And these commandments perdure even though the whole law and its meaning is summed up in the one commandment of love (*cf.* Rom. 13:8–10; 1 Cor. 6:9–10).

Hence love, too, is possible and necessary. "My children, in writing thus to you my purpose is that you should not commit sin" (1 John 2:1). "The man who does not love is still in the realm of death, for everyone who hates his brother is a murderer, and no murderer, as you know, has eternal life dwelling in him" (1 John 3:15).

Finally, we cannot overlook Christ's picture of the Last Judgment. There eternal life is given or denied, depending on whether one has fulfilled Christ's command to love his neighbor. And this love is extended to cover even his most material needs.

Section II

Moving on to a second level of analysis, however, we must recognize that all this, and especially the description of the Last Judgment, may well have fostered an oversimplified notion of man's potentialities for loving. Not surprisingly people, basing their ideas exclusively on such biblical passages, thought that Paul's description of divided man belonged to a past already superceded. They imagined that man, now endowed with Christ's grace, stood poised on the fence as it were—equally capable of giving or refusing food to the hungry, etc. In other words, man had ceased to be a being who did not understand what he was doing. He had been transformed into a being who did good or evil as he chose.

Once Christianity became a religion of the masses, this oversimplification took firm root in a legalistic morality. Only a few people, such as Saint Augustine in his fight against Pelagianism, continued to point out that man's liberty remains a perduring problem.

But it was due to the religious experience of Luther that this problem was converted into one of the most profound points of Christian reflection. To the detriment of unity perhaps. Or perhaps so that unity would be based on a deeper truth.

The experience of Luther is the experience of sin which is inherent in Christian existence. It is not that Luther was an extraordinary sinner. Rather, he possessed a keener and deeper awareness of what lies buried in the depths of every so-called "good" action. He knew, as any reflective person might have, how terribly tenacious our egotism is, how it creeps into our most "virtuous" actions in disguised form.

For Luther, in other words, Paul's description of a man divided between what he wills to do and what he does continues to be the description of the Christian. Only a superficial view could divide man's deeds into "good" and "bad."

Luther's experience did not lead him, at least right off, to deny the biblical message of the texts we just cited. Instead it led him to discover other equally biblical elements whose importance had been overlooked by the oversimplified outlook mentioned above.

The reading and interpretation of Paul's Epistle to the Romans was a decisive factor in the religious itinerary of the Reformation.[1] And this epistle does indeed contain passages which do not tie in with the picture of man carrying out good or evil acts of his own free will.

"For (again from Scripture) 'no human being can be justified [i.e., accepted as just or declared so] in the sight of God' for having kept the law; law brings only the consciousness of sin. But now . . . God's justice has been brought to light . . . It is God's way of righting wrong, effective through faith in Christ for all who have such faith . . . For all alike have sinned . . . and all are justified by God's free grace . . . What room then is left for human pride? It is excluded. And on what principle? The keeping of the law would not exclude it, but faith does. For our argument is that a man is justified by faith quite apart from success in keeping the law" (Rom. 3:20–28).

And this is not an occasional teaching (see, for example, Phil. 3:9; Eph. 2:9–10). A major text of the Epistle to the Galatians says the same thing in almost identical words: "It is evident that no one is ever justified before God in terms of law; because we read, 'he shall gain life who is justified through faith.' Now law is not at all a matter of having faith: we read, 'he who does this shall gain life by what he does' " (Gal. 3:11–12). "But Scripture has declared the whole world to be prisoners in subjection to sin, so that faith in Jesus Christ may be the ground on which the promised blessing is given, and given to those who have such faith" (Gal. 3:22). To this picture we must add several passages in the Gospel. One, for example, is the parable in which Christ tells us how it is impossible to root out the chaff from the wheat [i.e., to distinguish the good from the bad in human actions] before the harvest.

So we come to the point where Christian experience, enmeshed in a full-fledged theological controversy, tried to formulate a consistent line of thought that kept both aspects in mind and unified them.

These formulations arose during the disputes of the Reformation, and they bear its stamp. We shall try to set forth the most classical of these formulas that embodied the thought of the Reformation period, reminding the reader that our concise synthesis here does not exhaust by any means the rich connotations suggested by their creators.

1. We are justified by *Christ's righteousness alone*. In effect there is really only one righteousness, only one just man: Christ. In view of what he accomplished, God ceases to see our sins and pardons us.[2]

2. As far as man is concerned, his being was so profoundly corrupted by original sin that he truly sins in everything he does. With respect to the possibility of avoiding sin, then, he possesses not a free will but an *enslaved will*.[3]

3. But God's righteousness demands that man's salvation follow upon

a judgment in which man is declared just. In declaring him so, however, God does not really look at man and his conformity to to the law. He looks at the just Christ and declares man to be just without man ceasing to be what he is. So it comes down to a *forensic justification* in which, akin to that which occurs in a courtroom, the accused is declared innocent but is not converted into an innocent person.[4]

4. Thus the man justified by God is sinner and just man at the same time: *simul peccator et justus.* He is just through the applied righteousness (or justice) of Christ. He is a sinner in terms of his own deeds.[5]

5. Finally, *faith alone,* not works, unites man with the saving, justifying grace of Christ. Faith liberates man from useless, obsessive, impersonal concern about his personal righteousness and thrusts him confidently toward the Father.[6]

The Council of Trent, convened to counter this outlook which it judged to be incompatible with the doctrine of the Church, anathematized it in almost strictly parallel terms. Thus we can synthesize its position too. Again we remind the reader that this summary does not exhaust the rich connotations of more creative Catholic thinking at the Council.

1. "If anyone says that human beings . . . *are formally just by virtue of it* [i.e., Christ's justice or righteousness], let him be anathema" (Denz. 820).

2. "If anyone says that *man's free will was lost and extinguished* after the sin of Adam, or that it is a thing in name only, or a name without substance . . . let him be anathema" (Denz. 815).

3. "If anyone says that men are justified either *solely by the imputation of Christ's justice* or solely by the remission of sins, excluding grace and the charity which is diffused into their hearts by the Holy Spirit and which inheres there within them . . . let him be anathema" (Denz. 821).

4. "If anyone says that *the just man sins in all his good deeds* . . . hence merits eternal punishments, and that *he is not condemned solely because God does not impute these works to him* for condemnation, let him be anathema" (Denz. 835).

5. "If anyone says that the faith which justifies is nothing else but confidence in the divine mercy which pardons sins for Christ's

sake, or that *this confidence is the one and only thing by which we are justified,* let him be anathema" (Denz. 822).

We think it is useless, anachronistic, and somewhat counterproductive to try, as one brand of well-intentioned ecumenism does, to minimize these differences by saying that they are due to a colossal misunderstanding, that in fact the differing formulas really were trying to say the same thing. We feel it is worth admitting that both sides, to their credit, were perfectly aware that there was a profound problem here. If the cultural and religious resources of that epoch permitted them only to pose the problem without resolving it, then our task is certainly not to bury it. Our task is to bring to it the new possibilities which stem from the maturing of history. That is what we will try to do in the very next section.

Section III

So we come to the third level of our analysis. Here we shall consider the new elements that enter the picture today when we consider this whole question.

It seems to us that these new elements can be summed up in terms of three points, and that they are truly capable of bringing us to a deeper and more authentically ecumenical formulation of the problem. Once again let us recall our original question: Does grace really transform us?

The first datum to be affirmed here is the impossibility of giving a purely experiential response to the question. In other words, there is no possibility of deciding whether grace has transformed our existence or not by merely comparing our experiences as human beings.

As we pointed out early in this volume, and as our discussion of the unlimited breadth of grace in the last chapter made even more clear, it is impossible for us to decide this question by comparing some *before* and *after* in time, or *one* human being with *another* within the human race. Grace accompanies us all and always. If God's gift does transform us, this transformation is continual and universal.

Paul's *before* and *after* are not chronological but theological. They do not frame the transformation in time, but in relation to him who is its cause.

Now if we realize that the change effected by grace has dimensions that go far beyond the bounds of time or visible membership in Christ, we will realize at the same time that it is faith, supported by our personal experience of course, which assures us that we really can love and that we owe this possibility to grace.

John says: "We for our part have crossed over from death to life;

this we know, because we love our brothers" (1 John 3:14). Hence revelation calls our attention to the fact that God's decisive judgment on us will turn upon this love which is possible and obligatory for us.

As we shall see further on, this does not mean that the dividedness of which Paul speaks in Romans is a past or superceded reality. It is not that in looking at what we have done, we today, in contrast to other men or yesterday, recognize in it what we really willed to be and do interiorly.

A note of strangeness in our deeds and a lack of correspondence with our inmost decision continue to be radical characteristics of human existence, and hence of Christian existence. Christ did not erase them in his followers, or even in his saints. And he did not because they constitute the *concrete human condition.* And condition here means two things. It is both a conditioning and the necessary component for man to be man: i.e., for man to be free.

But it does not mean that the disparity between inner decision and outer deed is absolute, or that the two realities have no relationship save that of falsehood. There would be no liberty there either.

Let us take the familiar problem of the artist as an example. He, too, experiences the condition surrounding his work. Uncomfortably he notes that he cannot see his inner inspiration and ideal in the finished work. He, too, can and must say that he does not understand what he is doing, that he does not know at what moment his instruments got out of his control and went off on a path of their own.

The note of strangeness is felt by both the apprentice and the great artist. Yet man, without ceasing to feel this note, is capable of *art.* Something of his inner inspiration passes over into the finished work. And this something is real, inspiring, imperishable, and unmistakable.

Now someone might argue that the artist, in his creative capacity, does not have some artistic "original sin" to overcome. But the person who argues in this way forgets something. He forgets that redemption is not merely a juridical possibility offered but a reality operative in humanity. He forgets that its efficacity does not reside precisely in making us such and such, but in seeing to it that our liberty, like artistic inspiration, penetrates and suffuses the imposing wall of opposing forces which seem destined to wreck it. "I kneel in prayer to the Father . . . that out of the treasures of his glory he may grant you strength and power through his Spirit in your inner being . . ." (Eph. 3:16).

Thanks to Christ, then, and despite the dividedness of the human condition with all its weighty determinisms and snares which weight down our projects to a great extent, a little portion of love passes into our lives.

This is what the Catholic Church defended against Luther, or against those who would oversimplify the picture. But that should not lead us to fall into the opposite oversimplification with regard to man's situation after Christ, baptism, or the Church. We must not picture human liberty on some fantastically creative plane where love and egotism are placed before his free will for him to decide which shall guide his existence.

It is precisely here that we are offered *a second datum* by psychology, phenomenology, and the evolutionary conception of man. Human acts, insofar as liberty is concerned, are more complex than was pictured by the classical conception of philosophy and theology. The latter conception was a stationary, fixist one. It pictured man's free will standing firmly between a choice of good or evil and then deciding which would be carried out in reality. But if we, operating from an overall Christian conception,[7] inquire into modern depth psychology, it will show us a different picture. It will show us man barely emerging from the obscure world of the instincts. Under a thousand disguises they are unconsciously reintroduced into his motivations; they lie hidden in what would seem to be at first glance a freely chosen deliberation of our conscious will.[8]

If we inquire into phenomenology, it offers us a convergent picture. The activity of a human being is a constant battle with bad faith, which tries to pass off as a free decision our all too easy surrender to the law of minimum effort and its attendant reification.[9]

The evolutionary conception of man offers us a similar orientation. With the very birth of his liberty, man is situated on a difficult and critical borderline. He can shoulder the evolutionary process consciously, or he can allow his new reality to be fettered by the same blind forces that operate on everything else. In this conception liberty does not show up as a facility given fully and once and for all. It shows up as the possibility of shouldering, little by little and with repeated reverses, the control over an evolutionary process whose determinisms continue to remain in force.[10]

To sum up: the whole outlook of science and philosophy, which does not lean toward mechanism or determinism, has converged surprisingly over the last century toward Paul's description of a liberty opening out slowly and painfully through its own instruments of operation.

What consequence does all this have with respect to the use of human liberty? It has a variety of consequences that are most important.

1. Firstly, not all our actions of each day or our whole life proceed from our liberty, however conscious they may be. Many of them actually obey the law of minimum effort.

2. In addition, within the overall structure of *each act* one of the components is always egotism. It directs the finality of the act back to-

ward ourselves, using for its own convenience the law of minimum effort that governs every performance.

3. In other words, egotism is a component of all our actions. It takes the determinisms inherent in the carrying out of a human project and makes them serve our own convenience. Thus it causes man to lose his control over them continually, at least to some extent. It is not possible for us to take total control over the mechanisms we utilize in our activities. They are never totally ours.

4. Thus our liberty moves between these two poles or limit-concepts. On the one hand we are driven toward becoming simply one more *thing* by an egotism carried to its ultimate conclusion; the law of minimum effort replaces the *person* completely. On the other hand we are driven to become entirely creative by the absolutely free and personal utilization of all these determinisms; in love they will serve as the highest expression of our being.

5. In this context liberty, person, and love are identical even as they are in Paul's context. The most decisive moments of our existence cease to be given actions, which at bottom are only consequences—often undeliberated. The decisive thing is to take advantage of the (unstable) situations of psychic equilibrium to enlarge and deepen our capacity for feeling and living the lives of others as neighbors. Herein lies the one and only possibility, ever limited, of defending our liberty, person, and love from the inevitable doses of egotism that the law of minimum effort will inject into our every concrete act. We must continually seek to fashion and recover the nearness of others as neighbors.

Here we can also reflect on the fact that it is only in such a context that the parable of the wheat and the chaff takes on its full meaning. In fact it does not refer so much to the impossibility, on God's part, of separating good people and bad people during their lives, for such an impossibility could never be absolute. Instead it refers to the impossibility of separating *good and evil,* virtue and vice, love and egotism. To separate these two elements in the constructive efforts of man would be equivalent to putting an end to the constructive effort itself in the whole of human existence—at least in terms of man's present condition.[11]

This brings us to a third and equally important datum relating to the correct formulation of our question: What transformation does grace effect in our existence? This third datum is *a maturation in our idea of God's judgment.*

The classic conception of man's liberty, which saw it poised equally between good and evil, also pictured it moving successively in one direction or the other. The evildoing of today wiped out the good deeds of yesterday, and vice-versa. From this there came the notion that the decisive thing had to be one's *final act*. In the last analysis it was God who decided the fated destiny of each individual—not so much by predetermining it in advance but rather by marking him for death at a given moment, after he had performed a good act or a bad act.[12]

The controversy at the time of the Reformation presupposed the same fixist conception of liberty. It tried to say whether the balance between good and evil was modified fundamentally by grace during life. Left in the shadows is one of the most important data of the Christian message: the *essential disproportion* between the solidity and efficacy of love and that of egotism. Hence also left in the shadows is the secret of man emerging from evolution and personally shouldering the course of his own personal destiny and that of humanity.

Logically enough, the import of the human adventure was missed: "If I am to believe my parish priest and you people, this is the situation. The God which Saint Paul preached twenty centuries ago along the Mediterranean coast created human beings to place them in the most dangerous world a human mind could imagine. Man lives in a dark labyrinth, encountering forbidden temptations, sneaking through a trapdoor into eternal bliss unless he slips through the other trapdoor into an eternity of sufferings." [13]

The datum mentioned above is diametrically opposed to this outlook. The Epistle of James, for example, ends on this note: "Any man who brings a sinner back from his crooked ways will be rescuing his soul from death and cancelling innumerable sins" (James 5:20).

Whence springs this manifest disproportion? Does it have to do with a special promise made by God to the person who exercises this particular type of love? Undoubtedly it does not. Here we are dealing with a particular application of a principle which the apostolic Church knows and enunciates in a much more general form. Citing a verse of Proverbs (10:12), which takes on fresh meaning after Christian revelation, it tells us: "Above all, keep your love for one another at full strength, because love cancels innumerable sins" (1 Pet. 4:8).

What does that mean? Once again, whence the disproportion which here assumes its full dimensions? Why does love, any act of love, surpass the power of innumerable sins?

There is something here that cannot be translated into juridical or quantitative terms, something which points to another plane than the one we habitually use for such comparisons. Our way of thinking about this matter is juridical. Often it is aggravated by an infantile and pessimistic outlook which feels that no love can prevail when sin has taken possession of our soul. And any sin renders prior love useless! This is the outlook, despite the central but oft-forgotten statement of Paul:

"Where sin was thus multiplied [i.e, in all], grace immeasurably exceeded it" (Rom. 5:20).

In reality all these biblical citations are indicating what the three data cited earlier also indicated: The superabundance and victory of grace does not consist in improving the numerical ratio between acts of love and acts of egotism. Even though both love and egotism come under our responsibility, they are not on the same plane. Nor do they have the same ontological efficacy, so to speak. They are not situated vis-à-vis the absolute, the definitive, in the same way.

Remember that man emerges from nonliberty. Everything achieved by love is inscribed in the positive history of humanity. Everything effected by egotism is a return to the blind force of the prehuman. Like the shape of this world (*cf.* 1 Cor. 7:31; 1 John 2:17), the latter passes away without dragging along with it what love has constructed.

Paul presents this difference in effectiveness clearly when he says this about divided man: "For I know that nothing good lodges in me—in my unspiritual nature [i.e., my flesh], I mean—for though the will to do good is there, the deed is not . . . And if what I do is against my will, clearly it is no longer I who am the agent, but sin that has its lodging in me" (Rom. 7:18–20). That is the reason why we must give greater depth to the image of the last judgment in Matthew 25:31—preserving, of course, its essential point that the judgment will turn on the concrete love men have shown toward each other.

God's outlook on this being who is emerging from his determinisms with the divine potentiality for love takes into account the essential disparity between this love and that egotism. A more infantile outlook necessarily equates the two as weights on opposite ends of a balance scale.

Paul tells us that what is going on is a work of construction in which love and egotism are deeply intermingled. The solidity of the construct will depend upon the dosage of love and egotism it contains. "Or again, you are God's building . . . Let each take care how he builds . . . If anyone builds on that foundation with gold, silver, and fine stone, or with wood, hay, and straw, the work that each man does will at last be brought to light; the day of judgment will expose it. For that day dawns in fire, and the fire will test the worth of each man's work. If a man's building stands, he will be rewarded [i.e., with it]; if it burns, he will have to bear the loss; and yet he will escape with his life, as one might from a fire" (1 Cor. 3:10–15).

Christian maturity can understand this language. And hence it can appreciate that this inner transformation of our being by grace is precisely the wondrous center of rightful Christian hope.

"Then, with death overcome . . . what was sown in weakness and corruption will be clothed with incorruptibility. While charity and its fruits endure, all that creation which God made on man's account will be unchained from the bondage of vanity . . . For after we have . . . nurtured on earth the values of human dignity, brotherhood and freedom, and indeed all the good fruits of our nature and enterprise, we will find them again, but freed of stain, burnished and transfigured" (GS 39).

Perhaps the three data already mentioned, and the contribution they offer to the earlier formulation of the problem, will permit us to glimpse a fuller, more comprehensive and more ecumenical solution to the question that divided the Church four centuries ago. Perhaps, instead of leading us to denigrate what was defended by each side then, it will help us to appreciate better the truth that each side perceived and defended.

NOTES TO CHAPTER FOUR

1. Stanislas Lyonnet describes a present-day ecumenical "happening" that had to do with this same epistle. It was the publication of a French translation of the Epistle to the Romans, made and commented on by Protestant and Catholic exegetes. The original plan was that the notes would indicate points of divergence between the Protestant and Catholic exegetes. It was seemingly a wise provision on such a basic document surrounding the original division between Protestants and Catholics. In fact, however, it was practically never necessary to have recourse to such notes. A Spanish translation of Lyonnet's account is available: Stanislas Lyonnet, "Un acontecimiento ecuménico," in *Perspectivas de Diálogo*, 15:129–30.

2. Lest one might think these formulas belong only to some past stage, we will cite a few passages from the work of Henri Bouillard on the thought of Karl Barth: *Karl Barth: Parole de Dieu et existence humaine* (Paris: Aubier, 1957). The continuity between the formulations of Trent and the Catholic theology of our day is even more evident.

"Everything depends here on God, on the unique action He exercises, through Jesus Christ, in favor of man. Everything depends on what reaches man from above, nothing on what man brings from below. The grace of God is His grace. Hence it is ever new and alien to man, a free act of divine sovereignty. Barth makes the point that the error of Catholic doctrine consists in dividing up the unique and indivisible grace of Jesus Christ. Catholic doctrine does this by saying that it is certainly His grace in the first place, but then going on to say (and to stress) that it is also our grace (*Dog.* IV, 1, 88–89)." Bouillard, p. 28.

3. "The fact that Jesus Christ died for the reconciliation of man corrupted by sin 'establishes in decisive fashion that the corruption was radical and total. This means that the perversion of sin occurs in the depth and core of human existence, in the heart of man, and that the *state* of sinful perverseness which results is extended to his total way of being, with none of his traits excepted' (*Dog.* IV, 1, 548) . . . Within this situation man, by virtue of the unity of his being and action, goes from sin to sin. This is the corruption in which God encounters him" (Bouillard, *ibid.*, pp. 47–48).

4. "By virtue of the divine sentence, man is rooted up from his past as a sinner and advances towards his future as a just man. The positive verdict, his justification, consists of this passage, of this history in which he is at once sinner and just man in an irreversible succession (*Dog.* IV, 1, 634 and 639–40). At every moment of his existence, the human being who is absolved by God never ceases to be the sinner he was as well" (*ibid.*, p. 62).

5. See the preceding note.

6. "This must be kept clearly in mind, continues Barth, when one wants to understand the great negation of Paul and the Reformationists—particularly the *sola fide* ("by faith alone") of Luther. His doctrine of justification by faith opposes faith to all good works. It is summed up in two propositions: (1) no work of man as such can be or contain his justification; but (2) the believer is indeed the man justified by God. The second, positive proposition finds its true sense only when the first, negative proposition has created its field of action and purified the atmosphere in which it must live. One must maintain first and foremost that none of man's works, not even those which divine law prescribes and which must be called 'good,' can be or contain man's justification. Precisely as works which would claim to serve as this justification, they are not good (*Dog.* IV, 1, 693–94)." *Ibid.*, p. 66.

7. Here we do not mean to suggest some specific anthropology that would be Christian. We mean any sort of overall outlook that starts off from the Christian problematic and remains open to its message.

8. See Paul Ricoeur, *De l'interprétation: Essai sur Freud* (Paris: Ed. du Seuil, 1965), I, Chapters 1 and 2.

9. See Jean Paul Sartre, *Being and Nothingness*, Part I, Chap. II.

10. Emile Rideau, Eng. trans., *The Thought of Teilhard de Chardin* (New York: Harper & Row, 1967). Chapters 4 and 5 contain excellent unpublished material.

11. According to theology, even though Christ and his mother shared human *nature*, by virtue of their immunity from sin they were not subject to the human *condition* which results from it in the rest of humanity ("one who, because of his likeness to us, has been tested every way, only without sin," Heb. 4:15).

12. Not more than fifteen years ago, theology was teaching this thesis: "In addition to the special grace by which they *may be able* to persevere [in grace up to the point of death], the just need another grace: i.e., *the great grace of perseverance* by which they really do persevere [in the state of grace] up to the very end." The aim of this thesis was to prove that "the *interior* fact of having responded in one's last free act to God's grace, and the *exterior* act of being overtaken by death when one is in grace, constitute a grace of God." In other words, the principal grace of God was receiving death when one's life was oriented toward good by virtue of one's last act. In line with this outlook, one of the participants in a recent debate over medical revivification expressed his opposition to any cessation of revivification techniques, however useless and prolonged they might be. His reason: "I am a doctor. At the same time I believe in an eternal life which will be different, depending on whether I end my life in the state of mortal sin or not" (*Nouvel Observateur*, October 25, 1967, p. 28).

13. Armand Salacrou, *Théâtre VI*, 4th ed. (Paris: Gallimard, 1954), p. 210.

CLARIFICATIONS

I. SAVED HERE OR IN THE HEREAFTER?

The concept of "salvation" is so bound up with the gospel that the first Christians found it prophetically united with the very name of their founder: "You shall give him the name Jesus (Saviour), for he will save his people from their sins" (Matt. 1:21).

And when Christians, hiding from their persecutors, sought an identifying sign for themselves, they decided on the picture of a fish. Why? Because each of the letters of the Greek word for fish, *ichthus* (i-ch-th-u-s), was the first letter of a word in its own right. And the five words put together expressed the name, capacity, person, and function of the person in whom they believed: Jesus–Christ–Son of God–*Savior*.

In fact Jesus appeared within a cultural universe which in countless ways was searching for salvation in the religious realm, the latter being more or less mixed up with the ideological realm. Rites, cosmogonies, mythical images and ideas concerning God, and ethics were united in a hope. On the popular level this hope was translated into a question that sprang spontaneously to people's lips: "Masters, what must I do to be saved?" (Acts 16:30)

It is a fact, easily verifiable, that from the time of Jesus to that of the apostles the "good news" was preached in this climate of questioning so different from our own. In other words: the gospel was proclaimed and translated in terms of salvation.

Considering what we have seen in the two preceding chapters of this book, one might well ask whether we are faithful to this aspect of revelation? Is Christianity really a religion of salvation, of extraterrestrial salvation, of a salvation situated in the hereafter?

To answer this question we must first establish certain points. Let us consider the term *salvation* and how it was used.

1. The normal human use of the closely related words—*to save, savior, salvation*—already contained certain elements that predestined them, so to speak, for the religious realm.

Firstly, if we ask *from what* is one saved, we will find that any evil which threatens man, be it internal or external, be it sickness, error, sin, or death, can be the matter from which one is saved. They are not the object of salvation, strictly speaking, because man himself is really the object of salvation. Thus to be saved and to escape are somewhat synonymous in this respect. The notion of liberation is there.

Secondly, the picture changes somewhat if we go on to ask *who* does the saving. For while a person may escape or free himself, he is more a passive recipient of salvation. Man's activity seems to be decisive in the case of escape. But salvation seems to imply an unexpected deliverance from some threat of evil. And we find that the languages of antiquity, that of the New Testament for example, almost always used the passive voice: someone *is saved*.

Thirdly, if we ask *how* one is saved, we find that the manual of first aid tells us that the essential thing is to yield to the saving activity trustfully, not to oppose it or expend dangerous efforts. And this is a logical consequence of the fact that it is someone else who must save men. The only active thing I can do, so to speak, is to offer my submission, my trust, my faith. When the verb *save* is used in terms that are not strictly theological, it is interesting to note that the one time it is used actively in the Synoptics, the subject is not a person but faith: "Your faith has cured you" (Matt. 9:22. See especially Luke 7:50; 17:19; 18:42. Also see other passages that relate human salvation to faith: Matt. 14:30; Luke 8:50; Acts 14:9). In other words, when Christ saved the woman who touched his cloak, her *yielding* into his hands in faith was her only collaboration.

2. The "salvation" which the Jews of the Old Testament expected from Yahweh was almost exclusively the same type we have just seen. God saves his people on the one hand, and individuals on the other, to the extent that they trust in him. And this salvation covers all the physical and moral ills that occur within temporal existence—the only existence they recognize.

It is only very close to the end of the Old Testament, when the notion of life after death dawns on their religious horizon (especially in the Book of Wisdom), that the idea of salvation undergoes an important change. And this change will transform the vocabulary used in this respect in the writings of the New Testament.

Wisdom presents man as free before the law of God, which is set there to test him. It is up to the person to carry out the righteousness of this law. If he does so, a judgment will take place after death. The riches which the person renounced on earth, in order to be righteous, will be given to him as a reward in the hereafter. On the other hand, death will destroy all the temporal wealth accumulated unjustly by the wicked man.

Salvation from relative evils is here converted into absolute salvation. No longer is it necessary to add *from what* a person is saved. One is simply saved or not. We are in the realm of the absolute, and the religious vocabulary will register this transformation.

In this conception relating to the hereafter, the importance of man as an active agent also increases. For his liberty, tested by the law, is converted into the cause of his own salvation. God clearly continues to be the savior. But he is so in a more remote sense, in that he insures reward with his law and his judgment while leaving it all up to man. From this we can say that there arose a conception which finds some expression in the New Testament, but which becomes even more explicit in later spiritual treatises: i.e., the notion of "saving your soul" or "sending yourself to hell."

3. Now while the same vocabulary may not have been used, the re-

ligious outlook on salvation just described was the one which surrounded
Jesus. And it would provide the idiom in which the good news of
Christian salvation would be couched.

Some New Testament writings are closer to the mentality and outlook
of the Old Testament. In other words, their ideas seem less original, less
clearly marked by the radical newness of Jesus. If we read these writings,
we can hear an echo of the Book of Wisdom on many points. For Jesus
did not utter his message in some language he made up on the spot, one
that was impervious to the inadequacies and ambiguities of preceding tradition. Only gradually, by reflecting on the deeper recesses of his revelation, did his listeners come to see that his teaching ultimately meant the
dissolution of the old frames of langauge in which his message had first
been expressed.

On the surface at least, the terms referring to salvation in many
Synoptic passages clearly reflect the same conception found in the Book of
Wisdom. This is true even though one may debate whether certain passages, though framed in an eschatological context, refer to escaping evil
and destruction within this life or outside it (cf. Matt. 10:22; 24:13, 22;
and parallel passages).

In a passage of Luke's Gospel, someone asks Jesus if the number of
those saved will be few. His answer would seem to be the same as that
of the Book of Wisdom: "Struggle to get in through the narrow door; for
I tell you that many will try to enter and not be able. When once the
master of the house has got up and locked the door, you may stand outside and knock . . . but he will only answer, 'I do not know where you
come from . . . Out of my sight, all of you, you and your wicked ways!'
There will be wailing and grinding of teeth there, when you see Abraham,
Isaac, and Jacob, and all the prophets, in the kingdom of God, and yourselves thrown out" (Luke 13:23–28). There is no doubt that here Jesus
and his audience share the same language: salvation consists in being
admitted to some place *beyond,* where Abraham, Isaac, and Jacob are real
persons [i.e., a place beyond death].

And when the disciples, shaken by the exigencies of Jesus' morality,
ask themselves who can really be saved, it is evident that they reflect the
same conception of salvation. But the response of Jesus contains a subtle
difference here, for it does not seem to depend entirely on man's liberty
in the face of God's testing law: "For men this is impossible; but everything is possible for God" (Matt. 19:26).

Within the context of Jesus' response here, there is another important
shading. For Matthew, being saved is identified with entering the kingdom
(see Matt. 19:24). But does this refer to an earthly, ecclesial condition or
to a celestial, extraterrestrial one? The context of Mark and Luke is
clearer. When Peter asks Jesus what reward they will get for leaving all
things for the sake of Jesus, the latter replies by adding more concrete
content to the notion of entrance into the kingdom: "There is no one
who has given up home, brothers or sisters, mother, father or children, or
land, for my sake and for the Gospel (for the kingdom, according to
Luke), who will not receive in this age [i.e., at this time, or in this world,
or in goods of this world] a hundred times as much . . . and in the age
to come eternal life" (Mark 10:29–30; Luke 18:26–30). This shading is

important, for an appreciation of the present world and its benefits is placed on a continuous line with those of the future world. And this remains true, even though Christ's listeners were undoubtedly directing their attention toward some salvation that begins in the hereafter.

Above we noted that the expression "save your soul," as used today, is not properly biblical. In the language of the Synoptic Gospels, it is synonymous with "saving your life" or with the hereafter beyond death (see Mark 3:4 and the well-known text of Matt. 16:25–26; the latter text, often interpreted in a sense more spiritual than literal, is supposed to have converted Francis Xavier). Nonetheless, and starting this time with the "hereafter," we will find a shading in the teaching of Jesus that is equally important and significant. On several occasions Jesus indicated that he had come to "save what was lost." Now in his Gospel Luke or another author, introduces this statement into a context where some disciples of Jesus are asking him to bring fire down upon unbelieving towns. Jesus replies: "You do not know to what spirit you belong; for the Son of Man did not come to destroy men's lives but to save them" (Luke 9:55–56, note c in NEB). The context leaves no doubt that the reference is to destroying or saving "temporal" lives. But again, with a subtle shading, Jesus relates his mission of saving *absolutely* with that of saving *these earthly lives themselves*. Within the context of Jesus' salvation, life and eternal life acquire a mysterious continuity that the idiom of the Synoptic Gospels registers but does not develop.

Finally, we have the famous text of Mark's Gospel (16:16), which may or may not have been written by him: "Those who believe it and receive baptism will find salvation; those who do not believe will be condemned." Here, more clearly than ever, we have the absolute use of the terms "salvation" and "condemnation." It points to a judgment and reward beyond death, just as the context of the Book of Wisdom does. Yet here, too, we find an important shading. Consider another passage of Luke that is very similar. In the explanation of the parable of the sower, Luke adds something that is peculiar to him: ". . . the devil comes and carries off the word from their hearts for fear they should believe and be saved" (Luke 8:12). Obviously because, as Mark says, "those who believe . . . will find salvation." So in both texts it is *faith* that saves. The point here is, especially in the case of Luke, how can we help but see an echo of the numerous occasions when Christ, curing temporal ills, illnesses, and enslavement to sin, told the patient: "Your faith has saved you"? We get a clear shading which refers to the matter of *who* saves.

By virtue of the attitude of faith which makes it possible, total and absolute salvation shows up in mysterious continuity with all the intramundane deliberations accomplished, not by man's rigorous efforts under the law, but rather by his personal surrender to the Savior. In the two passages cited, it is certain that this submission must extend to "the gospel" and "the community" of Jesus (the allusion to the message and baptism); but the latter go to make up one single reality with the Savior himself.

4. What conclusions are we to draw from what we have said so far? The first is that in one part of the New Testament, that part which most faithfully reflects the environment in which Christianity was born, Christ's

message—with the exception of a few shadings—is translated in a salvation context which accords with the last stage of Old Testament thought.
In that context salvation is conceived as being extraterrestrial and as depending fundamentally on the free performance of religious and moral
duties during this life.[1]

But the divergent shadings are of great importance and open up
unsuspected vistas. Starting out from them, and hence presumably from
the central revelation of the message, Paul will go on to elaborate an
original idiom that is more appropriate for expressing the Christian conception of salvation.

As the reader may recall, these shadings were fundamentally three,
corresponding to the three questions we posed at the start regarding the
vocabulary of salvation. Let us sum them up in reverse order. *How* man
is saved through faith. Faith is the surrender of one's whole being to the
person, community, and teaching of God *who*, strictly speaking, saves
man with his grace *from the evils* which, here and now in this life, point
toward absolute paralysis, absolute enslavement, absolute death.

Thus the absolute, eschatological dimension of salvation is present,
not as something opposed to the present "age" but as its gratuitous and
actual, even though still invisible, absolutization.

We find both the content and the idiom of this conception, the
Christian conception, summed up in a remarkable passage of Romans:

> For all who are moved by the Spirit of God are sons of God. The Spirit you
> have received is not a spirit of slavery leading you back into a life of fear,
> but a Spirit that makes us sons. enabling us to cry "Abba! Father!" In that
> cry the Spirit of God joins with our spirit in testifying that we are God's
> children . . . For the created universe waits with eager expectation for
> God's sons to be revealed . . . Because the universe itself is to be freed
> from the shackles of mortality and enter upon the liberty and splendour of
> the children of God. Up to the present, we know, the whole created uni-
> verse groans in all its parts as if in the pangs of childbirth. Not only so,
> but even we, to whom the Spirit is given as firstfruits of the harvest to come,
> are groaning inwardly while we wait for God to make us his sons and set
> our whole body free. For we have been saved, though only in hope" (Rom.
> 8:14–24).

We have quoted this passage at length because it contains the elements
with which Paul restructures the idiom of the gospel regarding salvation.

If we start by asking, *firstly,* from what are we saved, we will find two
very important clues in this text and indeed in all of Paul's epistles.

The first clue is direct. It answers the question we have posed. Here
and elsewhere, to be sure, Paul talks about "being saved" without indicating the evils from which we are saved. At first glance this would seem
to contract his outlook back to the one in which salvation was absolutized,
hence situated beyond the concrete evils of existence in time. But it is
precisely the *hence* that is false for Paul. The context shows us in reality
that salvation, even when it is absolute, liberates us from here-and-now
evils. The passage cited is an example. At one point it does indeed say
that we "have been saved" without mentioning what we have been saved
from. Yet the passage mentions four specific, concrete evils from which
we have been saved: inner slavery and fear, the corruption of the sur-

rounding universe (destined for vanity otherwise), and the subjection of our body.

Consequently, salvation from these four evils leads into the reality *par excellence: our liberty*. If we look closely, we will see that the evils from which we "are saved" are nothing more nor less than the fetters on a creative existence.

Paul's letter to Titus also points out how the "generosity of God our Saviour" has rescued us from what we were before. "For at one time we ourselves in our folly and obstinacy were all astray. We were slaves to passions and pleasures of every kind. Our days were passed in malice and envy; we were odious ourselves and we hated one another" (Titus 3:3–6). This is more than a catalogue of sins; it is the description of an impersonal and noncreative existence. In another epistle Paul tells us something similar: "Grace, which was granted to us in Christ Jesus from all eternity . . . has now at length been brought fully into view by the appearance on earth of our Saviour Jesus Christ. For he has broken the power of death and brought life and immortality to light through the Gospel" (2 Tim. 1:10). Here, too, the universe is opened up to man's creative effort through this light. Without it man would lack motivation for using his creative liberty.

In this same order of things, perhaps the salvation which is most typically Paul's is that which liberates us from a religion that enslaves us in our very manner of seeking God: "My deepest desire and my prayer to God is for their salvation. To their zeal [i.e., quest] for God I can testify; but it is an ill-informed zeal. For they ignore God's way of righteousness, and try to set up their own, and therefore they have not submitted themselves to God's righteousness. For Christ ends the law and brings righteousness for everyone who has faith" (Rom. 10:1–4).

As one can see, Paul does not feel that the absolutization of salvation places it on an extraterrestrial plane. If in places he does not directly tie salvation to the elimination of concrete defects of liberty, it is because the immediate context and his overall doctrine allow one to establish the connection.

The *second* clue, enabling us to show that Paul saw salvation being carried out in our world without losing its absolute character, is indirect. It involves taking note of the tenses of the verbs which Paul uses when he discusses salvation.

The main passage cited earlier (Rom. 8:14–24) is a prime example: "The Spirit you have received . . . we are God's children . . . while we wait for God to make up his sons." The same reality is presented as past, present, and future; or, if you prefer, as already received in part and as still to come in part.

This should not surprise us—not only because Paul tends to intermingle the times of salvation in this way, but also because we are faced here with one of the most fundamental conditioning factors of Christian existence and its liberty. As Paul tells us: "We are saved (but) in hope." What is still lacking is "glory": i.e., the manifestation of the final outcome which, in and with us, has resulted from the divine sonship received as the firstfruits of the Spirit. In reality the Christian stands between two forms of knowledge, according to the first Epistle to the Corinthians: that which comes from the *witness* of Christ, and that which will come from his *manifestation* (or apocalypse). The consistency and firmness of the Christian (*cf.* 1 Cor. 1:4–8), that is, his solidity as a being neither wholly determined by the past nor wholly absorbed with the future, derives from these two poles of past and future.

Because of the first pole he knows that he has been saved (Eph. 2:4–6), and that this salvation suffuses and transforms his whole being. Because of the second pole he will see what this transformation into a son of God has permitted him to achieve in the total universe of beings and men: he will see his salvation. The last stage is already present in a certain way. The eschatological element is radically temporal; for Christian eschatology, far from threatening liberty as it might seem to do on the surface, is actually the eschatology of liberty.

Moreover, if we again pose the "who saves?" and "how are we saved?" to Paul, we shall again see the answers ending up with liberty. The main text we have been considering here presents salvation as the establishment of a new type of relationship between God and man, a relationship from which it is always possible to fall again. Only this kind of relationship befits a creative destiny. Liberty has its price. It entails the overcoming of servile fear. In other words, it entails *faith*.

Only the person who surrenders himself to the Father's love can be free on earth: "For it is by his grace you are saved, through trusting him; it is not your own doing. It is God's gift, not a reward for work done" (Eph. 2:8; *cf.* Titus 3:4–6). Hence Paul places the decisive step in the child's attainment of mature adulthood, wherein he can turn to God and call him "Father" (Gal. 4:4–7).

The Christian morality of love, the law of liberty, is possible only with the new religious outlook and attitude of faith, that looks less religious on the surface. In this new outlook, the "who" and "how" of salvation converge. If we wanted to sum up everything we have said in this CLARIFICATION, we would choose a statement by Paul Lehmann, giving it the full present and eschatological implications we have discussed here: "In short, maturity is salvation." [2] For it echoes the sentiments of Paul himself: "So shall we all at last attain . . . to mature manhood, measured by nothing less than the full stature of Christ" (Eph. 4:13).

II. LIBERTY AND ITS MOMENTS

The reader who has followed our discussion in this chapter will see clearly that we must significantly change our notion of the way liberty operates in our practical lives. We cannot picture it as functioning twenty-four hours a day, choosing between good and bad actions all the time. As Etienne de Greeff, a Catholic psychologist and a professor at the University of Louvain, puts it: "The majority of human beings are wholly in the dark with regard to their mental functions . . . Hence they do not evolve. They take their experience of interior liberty as an absolute, and do not derive further enrichment from it." [3]

But our inner activity is actually much more intricate. Even the fact that some action has been deliberated at the level of consciousness is not a sign that liberty has determined a concrete act.[4] Psychology knows very well that we often make subconscious use of such deliberations to justify some act as free and personally ours, when in fact we have been drawn into it by our passions.

In an earlier section (see Chapter I, CLARIFICATION I), we pointed out that a deeper and fuller, and even theological, awareness of the determinisms at work in our acts should not lead us to the erroneous conclusion that liberty is inoperative and can do nothing.[5] But it should also lead us to locate more accurately *the moments* of liberty. Let us first consider the question in more theoretical terms, which may entail some difficulty. Then we can offer an example which we feel will help to clarify the matter.

1. Our being has determinisms: i.e., different attractions. And as we saw earlier, we must not regard these as merely limiting things opposed to our liberty. They do indeed impose limits. But they also represent the precondition and corpus that make liberty itself possible.

We should also recall that liberty, in its positive sense, does not reside in the mere possibility of choosing this or that course. If that were the case, then the model of liberty would be the ass in the conundrum posed by the French scholastic philosopher, Buridan. The ass is placed between a pail of water and a bundle of hay. It is both hungry and thirsty, but it has no overriding reason to choose one or the other first, so it dies of hunger and thirst. In terms of this model, liberty would reside in indecision. Or, at the very least, it is only the person who has not yet decided that is truly free. For once a course is chosen, the other options fade away. Thus liberty as such would be radically opposed to its use, and would diminish with such use. Indeed the work of André Gide seems to offer grounds for upholding this notion of liberty as an ideal of life. It is criticized, in turn, in the *Caligula* of Albert Camus and *The Flies* of Jean Paul Sartre.

If, on the other hand, liberty consists in making one's own being into a creation that springs from our inmost depths, then the active (not passive) elimination of the possibility of choosing is something positive. To love—the creative action *par excellence*—is to deliberately choose to lose one's own autonomy. To do this, however, we must use and canalize the forces that are within us at the start as instinctive forces.

Consider sex, for example. For the vast majority of human beings, liberation from egoistic and passive solipsism is possible only insofar as self-giving utilizes the sexual instinct. In other words, the person liberates himself by stripping sex of its merely instinctive character and converting it into what it really is: a vehicle of personalization and hence of human community. Love will use the basic instinct of sex for self-giving. In so doing, it will mark both its power and its poverty.

What we have here is a very important dialectic. As we noted earlier, this kind of potentially creative force often dominates rather than being dominated. Interpersonal sexual union can be taken back by impersonal sexual drives and be submerged unnoticed. Marriage, or some other form of interpersonal sexual love, can degenerate into "mutual egotism" in which intimate sharing ceases to find expression.

So once again: How do we find our way to a creative kind of love? Normally people do this by utilizing new instinctive dynamisms. The instinct of motherhood and fatherhood comes into play, permitting further openings to others while maintaining love's control over the instinctive.

Here again, quite logically, there reappears the threat to personal expression that is inherent in the ambiguity of the instinctive realm. It tends to make of the family a closed circle in which children serve the egotism of their parents.

Presumably this tendency too will be offset by opening up to new instincts. These new instincts, more directly social and communitarian, will allow the family members to make their narrow circle the expression of persons in broader communitarian relationships.

The same thing occurs in the utilization and correction of class-based determinisms. And speaking in general, we can say that the same thing occurs in every area of human life.

The personal finds expression and fulfillment only through forces that threaten it even as they serve as its vehicle. And the possibility of dominating these forces is not to be found principally in a greater effort of will with the attendant struggle that is often sterile. Nor is it to be found in a continual backward look toward the idyllic start of it all, toward the honeymoon period of creative love. It is to be found in opening oneself up to new dimensions and dynamisms that restore a creative sense to what has turned into mere routine.

If we appreciate this dialectic, which we have sketched briefly here, we will also appreciate some other important facts about human life as suffused by grace. Recalling that grace signifies not only gift but also *youthfulness*, we can note the following.

a) A great majority of our actions are not so much free here and now as free more and more remotely. They escape our liberty to the extent that they move away from the focal point. In reality we perform them because, in the life or path we have chosen, they are dictated to us by some elemental logic that is not only, or even mainly, intellectual but also affective and subconscious.

b) The key point of our liberty resides in utilizing moments of equilibrium to open up our life and love here and now to new interests, new values, and new dimensions. The human person probably plays out his destiny much more in quiet, nonemotional decisions on his range of interests, relationships, and values, than in dramatic confrontations with temptations. The latter are often accepted from the start because they are the logical result of prior decisions.[6]

c) Thus man's destiny is not played out so much vis-à-vis what we would erroneously call "sin" or "failings." Though it may not seem true, it works out instead insofar as we keep opening up the love we already have to a greater or lesser degree. The option for love or egotism, for the personal or the impersonal, for grace or sin, is decided not so much vis-à-vis "evil" or the "forbidden" but rather within the "good."

2. We said earlier that we would offer a concrete example of all this. What could be better than an example from the Gospel itself? "A man was on his way from Jerusalem down to Jericho when he fell in with robbers, who stripped him, beat him, and went off leaving him half dead.

It so happened that a priest was going down by the same road; but when he saw him, he went past on the other side. So too a Levite came to the place, and when he saw him went past on the other side. But a Samaritan who was making the journey came upon him, and when he saw him was moved to pity. He went up and bandaged his wounds, bathing them with oil and wine. Then he lifted him on to his own beast, brought him to an inn, and looked after him there" (Luke 10:30–34).

The question to which Jesus is responding here is significant and worth noting: Who is my neighbor? In other words: Who is the object of my obligation to love?

The reply bears witness to the realism of the gospel, which goes right down to material concerns when it is a question of love: one's neighbor, *the person closest at hand.* Scripture knows well enough that it is not possible to have real love for someone we cannot see, for someone who is not tied to us by those basic dynamisms that are difficult to control but must be brought to fulfillment. The principle holds true with regard to God too. We do not love God if we do not love our neighbor: "If he does not love the brother whom he has seen, it cannot be that he loves God whom he has not seen" (1 John 4:20). Love must be genuine and show itself in action (1 John 3:18). To be and do this, it must proceed not only from a pure and intellectual willing but also from concrete emotions: i.e., from those that spring from the heart when it is moved by what the eyes see. Thus *proximity* is necessary to set our inner feelings in motion and start a train of concrete works of mercy. That is why the teacher of the law asked Jesus who his neighbor was? He wanted to know how far the range of proximity for love was to extend.

And Jesus' reply is clear. There is no neighbor as such, no fixed and defined limit. Who my neighbor will be depends on my capacity for drawing close to others, as the Samaritan did. Or better, it will depend on my ability to bring him close to me, to immerse him in my time, my world, and my range of interests.

The option open to the priest and Levite of the parable was not that of leaving their calling and becoming robbers. Yet, in the routine fulfillment of their lofty and respectable callings, they failed to take note of "the greatest commandment of the law." They were on a relatively long journey with no fixed time of arrival. They could have taken an hour longer. It was a moment when they could have opened up their love to a new dimension and drawn near to new realities. But they did not.

We can picture the examination of conscience of these two men sometime later, perhaps at the end of their life:

a) Firstly they would look for the "important" actions in which they had consciously deliberated and freely chosen. Their recollections would bypass the wounded man on the road, shoving him aside as irrelevant.

b) They would recall the crucial moments of their life when they resisted temptations to insubordination or unfaithfulness. But they would not even consider what happened in a quiet moment of peace when they were carrying out some duty, when their love could have added a new dimension and broken the egotism of virtuous routine.

c) They would certainly refuse to believe that the chain of sin and disguised self-interest began when this potential neighbor on the road was shoved out of their minds and preoccupations.[7]

III. IS HELL A CHRISTIAN DOGMA?

Both in this volume and Volume I we have had occasion to stress the inadequacy—which is not in itself falsity—of certain images of the realities presented by the Gospel. We have noted that these images were overly infantile. There is an overly childish image of heaven, and a corresponding image of divine judgment that is equally infantile. There is an equally childish image of hell.

We call these images "infantile" because they are the first stage of a deeper and richer revelation. They are not false, therefore. But one could not overstress the inauthenticity and the problems they are capable of introducing into an adult Christian life, if they do not undergo transformation as man's overall life grows and matures.

For example, it is not false that God is going to judge each individual on the basis of whether he has or has not practiced fraternal love in concrete form. But how much enslavement and alienation this can generate for a person if he takes salvation to be a quantitative inventory of good and bad deeds, or God's stepping in to end man's life after his last act of egotism or love and deciding his fate on the basis of that act!

The orthodoxy which the Church requires is that of a *human* truth: i.e., one which respects "the human way of approaching it," as Cardinal Lercaro once put it. Something is not *truth* in this full sense if it does not fit a mature level of life, if it directs the person's life back to dangerous and sometimes tragic infantilisms.

God's revelation took account of this fact, and the apostles followed the same course: "We have much to say, much that is difficult to explain, now that you have grown so dull of hearing. For indeed, though by this time you ought to be teachers, you need someone to teach you the ABC of God's oracles over again; it has come to this, that you need milk instead of solid food. Anyone who lives on milk, being an infant, does not know what is right. But grown men can take solid food; their perceptions are trained by long use to discriminate between good and evil" (Heb. 5:11–14).

Paul also talks about a contrast between "slaves of sin" and "slaves of righteousness" when he writes to the Romans, and he does so "to use words that suit your human weakness" (Rom. 6:19). He does the same thing in writing to the Corinthians (1 Cor. 3:1); but he points out to them that they cannot call themselves Christians if they do not continue to grow more mature (1 Cor. 2:14 ff.).

So let us briefly go back over the basic notions we have discussed in this volume, in our attempt to rescue them from an infantile framework and bring them to a level of mature Christianity.

Firstly, there is the notion of *grace* itself. Far from being a mechanism to multiply good acts and thus outstrip the production of evil acts, grace has shown up here as a great inner and personalizing force. Through it man fights against the depersonalizing law of minimum effort that fetters man to habit, be it licit or illicit, and to a state of liberty lost. Real liberty is thus conceived as man's possibility of defining his own person in the creative work of love.

Secondly, there is the notion of *judgment*. The New Testament presents a notion of judgment that contrasts sharply with an infantile notion of reward or punishment. It presents a notion of judgment that reveals the solidity of human endeavor, the solidity being its capacity for integrating the absolute and the indestructible with the object of its temporal creative work. To the extent that this work has been made personal and has overcome the lure of facile superficiality, its resistance to corruption, death, and destruction will be made manifest by the purifying fire of judgment.

Thirdly, this brings us to a mature notion of *heaven and eternal life*. It does not consist of a reward to replace what we have done or suffered. Rather, it situates on the plane of the absolute all that we have done freely out of love. It is the unexpected, but ardently desired, clothing of incorruptibility (2 Cor. 5:2–5) that is given to our adult person, now totally unified with its work in this life.

Fourthly, this logically affects the notion of *resurrection*. The latter is detached from the realm of deeds due to man's nature—in the more or less spiritual sense of the Greeks. Together with the notion of eternal life, it enters the realm of end results flowing from love, liberty, and the person. It is the gift whereby God takes hold of the overall work of human liberty and clothes it with divine incorruptibility, thus terminating and completing the impulse that began with grace's liberation of the personal in man.

As we have seen, in their mature version all these notions are injected with the dynamic impulse which is part and parcel of the action of grace, the great wind that picks us up and carries us aloft. Eternal life is not a reward waiting for us statically at the end of our life on earth; instead it is a fount of living water which is already bubbling up here from our liberated inner being (John 7:38). The resurrection is the terminal point of a course that begins here in this world and resembles the growth of a living plant. It consists in communing with the living Christ, which in turn is inseparable from communing with our fellow men (Phil. 3:10–11; John 6:50–51).

All this, then, is a dynamism which comes from on high—not in the manner of nature but as an end pole or goal for our willing. So it is only logical that the opposite pole, too, must necessarily figure in our image of existence if the latter is to be viewed in a Christian frame of reference. What is more, if man does have only one vocation (GS 22), then his line of march must stretch between two points which present directly opposite characteristics precisely because they are opposite limits. They are the *yes* and the *no* to the same reality, the same possibility, the same dynamism.

In other words, if the four positive and adult notions are to make human life in freedom comprehensible, then they should present corresponding negative notions *that are equally adult*. If a person talks about grace, life-affirming judgment, and resurrection, then he should be equally mature about facing up to the possibility of sin, life-destroying judgment,

death, and hell. In particular, if the adult notion of eternal life pictures
the definitive perdurance of love and its works (GS 39), then we as adults
cannot picture its opposite possibility as a simple pit of fire and sulphur.

If we look at the New Testament, we will note a fairly clear difference between the images of the Synoptic Gospels on the one hand and
the writings of John and Paul on the other.

In the former, *gehenna* and the more general terms alluding to hell
seem to refer to a place. But in contrast to the kingdom, which is also
conceived in terms of a place, it is not a place one enters but a place
one departs to, or better, is expelled to. In any case it is a place "out
there" (Matt. 25:30; 13:42) as opposed to the place "here" where Christ
is: i.e., the banquet feast where Israel is gathered together (Matt. 8:12;
25:41–46).

But it is also worth noting that the more simplistic images—the pit
of fire (Matt. 13:42), of thirst (Luke 16:23–28), of weeping and gnashing
of teeth (Matt. 3:12; 8:12; 25:30)—take in other imaginative elements
that point toward greater *depth* and *interiority:* e.g., expulsion from the
community into exterior darkness (Matt. 8:12; 25:30, 41), loss of everything as opposed to the loss of one part of the body (Matt. 18:8–9). Now
it is useless to debate the imaginative compatibility of these different
images, such as "fire" and "darkness." For the metaphors represent different levels of maturity. They move from the more infantile mentality of
physical, individual evil to the more mature level of psychic and social
evil. That does not alleviate the nature of hell at all; it does just the
opposite.

We must also point out another essential element in this terminology: the feature of *eternity* that is underlined repeatedly (Mark 9:44–48;
Matt. 3:12; 18:8–9; 25:41, 46). Before we saw that *eternal* life, viewed in
quantitative terms, seems out of all proportion to acts of concrete love
that are temporal and limited (Matt. 25:31–46). In like manner, insofar
as gehenna is conceived as a physical place, its eternity would appear to
make various Gospel passages incomprehensible. Consider, for example,
Luke's well-known story of the rich man and poor Lazarus (Luke 16:19–
31). When it comes to explaining the different fate of both men, Abraham
positively says that it involves the *reversal* of their life on earth. But the
image of some *definitive infernal place* is too simplistic and infantile to
make this explanation satisfactory as it stands. While the fire in the rich
man's place of torment may be comparable to the hunger and weakness
of Lazarus on earth, it certainly is not comparable in the light of its
absolute, inescapable, eternal dimensions.

Origen was not mistaken in noting this disproportion. His mistake
lay in trying to draw the logical consequence from this. He maintained
the notion of a place whose conditions had to correspond exactly to
man's temporal, relative decisions on earth. His idea of the *apokatastasis,*
of the temporal, noneternal nature of hell (Denz. 211), may well seem
to be attractive and merciful at first glance. But it is nothing more than
the incomprehension of the ultimate meaning of an image, an incomprehension that could be equally applied to eternal life and that would
end up by de-absolutizing man's existence and liberty.

Thus John prefers a more qualitative terminology to these physical and local images. His terminology is dominated by the notions of perdition (John 3:16), death in a deeper and more total sense than a merely physical one (John 6:50; 8:21; etc.), darkness and separation (John 12:46; 15:2,6). Through this type of image, we feel, hell ceases to be pictured as a place and to be conceived rather in terms of a final end. To use the Greek term of Paul, it is a *telos*: i.e., the distant and ultimate end. Just as eternal life appears simultaneously as continuity and discontinuous breakthrough, as an element that makes man's work whole and absolute.

Paul asks the Romans: "When you were slaves of sin, you were free from the control of righteousness; and what was the gain? Nothing but what now makes you ashamed, for the end (i.e., *telos*) is death. But now, freed from the commands of sin, and bound to the service of God, your gains are such as make for holiness, and the end (i.e., *telos*) is eternal life" (Rom. 6:20–22). Paul thus distinguishes the concrete results (gains) of both good and bad actions, which correspond directly with the contingency and relativity of the latter, from the two end terms (end) within which all possible human activity is framed and explained.

And this distinction is all the more important when one recalls that eternal life, presented as the final end and meaning-giving signpost of all activity in the Spirit, is not within the grasp of any human act; that through God's gift it is associated with an existence that can only be on route toward it. The "incorruptibility" which is proper to God, and which is passed on to man in his resurrection to eternal life, is not something that man "earns." It is something with which he is clothed (*cf.* 2 Cor. 5:2–5). But this of course does not rule out the possibility that one is hurrying toward it. Paul puts it neatly: "I have not yet reached perfection, but I press on, hoping to take hold of that for which Christ once took hold of me" (Phil. 3:12).[8]

But before approaching this aspect of the accessibility of the final ends to man's concrete and temporal decisions, we are interested in knowing what content we must give to the *telos* of hell in the light of what we have seen. Logically enough, it cannot be anything else but the negation of everything that is signified by the dynamism of grace. Realizing this, we make the same transition that John and Paul did. We move from a hell conceived in infantile terms of truth as an aid in carrying out the law, to a hell whose purpose, like that of all revelation, is to bring us "to the contemplation and appreciation of the divine plan" (GS 15) for our existence and history.

Paul conceives the action of grace in man just as Vatican II describes his doctrine: "The Christian man . . . receives 'the firstfruits of the Spirit' (Rom. 8:23) by which he becomes capable of discharging the new law of love. Through this Spirit, who is 'the pledge of our inheritance' (Eph. 1:14), the whole man is renewed from within, even to the achievement of 'the redemption of the body' (Rom. 8:23)" (GS 22). That is, to the point where the body itself ceases to be enslaved to frailty, corruption, and death (GS 39).

Conversely, the negation of the work of grace will be what we have already had occasion to see. It will be the negation of the creative liberty of love, the injection (or osmosis) of vanity and corruption into human activity which thus becomes incapable of resisting death or being offered the absolute. Thus for Paul death and consuming fire, more than thirst, weeping, and tormenting fire, become the images most capable of giving adult expression to the limit-notion at the opposite pole from eternal life.

The fact is that man can gradually lose his personhood and his effort by ceding control to external superficiality and the facile way: in a word, by ceding control to nature. Or, to put it in other terms: by becoming alienated, incomprehensible to his own inner self, enslaved to what is not rooted in inner creativity. We can readily see that for an adult human being this alienation is a thousand times more terrible—and sensible —than the idea of being hurled forever into a pit of fire for having died after overstepping the line into grave sin. John A. T. Robinson notes quite rightly: "It is this union-in-estrangement with the Ground of our being—what Paul Althaus once described as 'inescapable godlessness in inescapable relationship to God'—that we mean by hell. But equally it is the union-in-love with the Ground of our being, such as we see in Jesus Christ, that is the meaning of heaven. And it is the offer of that life, in all its divine depth, to overcome the estrangement and alienation of existence as we know it, that the New Testament speaks of as the 'new creation.' " [9]

Or it may be that hell, as an indispensable limit-concept that gives orientation and value to one possible dimension of our existence, appears to us as the synthesis of two meaningful and at the same time opposed components, as is the case with every limit-concept: (1) the extreme sensibility of man who is capable of perceiving and suffering his alienation and (2) alienation turned into a totality and set up indissolubly in the very depth of our existence.

Hence theology, in an effort to purify and bring maturity to the imaginative image, has long since placed the essential element in the idea of hell in what it calls "the pain of loss": i.e., in the absolute impossibility of relating oneself to God (who is love), and hence, of relating to any other person. In speaking thus, it does not picture hell literally as a *place*. One could imagine a damned human being in the very center of paradise, yet he still would be as incapable of relating himself to God as inert matter is. On the reverse side of the coin, the gate of hell is not an impassable barrier which prevents the damned person from heading out toward an absent God. God is there always, as he is in heaven. The element of hell resides in the fact that the condemned person is no longer master of the least part of his being so that he could communicate with God. The only *distance* that can exist vis-à-vis God anywhere is man's alienation.

So, the final question is: Can this gain of alienation, of which we are ashamed on earth, be converted into the *end* of a second, total death? In other words: Must we think that this limit-concept of a roadway on which one can always go farther can be humanly attainable? [10]

For the present we should correct our dangerous and infantile notion of a hell populated by people who were encountered by death and God's judgment *in mid-course* between love and egotism, between liberty and alienation. We hold such a notion, for example, when we think that a fault against love in one direction of our existence destroys all love in every other direction; when we think that the phrase, "love cancels innumerable sins" (1 Peter 4:8), must of course be understood with reference to sins committed *before* and not after this act of love; when we picture man passing alternately and continually from a state or totality of love to another state or totality of egotism.[11]

NOTES

1. Here, in addition to the Synoptics, we find the New Testament writings which are more indebted to the language and ambience of the Old Testament. See, for example, 1 Pet. 1:3–5; James 2:4,12; Heb. 6:7–9; etc.

2. Paul Lehmann, *Ethics in a Christian Context* (New York: Harper & Row, 1963), p. 99.

3. 1952 *Semaine* of Catholic Intellectuals: *L'Eglise et la liberté*, p. 78.

4. "What the psychoanalyst says is that all our choices are determined by similar (unconscious) stimuli which operate outside our control and consciousness; that they suggest decisions which our consciousness accepts, justifying them a priori one way or another while believing it has chosen them freely . . . Here we have the problem . . . Should the Catholic part with the psychoanalyst in scorn and indignation?" (*ibid.*, pp. 79–81).

5. "One cannot derive the voluntary from the involuntary. On the contrary, the primary thing in man is comprehension of the voluntary. I understand myself above all as someone who says: I will. The involuntary refers to willing as that which gives one motives, powers, bases, and limits" (Paul Ricoeur, Philosophie de la Volonté, Vol. I, *La voluntaire et l'Involuntaire* (Paris: Aubier, 1950).

6. After posing the question contained in note 4, Etienne de Greef answers "no." Then he goes on: "Would it not be better to accept discussion . . . and to explore how . . . one might investigate by what pathways the human being, effecting a balance of instinctive dynamisms, can reach a higher plane?" (*op. cit.*, p. 81).

7. Perhaps if Christian parents were to ponder the real nature of formation in liberty according to the greatest commandment of Christ, they would come to fear most what they seem to admire most today: habit and moral routine, the isolationism of class unanimity, their common outlook on problems or the lack of them, etc. Perhaps they would come to realize that being educated has meaning only if it means being prepared to be involved with others, to draw closer to a neighbor that once was distant.

8. Thus one cannot validly object that if one of the final terms is inaccessible, it is so because it is supernatural, while the other, being the negation of something offered gratuitously to man, must ever remain within the realm of concrete possibilities. If a person argues this way, then he is either picturing historical man on a purely natural plane and grace as some external addition, or else he is saying that redemption is much less universal than original sin because the latter changed our destiny without our personal intervention while the former is merely an offer that can only be turned into a reality by our dubious decision. That is not how Paul sees it, as the reader of this section will see.

9. J. A. T. Robinson, *Honest To God*, Chapter 4 (Philadelphia: Westminster Paperback edition, 1963) p. 80.

10. It would be worthwhile to ask oneself why this question must be asked and answered. Why does it pose a problem? Why isn't the Christian satisfied to know that this limit-concept has a clear, indispensable function to play as something that orientates and gives value to our free existence? Without any doubt

the urgency of the question and the anxiety it stirs up stems from the fact that hell, conceived as a well-populated prison, has not only been a traditional image in catechesis but also one of the elements that have gone to make up social stability among peoples with an "Occidental and Christian" culture. One thing unconsciously cries out for the other. In the same way the idea of *law* is a typically pre-Christian thing, for all its use as a preestablished category of what is permitted and what is forbidden.

11. It is not surprising that theologians like Karl Rahner and Piet Schoonenberg experience insoluble difficulties in trying to picture a totally and definitively egoistic act within the course of man's concrete, complex and divided existence—an act that would be totally given to egotism, impersonality, and hell. Schoonenberg says: "Thus, in the line of will too, we never meet *an act in which our person totally carries our nature along*" (our italics; *Man and Sin: A Theological View*, Notre Dame: University of Notre Dame Press, 1965, p. 23). And Rahner says: "It follows that the dualism of nature and person in its specifically human form, which we call concupiscence . . . is at work both in the case of a good decision of man's freedom . . . and also in the case of a bad free decision . . . Both the good and the bad moral decision encounter the resistance, the solidity, and the impenetrability of nature" ("The Theological Concept of Concupiscentia," in *Theological Investigations I*, Baltimore: Helicon, 1961, pp. 365–66).

This leads them to place the truly decisive act of man's destiny outside of history and its process of development—specifically, at the razor's edge of death, which is viewed as the apex of liberty and lucidity. Says Schoonenberg: "The first and only act in which the person disposes of his whole nature occurs at the moment of transition from time to eternity; it is the act by which man chooses his eternal attitude, thus definitively and irrevocably deciding his direction" (Schoonenberg, *op. cit.*, p. 34).

We feel that this position is difficult to sustain (1) in the light of human experience and (2) in the light of theological reasons. It is worth noting, for example, that Schoonenberg understandably vacillates between subordinating man's last decision to his earlier ones and making it independent of them. The first alternative would bring his view more in line with Matthew 25 and the subsequent tradition that frames the decisive element of man's destiny within the context of interpersonal relationships in history. The second alternative would tend to give man's ultimate decision the absolute and total quality attributed to it as a decision leading to an equally absolute and total destiny.

We have already said that Saint Paul speaks to us in an image that suggests a more mature outlook on God's judgment. There all man's work will be scrutinized and judged (*cf.* GS 39). Paul insistently assures us that grace and its results were and are superior to sin in the totality of mankind. Thus we can hope that his insistence on this point indicates his bedrock hope that all men, face to face with God, will commune personally with him and their brothers— using the being and life they have liberated from impersonality and death with the help of the Holy Spirit.

Conclusion

In one of the sections of Volume I we asked whether there was such a thing as a Christian anthropology. And our first response was that "every statement about God is at the same time a statement about man." *

In this volume, too, we have been dealing with a theological theme because "grace" is nothing but God's gift *par excellence:* i.e., God himself made into our existence. Grace is "the Spirit that dwells in us." With the help of revelation and our own experience we have tried to *locate* this great wind that takes hold of our existence and carries it much further than its innate gravity would permit it to reach.

Each chapter in this volume, operating from its own distinct viewpoint and approach, has led us to discover the same reality: the irresistible force that seeks to make us free, that transforms us into free men, and that turns us toward all free men so that we may collaborate in a common task. This task, which is both human and divine, is to create a history of love in all its fullness precisely by virtue of being free.

So here again we are led to the same response which we gave in the first volume to the question of a Christian anthropology. *No,* Christian theology does not constitute a Christian anthropology, if the latter is taken to mean a finished, readymade image of man that is to be grafted on to the material of history. But our *no* is a response welling up from richness not from penury.

Grace does not force us into a mold provided by God, nor does it tell us what sort of mold would represent the ideal man. It speaks to us, and offers us suggestions, and sometimes it even jolts us. So that we may understand that the one and only mold, the mold of the Son, is the liberty of the sons of God. So that we may realize that God has no other plan for us except to associate us with his creative work in the history of

---

*Cf. Volume I, Chapter II, CLARIFICATION I. This reply is in fact "the first response of the Council to the problem posed by the breach between faith and human living" (*ibid.*).

the universe. John's Gospel tells us that "the truth will set you free." If a person asks, "Free for what?" he has not understood a thing and must start over at the beginning.

Only the question of how has meaning here. In each of the four chapters we have seen something of this *how*, but admittedly not much. What we have seen is indeed simple even though fairly paradoxical. We have seen how to reform and revitalize what we believed we knew about sin and goodness, risk and security, heaven and hell, divine judgment and human history. We have seen how to view them in terms of the full measure and adulthood of Christ.

To repeat once again, it is only normal for this renewal to stir up new problems. But such problems will be welcome if they are the boon companions of true maturity.

Appendices

APPENDIX I

Introduction to the Series

FORMAT AND ORIGIN OF THIS SERIES

We have tried to make it easier for the reader to approach this series by using a coherent format. The essential aspects of our reflection on a given topic are contained in the initial article under each chapter. They are followed by a section entitled CLARIFICATIONS, in which we try to develop and apply more concretely the central lines of thought, to suggest study topics and related issues, and to go over one or more points in detail. Notes are given at the end of each of these two main divisions.

The notes are meant to be useful to the reader rather than to be erudite. Many of them are biblical, indicating other passages in Scripture which complement the thoughts presented or which can be used for related meditation. Instead of citing numerous scholarly works, we have limited ourselves to a few more accessible sources: e.g., the *Concilium* series. Our series was originally intended for a Latin American audience, and their needs were uppermost in our minds.

The type of theological reflection presented here can give rise to different discussion formats: full-length courses, study weeks, and the like. But we actually tested it in a seminar approach, involving intensive sessions of study, discussion, and prayer. It may interest the reader to know how our seminars actually operate.

As far as length of time is concerned, our experiences confirmed the feeling that the busy layman benefits more from short-term seminars in which he is actively involved than from long-term courses in which he is generally passive. So now we try to run seminars of three or four days that coincide with a holiday weekend. The aim is to provide five or six sessions of four hours each in a relatively short space of time. We also stress that enrollment in the seminar implies that the individual is willing to involve himself in it totally, to participate in all the sessions, and to remain until it is over. The seminar is meant to be a total experience, not mere attendance at a series of lectures.

Each four-hour session operates pretty much like this. It begins with a lecture (which is reproduced almost verbatim here as the initial section of each chapter). The lecture lasts about one hour, and at its conclusion one or two questions are proposed to the various study groups (see Appendix IV in this volume). But before they move into their discussion groups, the participants are asked to spend a few moments in personal meditation on the questions. In this way they can make an effort to formulate a personal solution, however provisional it might be, to the questions posed.

The various study groups then spend about forty-five minutes or an hour in discussing the questions. There are no more than ten persons in a given group, so that each individual will participate actively in the discussion. Herein lies the essential aim of the seminar itself, for the participants should move on from formulated truths to a truly interiorized truth. In other words, the discussion represents a confrontation between what they have heard and what they have learned from their real-life experiences; between that which they accepted uncritically as children and adolescents and that which they have put together into a coherent whole as adults.

Thus the questions proposed are not meant to serve as a review of the lecture. They are meant to foster a greater coherence between that which was provided in the lecture and other aspects or facts of Christian experience. To this end, it is highly desirable that the groups be somewhat heterogeneous in makeup, and that their discussion be stimulated by a pointed confrontation with things they may have read in the catechism or heard all their life from the pulpit.

It is also highly useful at this point to have the groups make an effort to reach unanimity on their answers and then write them up as a group project. Such a procedure obliges the participants to engage in real dialogue and to respect differences of opinion. When this period is over, the various groups reassemble at a roundtable forum and each group presents the answers it has formulated. The reply of the group may take one of three forms: a unanimous group response, a set of differing opinions, or a series of questions formulated by the group. It is our feeling that questions worked up by a group are more useful than those which an individual might formulate alone at the end of the lecture.

During the roundtable forum, the lecturer comments on the group replies, tries to respond to the questions of the various groups, and then takes up individual questions if he so desires.

The procedure varies for the final hour. Intellectual effort gives way to a period of prayer and recollection that is related to the theme under consideration. It may involve some form of paraliturgical service or a biblical reading that is not discussed in great detail (see Appendix III in this volume).

This pattern is repeated throughout the course of the seminar. As circumstances permit, the final four-hour session may be dedicated to a review of what has been covered and a discussion of possible concrete applications in the local or parochial sector.

As the reader will see from the text itself, our aim is not to move on to a wholly different topic in each four-hour session. Experience has shown that it is more useful to return to the same few basic ideas over and over again, relating them ever more deeply to real-life problems. It is useful, in this connection, to sum up what has gone before at the start of each session. One practical way of doing this is to refer to conciliar texts that relate to the material in question (see Appendix II in this volume). While we do not feel that these texts by themselves are enough to encourage this type of reflection, we do find that they are able to shore up and confirm the work already done. For they come from the universal Church gathered together in our day under the special action of the Holy Spirit.

Finally we would point out that this treatment of grace has been preceded by a volume on the Church and will by other volumes on fundamental aspects of the faith: God, the sacraments, sin and redemption, etc. Each year a seminar is held on a new topic, and seminars on old topics are held for those who have not yet attended them. In this way we hope to answer the needs of mature persons who are looking for a theology which is equally adult, which is open to exploring new pathways related to their temporal commitments.

Pertinent Conciliar Texts

It should be pointed out that none of the conciliar decrees or constitutions take grace as their theme. Explicitly at least, the major theme of the Council was the Church and her functions. So we cannot read conciliar passages referring to divine grace and Christian existence in the same way we can read passages dealing with the Church.

This notwithstanding, a revitalized vision of the Church presumes an equally revitalized vision of Christian existence, and hence of God's gift which is grace. It is not without reason that some theologians, whose ideas had a marked influence on the Council, have dedicated a portion of their written works to the theme that has occupied our attention in this volume. De Lubac and Rahner are two examples.

Hence we feel that it is possible to read various passages of the conciliar documents in search of an implicit theology of grace. But since this topic was not the major theme of the Council itself, it is obvious that such passages do not enjoy the probative force and authority specific to enunciations which flow from the main themes of the decrees and constitutions. Nevertheless they do form part of the roadway which the Spirit is inspiring the Church to undertake. Such a "spiritual" reading is what we propose to offer here. As the reader can understand, there will necessarily be a need for more extensive commentary on the passages cited.

Chapter One

A passage in *Gaudium et spes* sums up the doctrine of the Church on the human condition, identifying the human with the domain of *achieved liberty:*

> Only in freedom can man direct himself toward goodness . . . Authentic freedom is an exceptional sign of the divine image within man . . . Hence man's dignity demands that he act according to a knowing and free choice. Such a choice is personally motivated and prompted from within. It does not result from blind internal impulse nor from mere external pressure. Man achieves such dignity when, emancipating himself from all captivity to passion, he pursues his goal in a spontaneous choice of what is good, and

procures for himself, through effective and skillful action, apt means to that end. Since man's freedom has been damaged by sin, only by the help of God's grace can he bring such a relationship with God into full flower. Before the judgment seat of God each man must render an account of his own life, whether he has done good or evil (GS 17).

A. GRACE ON MAN'S ROADWAY

Human beings, be they Christians or not, are confronted with an historical order that unfolds and progresses in time. Another conciliar document answers the following questions:

1. What does the temporal order contain?

Many elements make up the temporal order: namely, the good things of life and the prosperity of the family, culture, economic affairs, the arts and professions, political institutions, international relations, and other matters of this kind, as well as their development and progress . . . (AA 7).

2. What value does all this have?

All of these not only aid in the attainment of man's ultimate goal but also possess their own intrinsic value . . . This *natural* goodness of theirs takes on a special dignity as a result of their *relation to the human person,* for whose service they were created (AA 7).

3. Is it, then, an ambiguous value? Yes, because it may not only serve the human person but also dominate and enslave him in a stifling way:

In the course of history, temporal things have been foully abused by serious vices. Affected by original sin, men have frequently fallen into multiple errors . . . The result has been the corruption of morals and human institutions and not rarely contempt for the human person himself (AA 7).

4. What sort of a task, then, can restore to history the due ordination of the temporal to man's service? A task that is at once historical and supernatural, because

It has pleased God to unite all things, both natural and supernatural, in Christ Jesus "that in all things he may have the first place" (Col. 1:18). This destination, however, not only does not deprive the temporal order of its independence, its proper goals, laws, resources, and significance for human welfare but rather perfects the temporal order in its own intrinsic strength and excellence and raises it to the level of man's total vocation upon earth (AA 7).

The next section of this decree returns to this fundamental task and describes it as follows:

1. A supernatural roadway

The greatest commandment in the law is to love God with one's whole heart and one's neighbor as oneself (cf. Matt. 22:37–40). Christ made this commandment of love of neighbor His own and enriched it with a new meaning. For He wanted to identify Himself with His brethren as the object of his love when He said, "As long as you did it for one of these, the least of my brethren, you did it for me" (Matt. 25:40). Taking on human nature, He bound the whole human race to Himself as a family through a certain supernatural solidarity (AA 8).

2. A roadway in history

At the present time, when the means of communication have grown more rapid, the distances between men have been overcome in a sense, and the inhabitants of the whole world have become like members of a single family, these actions and works (i.e., of charity and mutual aid) have grown much more urgent and extensive. These charitable enterprises can and should reach out to absolutely every person and every need. Wherever there are people in need of food and drink, clothing, housing, medicine, employment, education; wherever men lack the facilities necessary for living a truly human life . . . there Christian charity should seek them out and find them, console them with eager care and relieve them with the gift of help (AA 8).

3. A roadway of personalization

That the exercise of such charity may rise above any deficiencies in fact and even in appearance, certain fundamentals must be observed. Thus attention is to be paid to the image of God in which our neighbor has been created, and also to Christ the Lord to whom is really offered whatever is given to a needy person. The freedom and dignity of the person being helped should be respected with the utmost delicacy, and the purity of one's charitable intentions should not be stained by a quest for personal advantage or by any thirst for domination. The demands of justice should first be satisfied, lest the giving of what is due in justice be represented as the offering of a charitable gift. Not only the effects but also the causes of various ills must be removed. Help should be given in such a way that the recipients may gradually be freed from dependence on others and become self-sufficient (AA 8).

Gaudium et spes also attributes the same features to man's temporal task. *Firstly*, it is presented as a fully supernatural task motivated by the Holy Spirit that the risen Christ sent to us:

Appointed Lord by His resurrection and given plenary power in heaven and on earth, Christ is now at work in the hearts of men through the energy of His Spirit. He arouses not only a desire for the age to come, but, by that very fact, He animates, purifies and strengthens those noble longings too by which the human family strives to make its life more human and to render the whole earth submissive to this goal . . . He frees all of them so that by putting aside love of self and bringing all earthly resources into the service of human life they can devote themselves to that future when humanity itself will become an offering accepted by God (GS 38).

Secondly, the whole journey of humanity is meant in this description. In other words, it takes in the long and gradual history whereby the prehuman becomes fully human and converges, wittingly or unwittingly, toward Christ:

Human institutions, both private and public, must labor to minister to the dignity and purpose of man. At the same time let them put up a stubborn fight against any kind of slavery, whether social or political, and safeguard the basic rights of man under every political system. Indeed human institutions themselves must be accommodated by degrees to the highest of all realities, spiritual ones, even though meanwhile, a long enough time will be required before they arrive at the desired goal (GS 29).

Thirdly, as we have already seen, it has to do with the liberation of what is personal and creative in man (i.e., in man as a free being in the image of God):

> Man's social nature makes it evident that the progress of the human person and the advance of society itself hinge on each other . . . To be sure, the disturbances which so frequently occur in the social order result in part from the natural tensions of economic, political and social forms. But at a deeper level they flow from man's pride and selfishness, which contaminate even the social sphere. When the structure of affairs is flawed by the consequences of sin, man, already born with a bent toward evil, finds there new inducements to sin, which cannot be overcome without strenuous efforts and the assistance of grace (GS 25).

This effort starts from the fact that

> Man is split within himself. As a result, all of human life, whether individual or collective, shows itself to be a dramatic struggle between good and evil, between light and darkness. Indeed, man finds that by himself he is incapable of battling the assaults of evil successfully, so that everyone feels as though he is bound by chains. But the Lord Himself came to free and strengthen man, renewing him inwardly and casting out that prince of this world (cf. John 12:31) who held him in the bondage of sin. For sin has diminished man, blocking his path to fulfillment (GS 13).

Thus Christ, man's liberator, poses to his brothers a task in history wherein man's liberation to full humanity must confront three synonymous terms—*external superficiality, subjection, sin:*

> For this gospel announces and proclaims the freedom of the sons of God, and repudiates all the bondage which ultimately results from sin. The gospel has a sacred reverence for the dignity of conscience and its freedom of choice, constantly advises that all human talents be employed in God's service and men's, and, finally, commends all to the charity of all (GS 41).

Faced with this task, Christians know that

> The Lord left behind a pledge of this hope and strength for life's journey in that sacrament of faith where natural elements refined by man are changed into His glorified Body and Blood, providing a meal of brotherly solidarity and a foretaste of the heavenly banquet (GS 38).

B. GRACE ON THE WORLD'S ROADWAY

The world, the universe (i.e., the prehuman), thus shows up as material for the liberty of human beings. But it is a rebellious material, often enslaving man in the course of the history wherein he is trying to achieve his liberty in and with it:

> Today the human race is passing through a new stage in its history. Profound and rapid changes are spreading by degrees around the whole world. Triggered by the intelligence and creative energies of man, these changes recoil upon him, upon his decisions and desires, both individual and collective, and upon his manner of thinking and acting with respect to things and to people . . . Thus, while man extends his power in every direction, he does not always succeed in subjecting it to his own welfare (GS 4).

A particularly significant example is the progressive socialization of the universe. It is not simply a stage in the development of the world in history. What has already been said applies to it as well:

> This social life is not something added on to man. Hence, through his dealings with others, through reciprocal duties, and through fraternal dialogue he develops all his gifts and is able to rise to his destiny . . . In our era, for various reasons, reciprocal ties and mutual dependencies increase day by day . . . This development, which is called socialization, while certainly not without its dangers, brings with it many advantages with respect to consolidating and increasing the qualities of the human person . . . But if by this social life the human person is greatly aided in responding to his destiny . . . it cannot be denied that men are often diverted from doing good and impelled toward evil by the social circumstances in which they live and are immersed from their birth . . . When the structure . . . is flawed by the consequences of sin, man, already born with a bent toward evil, finds there new inducements to sin, which cannot be overcome without strenuous efforts and the assistance of grace (GS 25).

Thus the same split that Paul saw in the individual person between the task set for liberty and man's enslavement to the conditions surrounding its carrying out can also be attributed to humanity in history and society in general:

> Never has the human race enjoyed such an abundance of wealth, resources and economic power. Yet a huge proportion of the world's citizens is still tormented by hunger and poverty, while countless numbers suffer from total illiteracy. Never before today has man been so keenly aware of freedom; yet at the same time, new forms of social and psychological slavery make their appearance. Although the world of today has a very vivid sense of its unity and of how one man depends on another in needful solidarity, it is most grievously torn into opposing camps (GS 4).

Like humanity in history, the individual person is both the "cause and victim" (cf. GS 8) of this seemingly incomprehensible phenomenon. In such a situation we are bound to ask: Will it be possible for man to pave a new future for humanity with this second creation of his, if at the same time it gets out of hand for him? It is not easy to answer this question on the basis of the data we derive from the reality we sense around us:

> Because they are coming so rapidly, and often in a disorderly fashion, all these changes beget contradictions and imbalances, or intensify them. Indeed the very fact that men are more conscious than ever of the inequalities in the world has the same effect. Within the individual person there too often develops an imbalance between an intellect which is modern in practical matters, and a theoretical system of thought which can neither master the sum total of its ideas, nor arrange them adequately into a synthesis (GS 8).

However, revelation teaches us certain things. *Firstly*, it tells us that this world situation is not new. It is the human condition itself—or, the prehuman condition—which is the point of departure for grace. Hence the Council is aware that it must apply to the world the same analysis that Paul suggested with regard to this point of departure:

The truth is that the imbalances under which the modern world labors are linked with that more basic imbalance rooted in the heart of man. For in man himself many elements wrestle with one another . . . Indeed, as a weak and sinful being, he often does what he would not, and fails to do what he would. Hence he suffers from internal divisions, and from these flow so many and such great discords in society (GS 10).

Secondly, it tells us that the world too is assumed by a force which bears it continually from that situation toward salvation:

The Church believes that Christ, who died and was raised up for all, can through His Spirit offer man the light and the strength to measure up to his supreme destiny. Nor has any other name under heaven been given to man by which it is fitting for him to be saved (GS 10).

The Council does not see this salvation as something outside history. It sees salvation as the liberation of man in history. Thus the world is

emancipated now by Christ. He was crucified and rose again to break the stranglehold of personified Evil, so that the world might be fashioned anew according to God's design and reach its fulfillment (GS 2).

C. GRACE ON THE CHRISTIAN'S ROADWAY

What has been said up to now holds true for all men, as the Council makes clear repeatedly. Hence it also holds true for Christians.

Nevertheless, one might be able to say that, from the viewpoint of grace, Christians would be less comprehended within this description and analysis because, through faith and Christ's sacraments, they have the salvation we have just spoken about. Is that the way it is?

One can truly say of the Christian what the Council says of every religious human being:

Now man is not wrong when he regards himself as superior to bodily concerns, and as more than a speck of nature or a nameless constituent of the city of man. For by his interior qualities he outstrips the whole sum of mere things. He attains to these inward depths whenever he enters into his own heart. God, who probes the heart, awaits him there. There he discerns his proper destiny beneath the eyes of God (GS 14).

But this effective liberation of the interior man for a creative existence is not achieved solely in the act of establishing a religious relationship with God. It is a process that calls for a constant effort at liberation, which includes the religious and the rest of man's activities:

That is why Christ's Church, trusting in the design of the Creator, acknowledges that human progress can serve man's true happiness. Yet she cannot help echoing the Apostle's warning: "Be not conformed to this world" (Rom. 12:2). By the world is here meant that spirit of vanity and malice which transforms into an instrument of sin those human energies intended for the service of God and man. Hence, if anyone wants to know how this unhappy situation can be overcome, Christians will tell him that all human activity, constantly imperiled by man's pride and deranged self-love, must be purified and perfected by the power of Christ's cross and resurrection (GS 37).

In referring to Christ's cross and resurrection as the means of purifying all man's activities, the Council refers to a judgmental spirit. Etymologically this means a *critical* spirit that is capable of discerning when the instruments of liberty turn into man's master and enslaver. For

> Grateful to his Benefactor for these created things, using and enjoying them in detachment and liberty of spirit, man is led forward into a true possession of the world, as having nothing yet possessing all things. "All are yours, and you are Christ's, and Christ is God's" (1 Cor. 3:22–23) (GS 37).

If man does not have this detachment in using and enjoying things, which is not a fault but real liberty, and if he does not operate through the cross and resurrection of Christ, then religion itself, being a human activity, becomes enslaving rather than liberating.

1. As the Council sees it, then, the religious must not be converted into magic but rescued from it. To this end man must have a critical spirit. In other words, he must comply in faith with the judgment of God. Through detachment, this empties us and thus frees us:

> A more critical ability to distinguish religion from a magical view of the world . . . purifies religion and exacts day by day a more personal and explicit adherence to faith (GS 7).

2. As we have already seen, this liberation should penetrate everything and ultimately purify love and its designs as well. For here too we must face the crisis, and to do this we need the detachment that "daily" carries love through "the death and resurrection of Christ":

> That the exercise of such charity may rise above any deficiencies in fact and even in appearance, certain fundamentals must be observed . . . The freedom and dignity of the person being helped should be respected with the utmost delicacy, and the purity of one's charitable intentions should not be stained by a quest for personal advantage or by any thirst for domination . . . Help should be given in such a way that the recipients may gradually be freed from dependence on others and become self-sufficient (AA 8).

3. This spiritual poverty allows us to truly love. And it applies as well to the Church's activity in propagating its message to men. Thus everything said above can be applied as well to the apostolate. The Council alludes to this expressly when it says that

> The force which the Church can inject into modern society consists in that faith and charity put into vital practice, not in any external dominion exercised by merely human means (GS 42).

Chapter Two

Here again a passage in *Gaudium et spes* sums up for us the doctrine of the Church in this matter. It reminds us of the feature of elevation that God's gift has in our existence. In truth our destiny bears us to heights that surpass any human effort or pretension:

> But we are taught that God is preparing a new dwelling place and a new earth where justice will abide, and whose blessedness will answer and surpass all the longings for peace which spring up in the human heart. Then, with death overcome, the sons of God will be raised up in Christ. What was sown in weakness and corruption will be clothed with incorruptibility.

realization of creation and of redemption. The same idea is expressed in the Decree on the Apostolate of the Laity:

> Last of all, it has pleased God to unite all things, both natural and super-natural, in Christ Jesus "that in all things he may have the first place" (Col. 1:18). This destination, however, not only does not deprive the tem-poral order of its independence, its proper goals, laws, resources, and sig-nificance for human welfare but rather perfects the temporal order in its own intrinsic strength and excellence and raises it to the level of man's total vocation upon earth (AA 7).

Certain things are clear from this passage and the preceding ones: (a) the point of departure is the unity of all things in Christ; (b) the autonomy of the temporal perdures within this unity, so that any dialogue between the believer and other men should relate to the goals, laws, tools, and importance of the temporal for man; (c) since it does not abolish this autonomy, the supernatural should be viewed as being in the service of this autonomy, even though it is a divine gift coming from on high; (d) its purpose, in effect, is to permit the temporal order, more properly guided by its own dynamisms, to open out into life eternal and divine, into the full vocation of man and the universe.

This whole message can also be found in another passage of *Gaudium et spes* which speaks of Christ as the alpha and omega of the universe:

> For God's Word, by whom all things were made, was Himself made flesh so that as the perfect man He might save all men and sum up all things in Himself. The Lord is the goal of human history, the focal point of the long-ings of history and of civilization, the center of the human race, the joy of every heart and the answer to all its yearnings. . . . We journey toward the consummation of human history, one which fully accords with the counsel of God's love: "To re-establish all things in Christ, both those in the heavens and those on the earth" (Eph. 11:10) (GS 45).

So we can appreciate that:

> The expectation of a new earth must not weaken but rather stimulate our concern for cultivating this one (GS 39).

> A hope related to the end of time does not diminish the importance of intervening duties, but rather undergirds the acquittal of them with fresh incentives (GS 21).

C. CONCLUSION

What has been said tells us something about the distinction brought about by a grace that elevates the natural and the temporal to the realm of the supernatural and the eternal. It tells us that the distinction does not depend on some classification of activities and values. It depends rather on the recognition that *within* the human and the temporal there is operating God's own power and life; the latter is leading the one, unique history of the universe toward its full, definitive reality. For this reason, *Lumen gentium* exhorts lay people as follows:

> The faithful, therefore, must learn the deepest meaning and the value of all creation, and how to relate it to the praise of God. They must assist one another to live holier lives even in their daily occupations. In this

> While charity and its works endure, all that creation which God made on man's account will be unchained from the bondage of vanity (GS 39).

Through this elevation of man to the divine plane, his ephemeral activity becomes creative and eternal like that of God. This raises the problem of its relationship to that which man is and carries out on his own by mere human effort, or at least to that which man *could* carry out by such effort. So the Council goes on to point out that this elevation presumes a distinction between that which is a gift in the absolute and proper sense and that which is not (apart from the fact that creation itself is a gift). But the Council also takes great pains to point out that this distinction must not be turned into a separation:

> Therefore, while we are warned that it profits a man nothing if he gain the whole world and lose himself, the expectation of a new world must not weaken but rather stimulate our concern for cultivating this one. For here grows the body of a new human family, a body which even now is able to give some kind of foreshadowing of the new age. Earthly progress must be carefully distinguished from the growth of Christ's kingdom. Nevertheless . . . it is of vital concern to the kingdom of God (GS 39).

The document goes on to show why it is of such interest. It points out that it would be fatal to turn the distinction into separation, because the com-pleted kingdom of God will be composed precisely of the materials of history and human effort carried to their definitive goal by elevating grace:

> For after we have obeyed the Lord, and in His Spirit nurtured on earth the values of human dignity, brotherhood and freedom, and indeed *all the good fruits of our nature and enterprise*, we will find them again, but freed of stain, burnished and transfigured. This will be so when Christ hands over to the Father a kingdom eternal and universal (GS 39).

It is worth noting how the Council, in treating various central themes, spells out this distinction which is not separation, and which is in fact identified with the theme of grace elevating man to eternal life.

A. THE "NEW HUMANITY"

The human race has been profoundly transformed by grace:

> In the human nature which He united to Himself, the Son of God redeemed man and transformed him into a new creation (cf. Gal. 6:15; 2 Cor. 5:17) by overcoming death through His own death and resurrection (LG 7).

From this it is clear that grace is rooted in the death and resurrection of God's Son, and that its effect in man—or rather, in all those who share this same human nature—consists in a new, redeemed (i.e., liberated) existence. What is more, redemption is not a possibility granted to the individual in isolation. Through grace it is the goal of the human race as a whole.

> God did not create man for life in isolation, but for the formation of social unity. So also "it has pleased God to make men holy and save them not merely as individuals . . . but by making them into a single people . . ."

. . . This communitarian character is developed and consummated in the work of Jesus Christ. For the very Word made flesh willed to share in human fellowship. He was present at the wedding of Cana, visited the house of Zacchaeus, ate with publicans and sinners. He revealed the love of the Father and the sublime vocation of man in terms of the most common of social realities . . . He chose to lead the life proper to an artisan of His time and place (GS 32).

Christ himself teaches us that not confusing human progress with the kingdom is not achieved by recognizing two distinct spheres of interests and values and then looking for ways to unite them. Grace creates the new humanity, i.e., the new creature, carrying beyond any merely human potentialities the social relationships that unite men into one single humanity in history. This is not to say that we could tell precisely how far these human potentialities could go on their own:

> For the more unified the world becomes, the more plainly do the offices of men extend beyond particular groups and spread by degrees to the whole world. But this challenge cannot be met unless individual men and their associations cultivate in themselves the moral and social virtues, and promote them in society. Thus, with the needed help of divine grace, men who are truly new and artisans of a new humanity can be forthcoming (GS 30).

Thus when the Council affirms that the Church possesses things which do not come from men but from God, it does not affirm that these things have value independently of the construction of history:

> Christ, to be sure, gave His Church no proper mission in the political, economic or social order. The purpose which He set before her is a religious one. But out of this religious mission itself come a function, a light, and an energy which can serve to structure and consolidate the human community . . . (GS 42).

If by "religious" mission we meant a realm of means and activities whose working out did not go through the political, economic, or social orders, then human activity and the activity of grace would be not only distinct but separated. But this is not true:

> The promotion of unity belongs to the innermost nature of the Church, since she is, "by her relationship with Christ, both a sacramental sign and an instrument of intimate union with God, and of the unity of all mankind" (GS 42).

As is evident, the proper and innermost mission of the Church works toward the unity, not only of believers, but also of the whole human race. She has indeed received from Christ elements that will aid this unity and that are properly her own. For lack of a better word, the Council calls them "religious." But we must be careful to correct a false idea of what "religious" means. There are some people who erroneously

> think that religion consists in acts of worship alone and in the discharge of certain moral obligations, and who imagine they can plunge themselves into earthly affairs in such a way as to imply that these are altogether divorced from the religious life. This split between the faith which many profess and their daily lives deserves to be counted among the more serious errors of our age. . . . Therefore, let there be no false opposition between

professional and social activities on the one part, and religious [other (GS 43).

B. THE "NEW EARTH"

We can make the same observations with regard to anothe texts. They refer not so much to man in human society as to m with things and events (i.e., with the universe and the world).

Right at the outset, *Lumen gentium* talks about the un comes from the gift of Christ and which culminates in the unity procures in history through society, technology, and culture:

> The conditions of this age lend special urgency to the Churc bringing all men to full union with Christ, since mankind tod together more closely than ever by social, technical and cul (LG 1).

In reality, what we have in this passage is a parallel though l version of what we saw in the earlier passage about "neither cor separating" two distinct but united realities. We must contin that is already there, but its plenitude comes from somethin passes the power of the human means we may employ: the gif

This point is explicated even more clearly in a passage o constitution that describes the universality of the one and onl God:

> Since the kingdom of Christ is not of this world (cf. John Church or People of God takes nothing away from the temp of any people by establishing that kingdom. Rather does sh take to herself, insofar as they are good, the ability, resources, of each people. Taking them to herself, she purifies, strength nobles them . . . This characteristic of universality which add ple of God is a gift from the Lord Himself. By reason of it, Church strives energetically and constantly to bring all huma its riches back to Christ its Head in the unity of His Spirit (LG 1

Hence it is most important for us to realize that it is the very ities that help to advance both the order of creation and t redemption. This is what the Council tries to bring home to who works in the temporal arena:

> The laity, by their very vocation, seek the kingdom of God b temporal affairs and by ordering them according to the plan live in the world, that is, in each and in all of the secular p occupations . . . They are called there by God so that by e proper function and being led by the spirit of the gospel they the sanctification of the world from within, in the manner o It is therefore their special task to illumine and organize th such a way that they may always start out, develop, and per to Christ's mind, to the praise of the Creator and the Redeemer

We can therefore readily see that the distinction discussed i passages cannot be based on a classification of the tasks inv more insofar as they are declared to be united. It is *the wa* out the very same temporal tasks that ordains them to the p

way the world is permeated by the spirit of Christ and more effectively achieves its purpose in justice, charity, and peace. The laity have the principal role in the universal fulfillment of this purpose. Therefore, by their competence in secular fields and by their personal activity, elevated from within by the grace of Christ, let them labor vigorously so that by human labor . . . created goods may be perfected for the benefit of every last man, according to the design of the Creator and the light of His Word. Let them work to see that created goods are more fittingly distributed among men, and that such goods in their own way lead to general progress in human and Christian liberty (LG 36).

Chapter Three

(This Chapter in particular picks up perspectives that are presented in Volume I of this series: *The Community Called Church.* In that volume one will find a fuller panoply of pertinent conciliar texts and related discussions.)

Here again we find a passage in *Lumen gentium* that sums up the point about the breadth of grace. It does it, so to speak, by following the process we are trying to follow in this volume: i.e., moving from an awareness of "Christian" grace to an appreciation of "human" grace (that is, grace granted to humanity). The conciliar text says this:

At all times and among every people, God has given welcome to whosoever fears Him and does what is right (cf. Acts 10:35). It has pleased God, however, to make men holy and save them not merely as individuals without any mutual bonds, but by making them into a single people . . . (LG 9).

This people is the Church. But while it may seem to reduce humanity to a concrete group, in reality this group is not the end result but rather a seed destined to take on a total universality that transcends all time:

That messianic people has for its head Christ, "who was delivered up for our sins, and rose again for our justification" (Rom. 4:25), and who now, having won a name which is above all names, reigns in glory in heaven. The heritage of this people are the dignity and freedom of the sons of God, in whose hearts the Holy Spirit dwells as in His temple. Its law is the new commandment to love as Christ loved us (cf. John 13:34). Its goal is the kingdom of God, which has been begun by God Himself on earth, and which is to be further extended until it is brought to perfection by Him at the end of time. Then Christ our life (cf. Col. 3:4) will appear, and "creation itself will be delivered from its slavery to corruption into the freedom of the glory of the sons of God" (Rom. 8:21) (LG 9).

Thus there is a process of growth for the kingdom, one which is not quantitative but qualitative. It will keep growing until, at the end of time, the *Christic* quality of the whole universe shows that it embraces humanity and the entire universe, even quantitatively:

So it is that this messianic people, although it does not actually include all men, and may more than once look like a small flock, is nonetheless a lasting and sure seed of unity, hope, and salvation for the whole human race (LG 9).

So here we have the two essential elements of the theme under discussion right now:

a) The intrinsic *content* of this people, which represents the universal "sacrament of unity," is the freedom to put love in the service of the entire universe.

b) The ultimate but already assured *extent* of this people is the whole human race—even though "appearances" may not seem to bear that out "at the moment." The full flowering of the Church's perfection will be the appearance of its authentic reality which is now gestating in secret:

> The Church, to which we are all called in Christ Jesus, and in which we acquire sanctity through the grace of God, will attain her full perfection only in the glory of heaven. Then will come the time of the restoration of all things (Acts 3:21). Then the human race as well as the entire world, which is intimately related to man and achieves its purpose through Him, will be perfectly re-established in Christ (cf. Eph. 1:10; Col. 1:20; 2 Peter 3:10–13) (LG 48).

A. THE SUPERNATURAL SOLIDARITY OF HUMAN BEINGS

The Church's characteristic of universality will be made manifest— that is the technical meaning of the word *glory*, which the Council uses in imitation of Saint Paul—with the final recapitulation of the universe and its history in Christ:

> At the end of time she will achieve her glorious fulfillment. Then, as may be read in the holy Fathers, all just men from the time of Adam, "from Abel, the just one, to the last of the elect," will be gathered together with the Father in the universal Church (LG 2).

This passage indicates that the participation is already real even though hidden. In another decree, the Council sets forth the theological foundation of this participation. It is the "supernatural solidarity" that exists between Christ and human beings—hence between all human beings themselves, be they Christians or not:

> The greatest commandment in the law is to love God with one's whole heart and one's neighbor as oneself (cf. Matt. 22:37–40). Christ made this commandment of love of neighbor His own and enriched it with a new meaning. For He wanted to identify Himself with His brethren as the object of this love when He said, "As long as you did it for one of these, the least of my brethren, you did it for me" (Matt. 25:40). Taking on human nature. He bound the whole human race to Himself as a family through a certain supernatural solidarity . . . (AA 8).

When we understand this, we will draw the same conclusion that *Gaudium et spes* does from this premiss. By faith we know for sure what *our* Christian existence is:

> By His incarnation the Son of God has united Himself in some fashion with every man . . . The Christian man, conformed to the likeness of that Son who is the firstborn of many brothers, receives "the first-fruits of the Spirit" (Rom. 8:23) by which he becomes capable of discharging the new law of love. Through this Spirit, who is "the pledge of our inheritance" (Eph. 1:14), the whole man is renewed from within, even to the achievement of "the redemption of the body" (Rom. 8:23) . . . Linked with the paschal mystery and patterned on the dying Christ, he will hasten forward to resurrection in the strength which comes from hope (GS 22).

Now it is precisely when it arrives at this point that the Council realizes that faith goes even further and relativizes itself, so to speak. By this we mean that faith comes to recognize, through its own revealed content, that it is not necessary *to know* all this in order to participate actively in this reality. In other words: by virtue of faith insofar as it sees the breadth of saving grace—the grace of the Church—it goes beyond faith insofar as it is explicit recognition of revelation:

> All this holds true not only for Christians, but for all men of good will in whose hearts grace works in an unseen way. For, since Christ died for all men, and since the ultimate vocation of man is in fact one, and divine, we ought to believe that the Holy Spirit, in a manner known only to God, offers to every man the possibility of being associated with this paschal mystery (GS 22).

B. LIBERATING FAITH

There are, as it were, four stages in this conceptual incorporation of the man of good will into the universal reality of the Church through faith. They also represent the stages through which faith liberates the Christian from any possible alienation that may come from the religious itself.

1. The first stage is the realization that access to faith, insofar as it is inscribed in the concrete coordinates of history, is not in the hands of a huge number of human beings. And that this is not *in spite of* the plan of God but *within it*. For in this plan, nothing is asked of man but that which is given to him:

> Those also can attain to everlasting salvation who through no fault of their own do not know the gospel of Christ or His Church, yet sincerely seek God and, moved by grace, strive by their deeds to do His will as it is known to them through the dictates of conscience. Nor does divine Providence deny the help necessary for salvation to those who, without blame on their part, have not yet arrived at an explicit knowledge of God, but who strive to live a good life, thanks to His grace. Whatever goodness or truth is found among them is looked upon by the Church as a preparation for the Gospel (LG 16).

2. An "upright life," then, is the work of grace; it is the divine life in us. And the foregoing passage helps us to accept the fact that such an upright life entails an incipient faith: i.e., a knowledge of God, even though it be obscure, and a confident entrusting of oneself to this power that is God himself operating within. Hence the obligation to explicitly accept faith, and the Church takes effect only when faith and the Church are seen to be the next step in the fulfillment of the dynamism represented by upright living, love, and "supernatural solidarity."

> Whosoever, therefore, knowing that the Catholic Church was made necessary by God through Jesus Christ, would refuse to enter her or to remain in her could not be saved (LG 14).

3. Now some might think that this "necessity" is to be conceived in legal terms. But that is not the case. Following the inner logic of the idea, the same conciliar passage goes on to take a further step that explains and confirms the previous step. It points out that accepting faith

and the Church serves no purpose unless it is done within the framework
of growing love:

> He is not saved, however, who, though he is part of the body of the Church,
> does not persevere in charity. He remains indeed in the bosom of the
> Church, but, as it were, only in a "bodily" manner and not "in his heart"
> . . . If they fail moreover to respond to that grace . . . not only will they
> not be saved but they will be the more severely judged (LG 14).

4. This is precisely another one of the features of man's total liberation. In effect humanity knows that it stands before God, and hence before
all men. Thus, through faith, we receive the good news that faith does not
separate human beings from each other or subordinate one person to
another. Faith itself prevents us from accepting faith as some sort of magic
that gives some people privileges over others, and that justifies us in restricting the liberty of others for their own good. Quite the contrary is
true. Here faith and the Church are seen to be in the service of love, so
that man is liberated from the enslavement of religion. Insofar as religion separates human beings from one another and turns them into
mere instruments, it is just like any other form of enslavement. And the
Council rejects them all:

> Since they have the same nature and origin, have been redeemed by Christ
> and enjoy the same divine calling and destiny, the basic equality of all
> (men) must receive increasingly greater recognition . . . With respect to
> the fundamental rights of the person, every type of discrimination . . .
> whether based on sex, race, color, social condition, language, or religion, is
> to be overcome and eradicated as contrary to God's intent (GS 29).

Paradoxically enough, it is precisely the Christian faith which, in the
Council's words,

> manifests God's design for man's total vocation (GS 11).

Here we have the depth of grace that enables us to take an overview of
the entire course of human history:

> The Lord is the goal of human history, the focal point of the longings of
> history and of civilization, the center of the human race, the joy of every
> heart and the answer to all its yearnings. He it is whom the Father raised
> from the dead, lifted on high and stationed at His right hand, making Him
> judge of the living and the dead. Enlivened and united in His Spirit, we
> journey toward the consummation of human history, one which fully accords
> with the counsel of God's love: "To re-establish all things in Christ, both
> those in the heavens and those on the earth" (Eph. 11:10) (GS 45).

Chapter Four

Lumen gentium also sums up the deep transformation effected by the
grace of Christ, whose breadth has already suggested certain things to us:

> The followers of Christ are called by God, not according to their accomplish-
> ments, but according to His own purpose and grace. They are justified in
> the Lord Jesus, and through baptism sought in faith they truly become sons
> of God and sharers in the divine nature. In this way they are really made
> holy. Then, too, by God's gifts they must hold on to and complete in their
> lives this holiness which they have received. They are warned by the Apostle

to live "as becomes saints" (Eph. 5:3), and to put on "as God's chosen ones, holy and beloved, a heart of mercy, kindness, humility, meekness, patience" (Col. 3:12), and to possess the fruits of the Spirit unto holiness (cf. Gal. 5:22; Rom. 6:22). Since we all truly offend in many things (cf. James 3:2), we all need God's mercy continuously and must pray daily: "Forgive us our debts" (Matt. 6:12) (LG 40).

Paradoxically enough, the Council does not see any excuse for failure here; it sees only the surety of triumph:

Thus it is evident to everyone that all the faithful of Christ . . . are called to the fullness of the Christian life and to the perfection of charity. By this holiness a more human way of life is promoted (LG 40).

This passage reiterates the doctrine of Trent, but with a different stress. From it we can see several things:

a) Justification comes from God, not from any possibility of man being able to pass the test of his innocence before some criterion of the law. Moreover, it is evident that sin forms a structural, day-to-day part of our life; no holiness can exist without sharing in sin and being supported by mercy. Thus we are framed within gratuitousness.

b) Despite this fact, and by virtue of God's mercy, holiness does "really" exist. It is not a condition for the gift of justification but rather its fruit and end product. In other words, we are not only *objects* but also *subjects* of this gratuitousness. God's creative rather than juridic mercy is profoundly interiorized within us. His benignancy turns into a benign attitude in us, and his creative love for us turns into man's creative love for the new earth.

A. SIMUL PECCATOR ET JUSTUS (sinner and upright at the same time)

Seeking to bring the Church face to face with the world, the Council examines the profound reality of sin more in societal terms than in individual terms. This framework is valid for all times in any case, even though it is more apparent today with the growing socialization of the planet:

Man's social nature makes it evident that the progress of the human person and the advance of society itself hinge on each other (GS 25).

Thus man must face the fact that sin often forms an integral part of the very structure of his existence in society:

When the structure of affairs is flawed by the consequences of sin, man, already born with a bent toward evil, finds there new inducements to sin, which cannot be overcome without strenuous efforts and the assistance of grace (GS 25).

When we hear this last phrase, however, we must be careful not to understand this effort as the initiative of the individual who, starting from innocence, says no to temptation. The human person and society condition each other mutually. So the effort which grace sustains must be an effort to liberate from the structures of sin the society to which we belong and of which we are both "victims and causes" (GS 8).

What is more, on this terrain we cannot be victorious in a definitive

way or for an extended period of time. But neither are we to take the
track of Sisyphus, going back to the beginning and starting over again in
order to achieve some absolute purity in our work of societal construction:

> The social order and its development must unceasingly work to the benefit
> of the human person if the disposition of affairs is to be subordinate to the
> personal realm and not contrariwise. This is what Our Lord implied when
> He said that the Sabbath was made for man, and not man for the Sabbath.
> This social order requires constant improvement. It must be founded on
> truth, built on justice, and animated by love; in freedom it should grow
> every day toward a more humane balance . . . Widespread changes in
> society will have to take place if these objectives are to be gained (GS 26).

Thus these reforms cannot be made once for all time, no matter how
deep and thoroughgoing they may be. We must keep pushing forward to
find a balance that proves amenable to man's creative liberty. Or, to put
it another way, we must keep looking for a balance that makes man a
subject rather than an object of history.

Hence we could say that sin is not surmountable on either the individual or the social level, but that it is always possible to resurrect oneself from it, from its death:

> Hence if anyone wants to know how this unhappy situation can be over-
> come, Christians will tell him that all human activity, constantly imperiled
> by man's pride and deranged self-love, must be purified and perfected by
> the power of Christ's cross and resurrection (GS 37).

B. LOVE'S VICTORY

Despite all these obstacles, however, love will be victorious and the
resurrection will have the final word:

> In Him [i.e., Christ] God reconciled us to Himself and among ourselves.
> He delivered us from bondage to the devil and sin . . . The Christian man,
> conformed to the likeness of that Son . . . receives "the first-fruits of the
> Spirit" (Rom. 8:23) by which he became capable of discharging the new
> law of love. Through this Spirit . . . the whole man is renewed from
> within, even to the achievement of "the redemption of the body" (Rom.
> 8:23) (GS 22).

Here again it is not an individual victory but the victory of all history.
From this history of sin and holiness, which are ever united, there wells
up love and liberty. But is it not true that the latter will once more be
submerged by new waves of egotism and enslavement?

> Throughout the course of the centuries, men have labored to better the
> circumstances of their lives through a monumental amount of individual
> and collective effort. To believers, this point is settled: considered in itself,
> this human activity accords with God's will . . . Thus, far from thinking
> that works produced by man's own talent and energy are in opposition to
> God's power . . . Christians are convinced that the triumphs of the human
> race are a sign of God's greatness and the flowering of His own mysterious
> design (GS 34).

How can we arrive at such a judgment on the totality of history and
present it as the judgment of God himself? Whence derives this disproportionate evaluation of victory and success over against failures and

defeats? It derives from the *radical unbalance* between the constructive power of love and the destructive power of egotism—as seen by Christian faith. As the Council notes, love covers a multitude of sins (1 Pet. 4:8) on whatever level it operates, including the level of history:

> We are taught that God is preparing . . . a new earth . . . Then, with death overcome, the sons of God will be raised up in Christ, and what was sown in weakness and corruption will be clothed with incorruptibility. While charity and its works endure, all that creation which God made on man's account will be unchained from the bondage of vanity (GS 39).

The Council is sure about the disproportion between the end result of love and the end result of egotism. And the basis of this sureness is the text of Saint Paul that talks about God's judgment on what we have done with our life. The edifice we build will be composed of mixed elements. Only those fashioned by love and designed for eternity will withstand God's judgmental fire (1 Cor. 3:14).

APPENDIX III

A Biblical Tapestry

God's gift, grace, shows up first as a desire that God placed within the existence of his people. It was nourished and purified by the preaching of the prophets. Then, with the ushering in of the "now" that echoes through Paul's letters, it shows up as a fulfilled reality.

Here we shall examine each of the dimensions of grace that we have discussed chapter by chapter, indicating the ancient promise and its definitive fulfillment in the Bible.

Chapter One

A. PROMISE

1. **The remnant, universal law of God's gift-giving:** From Adam to the inception of the chosen people:

[God's] Wisdom it was who kept guard over the first father of the human race, when he alone had yet been made; she saved him after his fall, and gave him the strength to master all things . . . The earth was covered with a deluge, and again wisdom came to the rescue, and taught the one good man to pilot his plain wooden hulk. It was she, when heathen nations leagued in wickedness were thrown into confusion, who picked out one good man and kept him blameless in the sight of God, giving him strength to resist his pity for his child. She saved a good man from the destruction of the godless, and he escaped the fire that came down on the Five Cities . . . It was she, when a good man was a fugitive from his brother's anger, who guided him on the straight path . . . It was she who refused to desert a good man when he was sold as a slave; she preserved him from sin and went down into the dungeon with him . . . It was she who rescued a god-fearing people, a blameless race, from a nation of oppressors (Wis. 10:1–15).

Even for the chosen people, the same law of majority misdeeds applies:

The glory of [Israel's] forest and meadow shall be destroyed as when a man falls in a fit; and the remnant of trees in the forest shall be so few that a child may count them one by one. On that day the remnant of Israel, the survivors of Jacob, shall cease to lean on him that proved their destroyer, but shall loyally lean on the Lord, the Holy One of Israel. A remnant shall turn again, a remnant of Jacob, to God their champion. Your people, Israel, may be many as the sands of the sea, but only a remnant shall turn again, the instrument of final destruction, justice in full flood; for the Lord, the Lord of Hosts, will bring final destruction upon all the earth (Isa. 10:18–23).

This remnant is *a gift*, a product of divine love:

> The survivors left in Judah shall strike fresh root under ground and yield
> fruit above ground, for a remnant shall come out of Jerusalem and survivors
> from Mount Zion. The zeal of the Lord of Hosts will perform this (Isa.
> 37:31–32).

The remnant will be composed specifically of those who receive the gift
for what it is, a gift:

> On that day, says the Lord, I will gather those who are lost; I will assemble
> the exiles and I will strengthen the weaklings. I will preserve the lost as a
> remnant and turn the derelict into a mighty nation. The Lord shall be
> their king on Mount Zion now and for ever (Mic. 4:6–7).

> For then I will rid you of your proud and arrogant citizens, and never
> again shall you flaunt your pride in my holy hill. But I will leave in you a
> people afflicted and poor. The survivors in Israel shall find refuge in the
> name of the Lord; they shall no longer do wrong . . . (Zeph. 3:11–13).

2. The root germ, a new beginning ushered in by God's gift: Here is
the judgment that God passes on his people as a whole during the Exodus:

> Then the Lord said to me, "I have considered this people and I find them
> a stubborn people. Let me be, and I will destroy them and blot out their
> name from under heaven; and of you alone I will make a nation more
> powerful and numerous than they" . . . and I prayed to the Lord and
> said, "O Lord God, do not destroy thy people, thy own possession, whom
> thou didst redeem by thy great power . . ." (Deut. 9:13–14, 26).

So Yahweh does not decide to destroy his people and replace them with
another people. But he does decide to destroy what is recalcitrant in
them, and it is the task of the prophet to reveal this:

> This day I give you authority over nations and over kingdoms, to pull down
> and to uproot, to destroy and to demolish, to build and to plant (Jer. 1:10).

Now it is not a question of substituting one plant for another; it is a
matter of *renewing*. The new here does not signify "another," but the
same thing in a different state: a state quite different from its former
decrepitude and rigidity.

> Then I asked, How long, O Lord? And he answered, Until cities fall in ruins
> and are deserted, houses are left without people, and the land goes to ruin
> and lies waste, until the Lord has sent all mankind far away, and the whole
> country is one vast desolation. Even if a tenth part of its people remain
> there, they too will be exterminated like an oak or a terebinth, a sacred
> pole thrown out from its place in a hill-shrine* (Isa. 6:11–13).

Rigidity is replaced by vitality:

> I will sprinkle clean water over you . . . I will give you a new heart and
> put a new spirit within you; I will take the heart of stone from your body
> and give you a heart of flesh (Ezek. 36:25–26).

---

* Translator's note: The Hebrew of the last phrase is obscure. Closer to the
Spanish text here is the translation of the NAB: "As with a terebinth or an
oak whose trunk remains when its leaves have fallen. Holy offspring is the trunk."

The focusing and fulfillment of this renovation around this germ takes on messianic perspectives. Christ is the germ:

> Then a shoot shall grow from the stock of Jesse, and a branch shall spring from his roots. The spirit of the Lord shall rest upon him, a spirit of wisdom and understanding, a spirit of counsel and power, a spirit of knowledge and the fear of the Lord . . . He shall judge the poor with justice and defend the humble in the land with equity (Isa. 11:1–4).

B. FULFILLMENT

1. **Man's condition according to Paul:** In the writings of Paul, the universal perspective of majority misdeeds and saved remnant ceases to characterize historical groups of human beings. It becomes the inner, existential situation of each and every human being—a situation that is heartrending and incomprehensible:

> I do not even acknowledge my own actions as mine, for what I do is not what I want to do, but what I detest (Rom. 7:15).

Here, too, an ineradicable remnant remains. It is the portion of our being that wants to do good, but that is dominated by the might and reach of the other portion that performs evil deeds:

> But if what I do is against my will, it means that I agree with the law and hold it to be admirable. But as things are, it is no longer I who perform the action, but sin that lodges in me. For I know that nothing good lodges in me—in my unspiritual nature, I mean—for though the will to do good is there, the deed is not (Rom. 7:16–18).

This fleshly, unspiritual nature, this incomparable power that dominates what I actually do, is the impersonal in me:

> The good which I want to do, I fail to do; but what I do is the wrong which is against my will; and if what I do is against my will, clearly it is no longer I who am the agent, but sin that has its lodging in me. I discover this principle, then: that when I want to do the right, only the wrong is within my reach. In my inmost self I delight in the law of God, but I perceive that there is in my bodily members a different law, fighting against the law that my reason approves and making me a prisoner under the law that is in my members, the law of sin (Rom. 7:19–23).

God's liberating gift comes to us when we are caught in the trammels of this situation:

> Through Jesus Christ our Lord! Thanks be to God! . . . because in Christ Jesus the life-giving law of the Spirit has set you free from the law of sin and death (Rom. 7:25–8:2).

2. **Threats posed to the Christian outlook by the flesh (i.e., the human condition):** We must not think that the victory of grace signifies a suppression of the prior condition. Without God's continuing work in us, the human condition can disfigure, falsify and render vain the Christian way of life itself:

> But now that you do acknowledge God [i.e., are in a personal relationship with him]—or rather, now that he has acknowledged you [i.e., it is his gift] —how can you turn back to the mean and beggarly spirits of the elements?

> Why do you propose to enter their service all over again? You keep special days and months and seasons and years. You make me fear that all the pains I spent on you may prove to be labour lost (Gal. 4:9–11).

Paul describes the threat posed by the old to the new, by the human condition to God's gift, in various oppositional pairs. In all of them, the authenticity of Christianity is associated with a truly personal way of life while the fleshly, unspiritual attitude is associated with a surrender to the impersonal on the very plane of religious life. The first opposition is between the letter and the spirit:

> While we lived on the level of our lower nature, the sinful passions evoked by the law worked in our bodies, to bear fruit for death. But now, having died to that which held us bound, we are discharged from the law, to serve God in a new way, the way of the spirit, in contrast to the old way, the way of a written code (Rom. 7:5–6).

The second opposition, which explains the first, is between fear and a filial outlook:

> For all who are moved by the Spirit of God are [and act as] sons of God. The Spirit you have received is not a spirit of slavery leading you back into a life of fear, but a Spirit that makes us sons, enabling us to cry "Abba! Father!" (Rom. 8:14–15).

> This is what I mean: so long as the heir is a minor, he is no better off than a slave, even though the whole estate is his; he is under guardians and trustees until the date fixed by his father. And so it was with us. During our minority we were slaves to the elemental spirits of the universe, but when the term was completed, God sent his own Son, born of a woman, born under the law, to purchase freedom for the subjects of the law, in order that we might attain the status of sons. To prove that you are sons, God has sent into our hearts the Spirit of his Son, crying "Abba! Father!" (Gal. 4:1–6).

The same opposition, in almost the very same terms, is found in the first Epistle of John:

> Thus we have come to know and believe the love which God has for us. God is love; he who dwells in love is dwelling in God, and God in him. This is for us the perfection of love, to have confidence on the day of judgement, and this we can have, because even in this world we are as he is. There is no room for fear in love; perfect love banishes fear. For fear brings with it the pains of judgement, and anyone who is afraid has not attained to love in its perfection. We love because he loved us first. But if a man says, "I love God," while hating his brother, he is a liar. If he does not love the brother whom he has seen, it cannot be that he loves God whom he has not seen. And indeed this command comes to us from Christ himself; that he who loves God must also love his brother (1 John 4:16–21).

This opposition between fear and filial love is translated concretely into a third opposition between works and faith, or if you will, between enslavement and freedom with respect to the law:

> You stupid Galatians! You must have been bewitched—you before whose eyes Jesus Christ was openly displayed upon his cross! Answer me one question: did you receive the Spirit by keeping the law or by believing the

gospel message? Can it be that you are so stupid? You started with the spiritual; do you now look to the material to make you perfect? Have all your great experiences been in vain . . . (Gal. 3:1–4).

Christ set us free, to be free men. Stand firm, then, and refuse to be tied to the yoke of slavery again. Mark my words: I, Paul, say to you that if you receive circumcision Christ will do you no good at all . . . When you seek to be justified by way of law, your relation with Christ is completely severed: you have fallen out of the domain of God's grace . . . You, my friends, were called to be free men; only do not turn your freedom into licence for your lower nature, but be servants to one another in love (Gal. 5:1–4, 13).

From this we get a fourth opposition between contract and promise. The ancient law, as well as the full-blown Church, should not be taken as clauses of a contract but as fulfillments of God's promise—the former being a partial fulfillment, the latter its definitive fulfillment. The Church is not a condition of the gift, it is the gift itself.

My brothers, let me give you an illustration. Even in ordinary life, when a man's will and testament has been duly executed, no one else can set it aside or add a codicil. Now the promises were pronounced to Abraham . . . What I am saying is this: a testament, or covenant, had already been validated by God; it cannot be invalidated, and its promises rendered ineffective, by a law made four hundred and thirty years later (Gal. 3:15–17).

You are still on the merely natural plane. Can you not see that while there is jealousy and strife among you, you are living on the purely human level of your lower nature? When one says, "I am Paul's man," and another, "I am for Apollos," are you not all too human? After all, what is Apollos? What is Paul? We are simply God's agents in bringing you to the faith . . . So never make mere men a cause for pride. For though everything belongs to you—Paul, Apollos, and Cephas, the world, life and death, the present and the future, all of them belong to you—yet you belong to Christ, and Christ to God (1 Cor. 3:3—5:21–22).

Chapter Two

A. PROMISE

1. Relationship between history and morality: From the start of the preaching by the prophets, God uses the notion of covenant to turn the eyes of Israel toward a history whose end result is in accord with man's moral outlook. Thus fidelity to God is synonymous with success:

She [Israel, his bride] says, "I will go after my lovers; they give me my food and drink, my wool and flax, my oil and my perfumes." Therefore I will block her road with thorn-bushes and obstruct her path with a wall, so that she can no longer follow her old ways. When she pursues her lovers she will not overtake them, when she looks for them, she will not find them; then she will say, "I will go back to my husband again; I was better off with him than I am now." For she does not know that it is I who gave her corn, new wine, and oil . . . (Hos. 2:5–7).

From this there derives the idealistic image of a history that corresponds exactly to man's moral conduct:

Happy is the man who does not take the wicked for his guide nor walk the road that sinners tread nor take his seat among the scornful; the law of the Lord is his delight, the law his meditation night and day. He is like a tree planted beside a watercourse, which yields its fruit in season and its leaf never withers; in all that he does he prospers. Wicked men are not like this; they are like chaff driven by the wind (Ps. 1:1–4).

Obviously the biggest success is life, life in full measure and extended for a long time:

At this time Hezekiah fell dangerously ill and the prophet Isaiah, son of Amoz, came to him and said, "This is the word of the Lord: Give your last instructions to your household, for you are a dying man and will not recover." Hezekiah turned his face to the wall and offered this prayer to the Lord: "O Lord, remember how I have lived before thee, faithful and loyal in thy service, always doing what was good in thine eyes." And he wept bitterly. Then the word of the Lord came to Isaiah: "Go and say to Hezekiah: 'This is the word of the Lord, the God of your father David: I have heard your prayer and seen your tears; I will add fifteen years to your life. I will deliver you and this city from the king of Assyria and will protect this city' " (Isa. 38:1–6).

But as one comes to comprehend God's transcendence, it becomes more difficult to pray as sincerely as Hezekiah. Why?

A word stole into my ears, and they caught the whisper of it; in the anxious visions of the night, when a man sinks into deepest sleep, terror seized me and shuddering; the trembling of my body frightened me. A wind brushed my face and made the hairs bristle on my flesh; and a figure stood there whose shape I could not discern, an apparition loomed before me, and I heard the sound of a low voice: "Can mortal man be more righteous than God, or the creature purer than his Maker?" (Job 4:12–17)

2. Result: a more gratuitous-toned and eschatological perspective: If that is the case, then the covenant cannot be a contract. And experience confirms this:

There is an empty thing found on earth: when the just man gets what is due to the unjust, and the unjust what is due to the just. I maintain that this too is emptiness . . . I perceived that God has so ordered it that man should not be able to discover what is happening here under the sun . . . Everything that confronts him, everything is empty, since one and the same fate befalls everyone, just and unjust alike, good and bad, clean and unclean, the man who offers sacrifice and the man who does not (Eccles. 8:14–9:2).

Thus Israel's election by God (i.e., the covenant) cannot be anything but a gift. Ezekiel teaches this, using the image of a newborn babe:

The word of the Lord came to me: Man, he said . . . tell her [Jerusalem] that these are the words of the Lord God to her: Canaan is the land of your ancestry and there you were born; an Amorite was your father and a Hittite your mother. This is how you were treated at birth: when you were born, your navel string was not tied, you were not bathed in water ready for the rubbing, you were not salted as you should have been nor wrapped in swaddling clothes. No one cared for you enough to do any of these things . . . Then I came by and saw you . . . I spoke to you . . . and bade you live. I tended you like an evergreen plant, like something growing in the fields . . . (Ezek. 16:1–7).

Now knowledge of all this gratuitous treatment does not suppress the imperious desire for a full life and a just world. But now this perspective is framed in "the last days," on the eschatological plane. For each individual man there will be a judgment on the far side of death, as the Book of Wisdom and that of Daniel prophesy:

> At that moment Michael shall appear, Michael the great captain, who stands guard over your fellow-countrymen; and there will be a time of distress such as has never been since they became a nation till that moment. But at that moment your people will be delivered, every one who is written in the book: many of those who sleep in the dust of the earth will wake, some to ever-lasting life and some to the reproach of eternal abhorrence . . . I heard but I did not understand, and so I said, "Sir, what will the issue of these things be?" He replied, "Go your way, Daniel, for the words are kept secret and sealed till the time of the end. Many shall purify themselves and be refined, making themselves shining white, but the wicked shall continue in wickedness . . ." (Dan. 12:1–2, 8–10).

Now is it not natural that this finale should be conceived in the colors and things of this present existence? Following the passage cited earlier, which talks about a shoot from the stock of Jesse triumphing over the old, the new life is depicted in these terms:

> Then the wolf shall live with the sheep, and the leopard lie down with the kid; the calf and the young lion shall grow up together, and a little child shall lead them; the cow and the bear shall be friends, and their young shall lie down together. The lion shall eat straw like cattle; the infant shall play over the hole of the cobra, and the young child dance over the viper's nest. They shall not hurt or destroy in all my holy mountain; for as the waters fill the sea, so shall the land be filled with the knowledge of the Lord (Isa. 11:6–9).

In an almost identical passage with the same outlook, Yahweh sums up this ultimate prospect:

> For behold, I create new heavens and a new earth. Former things shall no more be remembered nor shall they be called to mind (Isa. 65:17).

The just man waits patiently for this final day:

> But the souls of the just are in God's hand . . . Though in the sight of men they may be punished, they have a sure hope of immortality; and after a little chastisement they will receive great blessings, because God has tested them and found them worthy to be his. Like gold in a crucible he put them to the proof, and found them acceptable like an offering burnt whole upon the altar (Wis. 3:1–6).

> Then the just man shall take his stand, full of assurance, to confront those who oppressed him and made light of all his sufferings (Wis. 5:1).

B. FULFILLMENT

1. Continuity between this earth and the new one: Christian revelation specifically seeks to show that the world of time is not simply a testing ground but also the building up of eternal life in history:

> Then the king will say to those on his right hand, "You have my Father's blessing; come, enter and possess the kingdom that has been ready for you since the world was made. For when I was hungry, you gave me food; when

thirsty, you gave me drink . . ." Then the righteous will reply, "Lord, when was it that we saw you hungry and fed you, or thirsty and gave you drink . . . ?" And the king will answer, "I tell you this: anything you did for one of my brothers here, however humble, you did for me . . ." The righteous will enter eternal life (Matt. 25:34–46).

In this perspective all the dynamisms of creation long to serve the cause. of eternal life; only thus will they fulfill their deeper destiny:

For the created universe waits with eager expectation for God's sons to be revealed. It was made the victim of frustration, not by its own choice, but because of him who made it so; yet always there was hope, because the universe itself is to be freed from the shackles of mortality and enter upon the liberty and splendour of the children of God. Up to the present, we know, the whole created universe groans in all its parts as if in the pangs of childbirth (Rom. 8:19–22).

2. Discontinuity: This is indicated by the word "new" and refers simply to the *gratuitousness* of the whole process.

From the second chapter of John's Gospel to almost the end of the fourth chapter we have what has been called "the new beginnings": the new cult, the new manna, the new purifications. It is not given to man to enter these new beginnings. It requires a new birth or a birth from on high (i.e., through elevating grace). The ambiguity of the latter phrase was probably consciously intended by John.

There was one of the Pharisees named Nicodemus, a member of the Jewish Council, who came to Jesus by night. "Rabbi," he said, "we know that you are a teacher sent by God; no one could perform these signs of yours unless God were with him." Jesus answered, "In truth, in very truth I tell you, unless a man has been born over again he cannot see the kingdom of God." "But how is it possible," said Nicodemus, "for a man to be born when he is old? Can he enter his mother's womb a second time and be born?" Jesus answered, "In truth I tell you, no one can enter the kingdom of God without being born from water and spirit. Flesh can give birth only to flesh; it is spirit that gives birth to spirit. You ought not to be astonished, then, when I tell you that you must be born over again. The wind blows where it wills; you hear the sound of it, but you do not know where it comes from, or where it is going. So with everyone who is born from spirit" (John 3:1–8).

Thus Paul calls Christian existence a "new creation." It is as if we had been created again, but as ourselves. Paul also calls it the "new man":

When anyone is united to Christ, there is a new world; the old order has gone, and a new order has already begun (2 Cor. 5:17).

Circumcision is nothing; uncircumcision is nothing; the only thing that counts is new creation (Gal. 6:15).

For he himself is our peace. Gentiles and Jews, he has made the two one, and in his own body of flesh and blood has broken down the enmity which stood like a dividing wall between them . . . so as to create out of the two a single new humanity in himself, thereby making peace. This was his purpose, to reconcile the two in a single body to God . . . (Eph. 2:14–16).

This new humanity, this new creation that already exists, will be consummated in the "new heavens and earth." Thanks to God's gift, the latter is the perfection of the former rather than a compensation for it. Here grace is the inception of the heaven and earth to come:

> But we have his promise, and look forward to new heavens and a new earth, the home of justice (2 Peter 3:13).

This is the vision of John in Revelation:

> Then I saw a new heaven and a new earth, for the first heaven and the first earth had vanished . . . I heard a loud voice proclaiming from the throne: "Now at last God has his dwelling among men! He will dwell among them and they shall be his people, and God himself will be with them. He will wipe every tear from their eyes; there shall be an end to death, and to mourning and crying and pain; for the old order has passed away!" Then he who sat on the throne said, "Behold! I am making all things new!" (Rev. 21:1–5).

Thus, thanks to grace which exalts our whole earth, a line of continuity runs from the bread we give to the humblest of men to the new heaven and earth.

Chapter Three

A. PROMISE

1. **Universal content of the covenant:** It is certain that their status as chosen people readily aroused sentiments of superficial exclusivism in the Israelites. But deep down this status contains evident elements of universalism. When Moses objected to God's desire to destroy sinful Israel and to fashion a new people from him, his reason was this:

> I prayed to the Lord and said, "O Lord God, do not destroy thy people, thy own possession, whom thou did redeem by thy great power and bring out of Egypt by thy strong hand. Remember thy servants, Abraham, Isaac and Jacob, and overlook the stubbornness of this people, their wickedness and their sin; otherwise the people in the land out of which thou didst lead us will say, 'It is because the Lord was not able to bring them into the land which he promised them . . . that he has led them out to kill them in the wilderness.' " (Deut. 9:26–28)

The fulfillment of the covenant and the success of Israel are thus turned into the universal manifestation of Yahweh:

> Have pity on us, O Lord, thou God of all; look down, and send thy terror upon all nations. Raise thy hand against the heathen, and let them see thy power. As they have seen thy holiness displayed among us, so let us see thy greatness displayed among them. Let them learn, as we also have learned, that there is no God but only thou, O Lord . . . Crush the heads of hostile princes, who say, "There is no one to match us." Gather all the tribes of Jacob, and grant them their inheritance, as thou didst long ago. Have pity, O Lord, on the people called by thy name, Israel, whom thou hast named thy first-born . . . Fill thy people with thy glory. Thou didst create them at the beginning; acknowledge them now and fulfill the prophecies spoken in thy name. Reward those who wait for thee; prove thy prophets trustworthy. Listen, O Lord, to the prayer of thy servants, who claim Aaron's blessing upon thy people. Let all who live on earth acknowledge that thou art the Lord, the eternal God (Eccles. 36:1–17).

This perspective is still exclusivist, but it evinces a certain universalism and even humility: Israel is a small instrument in the midst of the universe, which in those days was really Egypt and Assyria:

> The Lord will make himself known to the Egyptians; on that day they shall acknowledge the Lord and do him service with sacrifice and grain-offering, make vows to him and pay them . . . When that day comes there shall be a highway between Egypt and Assyria; Assyrians shall come to Egypt and Egyptians to Assyria; then Egyptians shall worship with Assyrians. When that day comes Israel shall rank with Egypt and Assyria, those three, and shall be a blessing in the centre of the world. So the Lord of Hosts will bless them: A blessing be upon Egypt my people, upon Assyria the work of my hands, and upon Israel my possession (Isa. 19:21–25).

2. Transcendence and universality: In the desert Israel begins to comprehend the whole import of God's creative work. The whole world is his creation. He governs all, and he expects from all the tribute of adoration and thanksgiving that befits a creature:

> God be gracious to us and bless us, God make his face shine upon us, that his ways may be known on earth and his saving power among all the nations. Let the people praise thee, O God; let all peoples praise thee. Let all nations rejoice and shout in triumph; for thou dost judge the peoples with justice and guidest the nations of the earth. Let the peoples praise thee, O God; let all peoples praise thee. The earth has given its increase and God, our God, will bless us. God grant us his blessing that all the ends of the earth may fear him (Ps. 67).

And the final vision of Deutero-Isaiah also opens up the same universal panorama to us:

> For, as the new heavens and the new earth which I am making shall endure in my sight, says the Lord, so shall your race and your name endure; and month by month at the new moon, week by week on the sabbath, all mankind shall come to bow down before me, says the Lord (Isa. 66:22–23).

B. FULFILLMENT

1. Breadth of grace's operation and effect: It is operative even where only an insignificant gesture would seem to be involved: e.g., offering a glass of water even without conscious reference to Christ (Matt. 25:40). For that which may frequently seem to be natural to us is already the byproduct of grace and the new creation:

> We for our part have crossed over from death to life; this we know, because we love our brothers (1 John 3:14).

The resurrection, for example, might seem to be a natural thing since it affects all men. But for Paul, it too is an effect of grace and its victory over sin:

> Then comes the end, when he delivers up the kingdom to God the Father, after abolishing every kind of domination, authority and power. For he is destined to reign until God has put all enemies under his feet; and the last enemy to be abolished is death (1 Cor. 15:24–26).

> And when our mortality has been clothed with immortality, then the saying of Scripture will come true: "Death is swallowed up; victory is won!" "O Death, where is your victory? O Death, where is your sting?" The sting of

death is sin, and sin gains its power from the law; but, God be praised, he gives us the victory through our Lord Jesus Christ (1 Cor. 54–57).

2. Breadth of grace's victory: It is victorious even where everything still depends on man's liberty. Thus it does not jeopardize the sureness of resurrection (which is a victory over sin) even though the latter too depends upon man's liberty. In Paul's case, for example:

> I count everything sheer loss, because all is far outweighed by the gain of knowing Christ Jesus my Lord . . . All I care is to know Christ, to experience the power of his resurrection . . . if only I may arrive at the resurrection of the dead. It is not to be thought that I have already achieved all this. I have not yet reached perfection, but I press on, hoping to take hold of that for which Christ once took hold of me (Phil. 3:8–12).

Thus, even with this conditional factor of freedom, Paul can assure us of the victory of grace. And its breadth is equivalent to the earlier victory of sin: i.e., it is universal. Let us read three comparisons that Paul makes in Romans: In the first comparison, he notes the breadth:

> But God's act of grace is out of all proportion to Adam's wrongdoing. For if the wrongdoing of that one man brought death upon so many [i.e., all], its effect is vastly exceeded by the grace of God and the gift that came to so many [i.e., all] by the grace of the one man, Jesus Christ (Rom. 5:15).

In the next verse, he compares the consequences. And he is not talking about possibilities, since the past tense of the preceding verse already excludes that interpretation:

> And again, the gift of God is not to be compared in its effect with that one man's sin; for the judicial action, following upon the one offence, issued in a verdict of condemnation, but the act of grace, following upon so many misdeeds, issued in a verdict of acquittal (Rom. 5:16).

In the next verse, he compares the final consequences: death or life. Here we shall add a similar passage from Corinthians where the theme of resurrection enters the picture:

> For if by the wrongdoing of that one man death established its reign, through a single sinner, much more shall those who receive in far greater measure God's grace, and his gift of righteousness, live and reign through the one man, Jesus Christ (Rom. 5:17).

> For since it was a man who brought death into the world, a man also brought resurrection of the dead. As in Adam all men die, so in Christ all will be brought to life; but each in his own proper place (1 Cor. 15:21–23).

The following verses in Romans compare the two deeds once again and lead to a general summation of the whole comparison:

> It follows, then, that as the issue of one misdeed was condemnation for all men, so the issue of one just act is acquittal and life for all men . . . Where sin was thus multiplied, grace immeasurably exceeded it [i.e., was victorious] (Rom. 5:18–20).

It is in this same framework, with due attention paid to the actual dependence of this plan on human liberty, that Paul develops the notion of the cosmic Christ who recapitulates and takes in the whole universe:

> When all things are thus subject to him, then the Son himself will also be made subordinate to God who made all things subject to him, and thus God will be all in all (1 Cor. 15:28).

And God will be all in all through the Word who is the culmination of the dynamism in every being:

> He is the image of the invisible God; his is the primacy over all created things. In him everything in heaven and on earth was created, not only things visible but also the invisible orders . . . the whole universe has been created through him and for him. And he exists before everything, and all things are held together in him (Col. 1:15-17).

The plan of grace, already victorious, is therefore this:

> He [God] has made known to us his hidden purpose—such was his will and pleasure determined beforehand in Christ—to be put into effect when the time was ripe: namely, that the universe, all in heaven and on earth, might be brought into a unity in Christ (Eph. 1:9-10).

> Through him God chose to reconcile the whole universe to himself, making peace through the shedding of his blood upon the cross—to reconcile all things, whether on earth or in heaven, through him alone (Col. 1:19-20).

Chapter Four

A. PROMISE

When Israel decides to take Yahweh as its one and only God and to live by the covenant, Joshua points out the great difficulty of this undertaking:

> Joshua answered the people, "You cannot worship the Lord. He is a holy god, a jealous god, and he will not forgive your rebellion and your sins. If you forsake the Lord and worship foreign gods, he will turn and bring adversity upon you and, although he once brought you prosperity, he will make an end of you." The people said to Joshua, "No; we will worship the Lord." He said to them, "You are witnesses against yourselves that you have chosen the Lord and will worship him." "Yes," they answered, "we are witnesses" (Josh. 24:19-22).

But Joshua was right. They were not able to serve Yahweh:

> He [Yahweh] laid on Jacob a solemn charge and established a law in Israel, which he commanded our fathers to teach their sons . . . He charged them to put their trust in God . . . not to do as their fathers did, a disobedient and rebellious race, a generation with no firm purpose, with hearts not fixed steadfastly on God . . . In spite of all, they persisted in their sin . . . When he struck them, they began to seek him, they remembered that God was their Creator, that God Most High was their deliverer. But still they beguiled him with words and deceived him with fine speeches; they were not loyal to him in their hearts nor were they faithful to his covenant. Yet he wiped out their guilt and did not smother his own natural affection; often he restrained his wrath and did not rouse his anger to its height. He remembered that they were only mortal men, who pass by like a wind and never return (Ps. 78:5-39).

So in the religious depths of Israel there wells up hope in a new covenant that will provide God with a people whose heart is faithful:

> The time is coming, says the Lord, when I will make a new covenant with
> Israel and Judah. It will not be like the covenant I made with their fore-
> fathers when I took them by the hand and led them out of Egypt. Although
> they broke my covenant, I was patient with them, says the Lord. But this is
> the covenant which I will make with Israel after those days, says the Lord;
> I will set my law within them and write it on their hearts; I will become
> their God and they shall become my people (Jer. 31:31–33).

The logical consequence is that this new pact, being a grace, will be
definitive and eternal:

> They shall become my people and I will become their God. I will give
> them one heart and one way of life so that they shall fear me at all times,
> for their own good and the good of their children after them. I will enter
> into an eternal covenant with them, to follow them unfailingly with my
> bounty; I will fill their hearts with fear of me, and so they will not turn
> away from me (Jer. 32:38–40).

From this new heart will well up a real knowledge of the truth, that is,
of Yahweh's revelation:

> No longer need they teach one another to know the Lord; all of them,
> high and low alike, shall know me, says the Lord (Jer. 31:34).

The whole nation will be a nation of prophets: i.e., men who possess
another sense of sight to ken Yahweh's plan for beings and events:

> This, says the Lord, is my covenant, which I make with them: My spirit
> which rests upon you and my words which I have put into your mouth shall
> never fail you from generation to generation of your descendants from now
> onward for ever. The Lord has said it (Isa. 59:21).

B. FULFILLMENT

1. **Interior transformation: the commandment and the mystery of
Christ:** Both for John and for Paul union with Christ makes possible and
calls for fulfillment of the new commandment and experiential knowledge
of the mystery:

> Here is the test by which we can make sure that we know him: do we keep
> his [Christ's] commands? The man who says, "I know him," while he dis-
> obeys his commands, is a liar and a stranger to the truth; but in the man
> who is obedient to his word, the divine love has indeed come to its perfec-
> tion. Here is the test by which we can make sure that we are with him:
> whoever claims to be dwelling in him, binds himself to live as Christ him-
> self lived. Dear friends, I give you no new command. It is the old command
> which you always had before you; the old command is the message which
> you heard at the beginning . . . As for you, the initiation which you re-
> ceived from him stays with you; you need no other teacher, but learn all
> you need to know from his initiation, which is real and no illusion. As he
> taught you, then, dwell in him. Even now, my children, dwell in him, so
> that when he appears we may be confident and unashamed before him at
> his coming. If you know that he is righteous, you must recognize that every
> man who does right is his child (1 John 2:3–7, 27–29).

And Paul says:

With this in mind, then, I kneel in prayer to the Father . . . that out of the treasure of his glory he may grant you strength and power through his Spirit in your inner being [which without grace was subject to the law of its bodily members], that through faith Christ may dwell in your hearts in love. With deep roots and firm foundations, may you be strong to grasp, with all God's people, what is the breadth and length and height and depth of the love of Christ [i.e., the full dimensions of the mystery, see Eph. 3:9], and to know it, though it is beyond all knowledge. So may you attain to fullness of being, the fullness of God himself. Now to him who is able to do immeasurably more than all we can ask or conceive, by the power which is at work among us, to him be glory in the church and in Christ Jesus from generation to generation evermore! Amen (Eph. 3:14–21).

2. But since sin coexists in us with grace, how will God judge our life? Christ gives us a picture of judgment in Matthew 25. There a glass of water granted leads to eternal life, while a glass of water denied leads to eternal death. But every human being has done both. Saint Paul adds:

> Make no mistake: no fornicator or idolater, none who are guilty either of adultery or of homosexual perversion, no thieves or grabbers or drunkards or slanderers or swindlers, will possess the kingdom of God (1 Cor. 6:9–10).

But no one is just a drunkard. He may also give food to the hungry and drink to the thirsty. Man's life is more complicated, as John points out at the beginning of his epistle:

> If we claim to be sharing in his life while we walk in the dark, our words and our lives are a lie [i.e., we are not authentic]; but if we walk in the light as he himself is in the light, then we share together a common life, and we are being cleansed from every sin by the blood of Jesus his Son. If we claim to be sinless, we are self-deceived and strangers to the truth. If we confess our sins, he is just, and may be trusted to forgive our sins and cleanse us from every kind of wrong; but if we say we have committed no sin, we make him out to be a liar, and then his word has no place in us (1 John 1:6–10).

Thus it is clear that each of the sins mentioned by Paul and the refusals depicted in Matthew 25 are a "no" to Christ and the kingdom. So the question is: Within the whole human complex, what determines God's judgment? Since good and evil are equal in power, will the latter have the final say? Nothing in Scripture points us in that direction. The texts tell us about a process of building in which both are at work, and from which God's judgment will weed out what is worthless:

> Or again, you are God's building. I am like a skilled master-builder who by God's grace laid the foundation, and someone else is putting up the building. Let each take care how he builds. There can be no other foundation beyond that which is already laid; I mean Jesus Christ himself. If anyone builds on that foundation with gold, silver, and fine stone, or with wood, hay, and straw, the work that each man does will at last be brought to light; the day of judgement will expose it. For that day dawns in fire, and the fire will test the worth of each man's work. If a man's building stands, he will be rewarded; if it burns, he will have to bear the loss; and yet he will escape with his life, as one might from fire (1 Cor. 3:10–15).

The same applies to the resurrection:

> As in Adam all men die, so in Christ all will be brought to life; but each in his own proper place (1 Cor. 15:22–23).

Love builds up and perdures. It is not in the same straits as evil. Thus we get an oft-repeated phrase that seems to have been a proverb of the primitive Church:

> Any man who brings a sinner back from his crooked ways will be rescuing his soul from death and cancelling innumerable sins (James 5:20).

Or put more generally:

> The end of all things is upon us, so you must lead an ordered and sober life . . . Above all, keep your love for one another at full strength, because love cancels innumerable sins . . . Whatever gift each of you may have received, use it in service to one another (1 Pet. 4:7–10).

APPENDIX IV

Springboard Questions

Here we should like to repeat what we said in the first volume of this series. There we noted that we found it absolutely necessary to prepare questions for the discussion periods which were an integral part of our seminars. Only in this way were the participants able to engage in probing discussions that took a direct look at accustomed images and concepts.

The questions were not meant to encourage passivity on the part of the participants. Their purpose was not to get the participants merely to "recall" or "review" what had been said in lectures or texts. They were meant to broaden the outlook of the participants by getting them to think out the logic of what they had heard in terms of real-life problems and situations. In short, they were meant to produce a confrontation between real life and what the participants believed they knew.

We felt that our readers might like to see the type of question we proposed and the rationale behind it. So here we offer some of the questions we proposed in connection with each chapter topic, together with an explanation accounting for our choice of these questions.

Chapter One

QUESTIONS

Can "mass-directed" media be put in the service of grace, the Church, and salvation? If no, why not? If yes, temporarily or permanently? In any case, how do you feel about this alternative: either Christianity reaches everyone through mass-directed media or else it is not universal at all?

EXPLANATION

The object of the question is to get across the point that we can obtain a specific line of conduct from human beings in one of two ways. We can appeal to his liberty on the one hand. Or, on the other hand, we can pressure him with one of the various instruments available to present-day society: propaganda, advertising, linking certain values with standards of prestige, comfort, etc. The stress is placed on the masses of humanity as a whole rather than just a multitude, precisely to make the definitive opposition between grace and mass-directed media as sharp as possible.

What we said in the first chapter, however, compels us to admit that pure liberty does not exist in man. Christianity of itself cannot be an object of propaganda or pressure. But the preparation of man for it, as for freedom in general, requires the use of mass-directed media to the same extent that human progress demands it. In the very idea of Christ's "good news" we may be able to find "mass-directed" elements that will be corrected and purified later. Note, for example, the "messianic secret" of Mark's Gospel.

QUESTIONS

What meaning or meanings does the word *poverty* have? Wherein can its Christian value lie?

EXPLANATION

Complementing the previous question, this one seeks to suggest that liberty does not depend on the use or non-use of certain means, but on using *only* those means which can be adopted in a personal, creative way *so long as* they can be used in this way (see Appendix II, Chapter I, C, and GS 37).

QUESTION

Does more frequent communion produce greater grace?

EXPLANATION

Grace is a gift that God gives us on his own initiative, but our liberation admits of progress and retrogression. This is something which should now be clear to us. The point of the question is to make us aware of the fact that the "poverty" mentioned in the previous question should have a rightful place in every sphere, including the religious one. The fact is that on the pathway to liberty all elements are ambiguous. They all shift imperceptibly from instruments to determinisms. The religious realm does not escape this fate. Nothing is automatic in the order of grace, not even the sacramental order.

Chapter Two

QUESTIONS

"A large number of active Christian vocations are made up more of natural generosity than of a supernatural spirit." Judging by the accustomed Christian terminology, what do you think the author of this phrase means by it? Do you agree with this *way of expressing it?* If yes, why? If no, how would you express it?

EXPLANATION

The statement comes from Canon Jacques Leclerq (*Vivre chrétiennement notre temps; Christians in the World*). Our question is meant to stimulate reflection on a preliminary question that should precede any in-depth study of this matter: How are the terms *natural* and *supernatural* used in current-day language? This should also help us to see their fateful equivocations when the activities denoted by these terms are tied up with their effectiveness for man's one and only (supernatural) destiny: eternal life.

QUESTION

"A Mass is infinitely more efficacious for the welfare of humanity than the sum total of human efforts to build history." Give reasons for or against this assertion.

EXPLANATION

This statement by Cardinal Jean Daniélou (*Essai sur le mystère de l'histoire*) is useful to start a discussion aimed at going beyond mere terminology and clarifying the real relationship between the "sacred" and the "profane" in connection with the kingdom of heaven. His statement alludes to an element of automaticity, which was already brought up in the third question of Chapter I. It also presupposes two parallel, though profoundly unequal, orders of efficacity.

It would be worthwhile to suggest that this question could be reformulated, replacing the notion of "a Mass" with the notion of "the Mass par excellence," that is, Christ's own sacrifice. It would also be worthwhile to relate this question, and the subsequent discussion, to concrete cases of all sorts: e.g., motivations which accompany the decision for or against the "religious state"; dividing up the "religious" and the "profane" tasks of the laity; and even the pastoral options of the Church in general vis-à-vis cult, pastoral work, dialogue with nonbelievers, etc.

QUESTIONS

Do Christian hope and man's hopes for history coincide? If yes, then why must we "distinguish carefully between temporal progress and the progress of the kingdom"? If no, what practical difference will there be between the Christian and the non-Christian in their respective commitments, by virtue of the hope of the former?

EXPLANATION

This question seeks to promote a discussion about the concrete attitude a Christian will tend to adopt on the basis of his own hope when he dialogues with nonbelievers. It may also be advisable to get people to spell out their social and political attitudes in the concrete. Here we have in mind such things as the problem of violence. In more general terms, such a discussion will concretize and specify the conciliar texts relating to this chapter (see Appendix II).

Chapter Three

QUESTIONS

Since the time of Saint Augustine there has been much talk about a "city of God" and a "city of man." The former is consecrated to the supernatural, the spiritual, and the sacred. It seeks to carry out God's plan. It is inscribed within the order of grace. The latter, inscribed within the order of nature, is consecrated to the service of the temporal, the natural, and the profane. It seeks to realize man's human designs. Have you heard these terms used recently? What do you think about this? How are the two cities related to each other: opposed? convergent? complementary? parallel? autonomous? Decide between these alternatives or propose others.

EXPLANATION

This question differs in two ways from those of the preceding chapter, despite their seeming resemblance. 1. It calls attention to various forms of expression, even conciliar ones (see CLARIFICATION V in this chapter), which talk about a religious function that is "distinct" even though not "separate" from temporal functions even while they proclaim the autonomy of the latter. 2. It then proceeds to query people about the way the religious dimension (which other people apparently lack) is to be injected into the common history of mankind and in the face of the problems posed by all. Needless to say, we are talking here about the Christian religious dimension, not about just any religious dimension.

QUESTION

How will the *political* consequences tend to differ if Christian hope is framed in terms of the soul's immortality rather than in terms of resurrection?

EXPLANATION

This question tries to call conscious attention to the genuine "autonomy" of the temporal, which is destined to reach its fulfillment in the resurrection. In a mental outlook dominated by the notion of the soul's immortality, by contrast, the temporal seems to be merely an aspect of man's testing period; as a result, the life to come seems to be a *wholly different* life, a reward rather than a fruition. Thus the question tries to get people thinking about the two possible interpretations of the word *ideology* as applied to Christianity.

Depending on the cultural level of the participants, the notion of ideology could be injected into the question itself. And one might also pose this question: How would this difference be affected, depending on whether Christianity is or is not considered an "ideology"? In a positive sense, the participants would try to figure out to what extent Christian hope in the resurrection of historical effort itself would constitute an ideological element in political platforms. In a negative sense, the ideological aspect of Christianity would refer to its disincarnated focus on some hereafter, which concealed an attitude of social and political conformism.

QUESTION

Considering the breadth of grace, what is the sense of the command to go throughout the world and preach the gospel to every creature, so that he who is baptized may be saved and he who does not believe may be condemned? Why go and preach the gospel?

EXPLANATION

This question may well be senseless if one has already reflected on the ideas put forth in the preceding volume of this series (see especially Volume I, Chapter III). But each volume of this series is independent too, and many will begin their work of reflection from the starting point of grace. So there will be good reason to raise this problem, which was already hinted at in the previous question: i.e., What does Christian faith (and also the sacraments) add to a grace that is operative on the scale of humanity itself? The consideration—for many, the discovery—of grace's breadth often tends to bring the idea of "mission" into crisis. Their first reaction is to wonder about the specific function of faith and the Church.

Chapter Four

QUESTION

What response would you make to someone who voiced sentiments like those of King Claudius in *Hamlet* (Act III, Scene III)?

> O, my offence is rank, it smells to heaven; it hath the primal eldest curse upon't—a brother's murder! Pray can I not, though inclination be as sharp as will. My stronger guilt defeats my strong intent and, like a man to double business bound, I stand in pause where I shall first begin, and both neglect . . . Then I'll look up; my fault is past. But, O, what form of prayer can serve my turn? Forgive me my foul murder!—That cannot be, since I am still possessed of those effects for which I did the murder—my crown, mine own ambition, and my queen. May one be pardoned and retain the offence? In the corrupted currents of this world, offence's gilded hand may shove by justice. And oft 'tis seen the wicked prize itself buys out the law: but 'tis not so above.

EXPLANATION

The purpose of this question is to underline the unreal nature of an outlook which sees Christian (and human) existence as a series of successive and incessant entries into "global states" of sin or innocence. Within this mental outlook, grace seems to be a return to some utopian fresh start, outside of sin and its occasions. It is highly advisable that the discussion here go beyond consideration of individual sins to another area: i.e., the possibilities of showing effective love in a society where we are all accomplices within sinful structures, and where concrete action is a continual occasion of sin even as it is the unique condition for creation.

QUESTIONS

Protestants insist on an awareness of sin. Do we Catholics possess a comparable awareness? Is the sacrament of penance normally an expression of this awareness? If yes, why? If no, why not?

EXPLANATION

This question may help the participants to realize that the enumeration of sins in the confessional usually has to do with mere end results; that it leaves out of account and awareness the real sinful structures in our individual and social life. These structures are not manifested in deeds and events that can be readily ticked off.